D1071835

A Pride of Lions

THE ASTOR ORPHANS

ALSO BY LATELY THOMAS

Storming Heaven

The Mayor Who Mastered New York

The First President Johnson

The Vanishing Evangelist

A Debonair Scoundrel

Sam Ward: King of the Lobby

Delmonico's: A Century of Splendor

Between Two Empires

THE ASTOR ORPHANS

A Pride of Lions

The Chanler Chronicle
by Lately Thomas

William Morrow & Company, Inc., New York   1971

Copyright © 1971 by William Morrow and Company, Inc.

Grateful acknowledgment is made to Houghton Mifflin Company for permission to quote from *John Jay Chapman and His Letters*, edited by M. A. DeWolfe Howe, and to Harvard University Press for permission to quote from *The Letters of Theodore Roosevelt*, edited by Elting E. Morison.

Unless otherwise indicated, all pictures are from the Rokeby Collection.

All rights reserved. No part of this book may be reproduced or utilized in any form or by any means, electronic or mechanical, including photocopying, recording or by any information storage and retrieval system, without permission in writing from the Publisher. Inquiries should be addressed to William Morrow and Company, Inc., 105 Madison Ave., New York, N.Y. 10016.

Printed in the United States of America.
Library of Congress Catalog Card Number 73–151918

". . . As for what is popular, and what people like, and so forth, it is all a joke. . . . Do the thing well, and the only difference will be, that people will like what they have never liked before, and will like it so much the better for the novelty of their feelings towards it. Dulness and tameness are the only irreparable faults . . ."

—*Sir Walter Scott to his publisher*

To Fantasy

Contents

PART THREE

Arms and the Man

1862-1901

In Pursuit of the Patrician Ideal

A gaggle of geese, a covey of quail, a drove of cattle, a wisp of snipe, a flock of sheep, a swarm of bees, a herd of deer, a nye of pheasants, a school of herring, a padding of ducks, a murmuration of peacocks, a skulk of foxes, a fall of woodcock, a pipe of wine, a clutch of eggs, a peck of trouble, a pride of lions, and an exaltation of larks . . .

And then there were the Chanlers . . .

"Was it one of the last of the eighteenth-century graces—some errant sister lingering miraculously in the democratic fastnesses of Dutchess County—who presided over the family of eccentric patricians at Rokeby? Or was the Chanler inspiration only a flower of the more fragile, more complex, and more fleeting aristocratic ideal which illuminated the dying years of nineteenth-century imperialism? It possessed the grand manner . . . But there was a touch of the Beerbohmian in its elegance, and rather more than a touch of Mr. Rudyard Kipling in its chivalry. It rode to hounds, it painted, it fought, it explored, it was cosmopolitan. Its oddity belonged definitely to the great century of skeptical individualism —even though when it ran for office it chose the Tammany ticket, in the grand ironic manner. . . . A salty, eccentric, and justly proud family . . ."

—Fragment of an obituary notice

PART ONE

Wild Seeds Planted

A Foothold in Time

To the little girl in the carriage, the great white house disclosed itself suddenly, emerging from its darkling screen of trees, solid and sedate against the blue spring sky. As the wheels crunched to a halt on the gravel her father lifted her down, and she clutched his hand tightly for reassurance. Together they walked toward the broad stone steps sweeping up in a double curve to the wide piazza that stretched across the front of the house and jutted out at either end. Squarely in the center of this piazza, both leaves of the lofty entrance door stood open, waiting. Looking up at the somnolent dwelling, with its observant windows, which she was seeing for the first time, the child had a feeling—not a thought, but a feeling that came over her—and it was that she was going to be in that house for a long time.

Had this child realized that Rokeby harbored ghosts, her premonition might have been keener. Indeed the grounds did harbor legends, and vestiges of ancestors pervaded the rooms and corridors of the mansion. There was even a domesticated fairy that manifested itself at long intervals, dressed in the garments of a bygone age. "Probably came over with the family from England," was the matter-of-fact surmise; since it had been seen, nobody could doubt the creature's existence.

But these aspects of Rokeby were hidden from the prescient child as she was introduced to the estate on this day in May, 1876 —the centennial year of the nation. And the date would come to have special meaning for the little girl because her own roots were sunk deep into the nation's history, as her name indicated. That name was Alida Beekman Chanler, an ancestral name, as were the names of all her brothers and sisters: Stuyvesant, Winthrop, Livingston, Armstrong, Ward, Astor, all were represented among the youngsters who tumbled out of farm wagon and carryall to take possession of their new home. The names had weighty associations, though the children appeared to be burdened with no sense of portentousness. Noisily they ran here and there in their excitement, one girl stooping to pluck some of the pretty flowers that lined the drive. A brother called to her to stop, but the gardener standing by exclaimed genially:

"No, let her; she owns the place as much as any of you."

Which was true: the manor house and its three hundred acres of surrounding park and farmland were these children's property, owned by them all, share and share alike. And the reason for their high-spirited invasion on this May day was the recent death of their mother, who had bequeathed to them jointly the estate on the Hudson. The situation was superb: high on the eastern bank overlooking a broad reach of the river and commanding a panorama sweeping westward to the Catskill Mountains, looming mistily in the blue distance.

These new owners of Rokeby were young, ranging in age from thirteen to infancy. They were no ordinary group. Already heritage had endowed them with an extraordinary mixture of conflicting genes, and circumstances equally extraordinary were to work upon this combustible material to produce often striking and sometimes pyrotechnic effects. To understand the multiple influences that were to shape and impel these Chanlers, a glance at their antecedents is vital: for in both a practical and a mystic sense, these children were captives of the past even in their toddling years.

First and foremost, Rokeby was an Armstrong demesne. Founded by an Armstrong, it was impregnated with Armstrong influences, just as Armstrong character traits persisted in their posterity. The story began with two Armstrongs named John, father and son. The family was border Scottish, but had retreated to Ireland in Cromwell's time as a result of favoring the royalist cause. The elder John Armstrong immigrated to America from Northern

Ireland sometime before 1748; arriving in Pennsylvania, he took up land on the colony's western frontier, where Scots-Irish were congregated. It was a region full of risks and hardihood. The Indians were a constant menace, and during the French and Indian War the settlements suffered cruelly from scalping parties of the Delawares, allied with the French. The Indians' headquarters was at Kittanning, a Delaware town in extreme western Pennsylvania. Bent upon retaliation, a band of three hundred Scots-Irish under the leadership of John Armstrong penetrated the wilderness, surprised the stronghold, killed fifty braves including their chief, and burned the community before beating a successful retreat.

The blow was disastrous to the Delawares, and the dying chief was said to have placed a curious curse upon John Armstrong and all his line, to the last descendant. Since the raid brought comparative peace to the frontier, the victorious leader was viewed in a different light by his own people, and Armstrong became celebrated in the colony as "the hero of Kittanning." Being Pennsylvania's outstanding military figure, he was commissioned a brigadier general upon the outbreak of the Revolutionary War, and served under Washington throughout that conflict. He failed, however, for whatever reason, to achieve distinction in that war comparable to his earlier exploits.

His son, the younger John Armstrong, had been born in the town of Carlisle, then virtually in the heart of Indian country, and was a student in what would become Princeton University when the war with England started. Enlisting immediately, young Armstrong, helped by his father's influence, obtained a captain's commission, although he was only seventeen. He served on the staff of General Mercer, a valorous Virginian, until Mercer was killed; then transferred to the staff of General Horatio Gates.

For a junior officer in the Continental Army, this was about as injudicious a choice as could be made. Gates's headquarters was a hotbed of intrigue, and young Armstrong was bound to become involved in Gates's plotting to supersede Washington.

After the cessation of hostilities, during the interval until a formal peace was signed, Armstrong's acquired taste for intrigue led him into further indiscretions, which culminated in his responsibility for the once notorious "Newburgh Letters." These

were "addresses," circulated anonymously among the officers of
Washington's army stationed at Newburgh, New York, reciting
the just grievances of the officers left without pay or adequate
provisioning by Congress, and hinting at a military coup, if necessary, to take over the government. They so angered Washington
that he threatened to hang their author, if he could be identified,
for inciting to mutiny. In later years Armstrong candidly admitted his authorship, while Washington, on his part, conceded
that the plight of his officers had not been overstated. Armstrong's
extreme pugnacity was remarked by his contemporaries even
then, as well as his tendency to overestimate his powers.

Retiring from the army with the rank of major, the young man
improved his social position by marrying a Livingston heiress—
Alida, sister of the redoubtable Chancellor Livingston and the
almost equally influential Edward Livingston, who would be both
minister to France and President Andrew Jackson's Secretary of
State. The Livingstons were potent in both state and national
affairs. Holders of vast land grants along the upper Hudson, they
lived on their estates in feudal grandeur, and their daughters
were customarily dowered with portions of the family lands. Alida
Livingston brought to her marriage with John Armstrong the
riverfront acreage in the Red Hook district of Dutchess County,
north of Rhinebeck, which would be given the name Rokeby.

Through his Livingston connections, John Armstrong was twice
elevated to the United States Senate, and in 1804 was named to
succeed his brother-in-law, Chancellor Livingston, as United States
minister at the court of Napoleon. As a diplomat, Armstrong
showed little aptitude, and although he lived in great style in
Paris, he failed to impress the emperor. His dispatches, although
vigorously phrased, for he had a marked literary gift, were too
often wide of the mark, and in 1810 he returned home determined to devote himself to the development of his Hudson River
property.

The War of 1812 intervened, again with unlucky consequences
for John Armstrong. Handicapped by a hopelessly incompetent
Secretary of War, President Madison, for purely political reasons,
offered the post to Armstrong, although the two men mutually
disliked and distrusted each other. But New York was unfriendly
to "Madison's war," which was crippling its commerce; and the

President hoped that his choice of a New Yorker for the all-important position would bring him support from that state. Characteristically overestimating his abilities, Armstrong (who by now held a general's commission in the New York state militia) accepted the appointment. For the disasters that followed—the overrunning of Washington and the burning of the Capitol and White House by British troops—Armstrong was bitterly blamed, although the incompetence displayed generally in high quarters was equally at fault. In the debacle, Armstrong's public career collapsed, and even the few wise decisions that he had made brought him no commendation. Yet it was he who had jumped Winfield Scott and Andrew Jackson to important commands over the heads of bumbling superiors. In a sour mood the disappointed politician withdrew to private life, and for the rest of his days his temperament would be what his children tactfully called "difficult."

Armstrong had set about providing his estate with a suitable manor house directly upon returning from France. A local carpenter, Warner Richards, was engaged to carry out the construction. Armstrong stipulated for a country house, not a mansion—nothing showy or extravagant—but a comfortable, commodious, dignified gentleman's home. That was the kind of house he got, large, solid, and practical, although the interior, it is true, was distinguished by touches of French taste which set the dwelling off from the other great houses along the river. Because of the interruption of the war and his being summoned to Washington, he was not able to move into the new home until 1815, and even then the builders were still at work.

General Armstrong and his wife had five sons and one daughter, named Margaret Rebecca. This daughter was expected to marry well, but her choice of a husband at first was not entirely to the liking of her parents. She met William Backhouse Astor, son of John Jacob Astor, the founder of the fortune, in Albany at a reception given by Governor De Witt Clinton; she was visiting friends there, and Astor was on a lobbying errand for his father.

The Knickerbocker gentility looked askance upon the Astors, despite the latter's great and growing wealth; and certainly the Astor antecedents were not impressive. John Jacob's father had

Rokeby as built by General Armstrong and as it appeared before the third story and tower were added by William B. Astor. Painted from a drawing by Alida Astor Carey, daughter of William B. Astor and great-aunt of the Chanler children.

been the village butcher in Walldorf, Germany, and while John Jacob himself was not ashamed of his origins, some of his descendants would be at pains to overlook them.

Margaret Rebecca Armstrong was a Livingston, and the Livingstons, while by no means as rich as the Astors (John Jacob already was rated the richest man in America), were immensely influential socially and politically. The advantages to the Astors of such a match were obvious, and William B. lost no time falling in love with Margaret's peach-bloom complexion. (The only display of romantic feeling ever observed in William B. Astor was his pet name for his wife, "Peachy.") There was some backing and filling, aimed, on the Astor side, at safeguarding their fortune from rapacious in-laws; but an understanding was finally reached, and the couple was married in 1818. And it was at Rokeby that their first child was born, a girl, whom her mother, an avid reader of romances, named Emily, after the heroine of *The Mysteries of Udolpho.* Five more children followed little Emily—three sons, named John Jacob III, William B., and Henry, and two daughters, Laura and Alida. Another daughter, Sarah, and a son, Robert, died as infants.

As a wedding present to his son and daughter-in-law, old John Jacob had purchased an interest in the Hudson River estate, all that Armstrong would part with, and for several years the young Astors spent their summers at Rokeby as guests of the general. But Alida Livingston Armstrong died in 1822, and when John Jacob Astor raised his offer to $40,000—a formidable sum for those days—Armstrong could hold out no longer, and the property passed entirely into Astor hands; in spite of which, the general continued to sit at the head of the table whenever he was at Rokeby for as long as he lived.

It was Margaret Astor who gave the estate its name. Armstrong had called it La Bergerie (The Sheepfold), having intended to engage in sheep raising; on the personal advice of Bonaparte, he had imported merinos, but the breed did not prosper, and the general turned to other experiments. Margaret Astor, fancying a resemblance to a glen described by Sir Walter Scott in his fashionable poem, *Rokeby,* bestowed the name on the house and grounds, and it stuck.

Both the Astors were assiduous readers, Margaret's taste running to romances and works of piety, while her husband perused encyclopedias. He had been educated at Heidelberg and Göttingen Universities, having Christian K. J. Bunsen, the celebrated scholar and diplomat, as his tutor, and often conversing with a moody classmate named Arthur Schopenhauer. On his return home William had bowed to his father's wish that he enter the family business, and thereafter passed his life poring over the estate's interminable rent-rolls. Yet he never lost his taste for scholarship, and the shelves by the fireplace in the library at Rokeby, within easy reach of his favorite chair, were stacked with books of reference, dictionaries and encyclopedias, many of them in German. An insatiable collector of facts, he eschewed books of imagination.

It was the steady accumulation of books in the house that had led to the addition of Rokeby's octagonal tower, the lower floor of which became the main library. And the increase in the number of children, requiring extra attendants, caused Astor to add a third story to the house, under a mansard roof. By this means six bedrooms were added, while an entire wing was built at the back to house a larger kitchen and offices.

Rokeby after the addition of third story and tower. Western side, overlooking the river. The tower contained the library, on ground floor, billiard room, boys' schoolroom, and a railed observation gallery called The View.

Although William B. Astor had deep affection for his family, his habitual expression was dour and morose, and when still quite young he assumed the care-worn air that never left him. Although he employed a valet, he always looked seedy. He was as parsimonious of words as he was of pence, old John Jacob having summed up his son's character exactly when he said:

"William will never make a dollar, but he will never lose one that he has."

In the city, the Astors lived in a setting of dreary elegance, at first on lower Broadway, and then in a red brick mansion in fashionable Lafayette Place. Their social life was colorless and correct; Margaret Armstrong Astor was too country-bred to take on city glitter, and William's demeanor as a host was dismayingly funereal. Rokeby was hardly more cheerful, although it was open, sunny, and hospitable. An air of provinciality and eighteenth-century formality pervaded it. The manners of another age were imposed by the presence of General Armstrong, and the Astors transmitted the same stiff decorum to their household. No Armstrong or Astor child ever turned his back upon his elders when leaving the room after bidding them good-night, and in the dining room the strict rule was "no speaking at table." The slightest suggestion of anything indecorous distressed and alarmed Mrs. Astor exceedingly.

Into this somber respectability Emily Astor brought a bit of sunlight. She had none of the dour taciturnity of her father, but inherited the delight in music and jolly, witty company so marked in her grandfather, John Jacob the Founder—when there was no question of business, *entendu*. She had a clear soprano voice of exceptional range and brilliance, extending over three octaves, and on her sheet music (preserved at Rokeby) she wrote dazzling cadenzas. Her grandfather doted on her singing of old German songs, in which he would sometimes join, in a thick accent. Her parents, on the other hand, preferred to hear her in hymns, accompanied on the harp by a sister.

Emily was easily her grandfather's favorite, and she could look forward to receiving a handsome *dot* upon her marriage. That event occurred in 1838, and with it a change came over Lafayette Place and Rokeby. Emily's husband was Samuel Ward, Jr., fourth of that name in a distinguished family of Rhode Island and New York. His family tree included two governors, Revolutionary patriots, and the Marions of South Carolina, who claimed collateral kinship with Charlotte Corday. He was witty, gay, and rich, had just turned twenty-four, and was one of those rare persons who seem to have been blessed with every gift and endowed with all the talents. Charming and affectionate, he was a fluent linguist, a more than passable writer, and a brilliant mathematician, as well as a polished dancer. He had traveled widely in Europe, where he seemed to have met everybody who counted, from youthful Henry Wadsworth Longfellow, at Heidelberg, to the Duchesse d'Abrantès, Liszt, Paganini, and the astronomer-physicist François Arago, at Paris. He had been honored by learned societies, and was already a gourmet and connoisseur of wines. As the eldest son of the most prominent banker in New York, he was prospectively a millionaire.

Sam was a decided catch for the Astors. His personality was enchanting, and the Astors applauded when he joined his clear tenor with Emily's soprano in the student songs he had brought back from Heidelberg. The harp stayed in its case when his jeweled fingers danced over the piano in the waltzes and mazurkas he had learned at the court of the King of Saxony, or the fashionable airs he had picked up in Paris. Emily and he fell blissfully in love, and Emily's dropsical old grandfather found young Sam the most obliging of possible sons-in-law, although their views on matters of money did not coincide. To the younger Astor sisters, Laura and Alida, Sam Ward appeared as a knight-rescuer from boredom.

Under Sam Ward's touch, Rokeby took on a new livability. Drives were cut through, gardens laid out, and a landscape architect was brought from Germany to beautify the estate. A hillock that partially blocked the river view was leveled off. Austerity seemed to depart from the rugged house when Sam came singing along the road, the only visitor who ever heralded his approach that way.

Summers found Emily and Sam at Rokeby, and the second summer they brought with them their first-born, a girl whom they had named Margaret Astor Ward for her grandmother. That summer Rokeby echoed with unaccustomed laughter when Sam's three sisters, Julia, Louisa, and Annie Ward, came visiting. The contrast between the lively Ward temperament and the stiff reticence of the Astors was not lost upon keen-witted, fun-loving Julia (who would become Julia Ward Howe), while Louisa Ward little guessed that her own daughter one day would serve as Rokeby's chatelaine.

Sam and Emily's halcyon days lasted less than three years. Then tragedy struck. Emily died in childbirth, the baby not surviving her, and motherless Margaret was brought back to Rokeby alone. From then on the child, called "Maddie" by the family, would live with the Astors, while they and her father became increasingly estranged. A complete break occurred when Sam fell in love with a luscious Creole, Medora Grymes, about whose family scandal hovered, and married her. In the Astors' eyes this was a desecration of Emily's memory, and all connection with Sam Ward was severed. Pressing the vendetta without quarter, the Astors did not scruple to bring Maddie's inheritance into question, threatening legal action unless Sam relinquished the child to her grandparents. Rather than jeopardize his daughter's prospects, he consented, and Maddie would grow up amidst the strict conventions, heavy piety, and somber luxury of Lafayette Place, relieved only by the simpler austerity of Rokeby. Sam Ward, meanwhile, would compound his turpitude, in Astor opinion, by losing his fortune. Although he went on to win and lose two fortunes more, and to scintillate through a career of friendships and adventures incomprehensible to his first wife's family, the breach was never healed.

Maddie Ward's girlhood was not gay. Thrown into the company of elderly cousins and uncles, she had few friends of her own age. Now and then she was permitted to see her scapegrace father briefly, but only in the severe custody of Nancy Richards, her mother's nurse, and she was never able to establish any satisfactory relationship with him. Her upbringing was largely in the hands of Nancy, who was one of the six daughters of the carpenter who had built Rokeby; five of these women had taken service with the Armstrongs and Astors. Maddie's was a feudal upbringing, filled with duties and the rigid enforcement of social gradations. She was drilled in Mrs. Astor's rubric of good manners, reserve, and decorum, many of the rules being vestiges of the previous century. Time often seemed to lag in that lumbering household; yet in spite of everything, Maddie was not unhappy, and at Rokeby she was sometimes almost carefree.

Two breaks in the regularity of those years were provided by the marriages of her two Astor aunts. Laura was married to Franklin Hughes Delano, member of a family of Belgian origin that had amassed a moderate fortune in the China trade, an early source of the Astors' wealth, too. The match so pleased old John Jacob Astor that he gave the bride $200,000 in trust as a wedding present. Uncle Frank Delano, given to easy ways as long as his inflammable temper was not crossed, became a favorite with Maddie Ward, and Laura always treated her niece like a sister.

Alida, the youngest Astor daughter, declined to be rushed into marriage. Her choice finally fell upon John Carey, Jr., an unpretentious but unobjectionable Englishman. Gentle and serious-minded, Alida became distressed over the want of any means of caring for orphaned girls in the county, and she begged her father to endow a home. It happened that Mrs. Astor, whose chief pleasure was gardening, had been expressing a wish to have a greenhouse, which would involve a considerable outlay of money, and Astor put the question to Alida, whether she would rather have her orphanage, or let her mother have her greenhouse? Although devoted to her mother, Alida held out for the orphanage; whereupon her father, commending her fidelity to principle, announced that both she and her mother should have their wishes granted. While the greenhouse was building, St. Margaret's home for girls was established in nearby Red Hook, where it would continue to be maintained as a privately supported charity until well into the twentieth century.

Meanwhile Margaret Astor Ward had grown into a very pretty young woman, and as the time for her marriage approached, her grandparents guarded her with watchful solicitude. Fortune-hunters were to be fended off, and Maddie herself felt that the more sensitive young men of her acquaintance shrank from an Astor alliance, disliking to be suspected of casting covetous eyes upon their wealth.

John Winthrop Chanler, a very proper and serious-minded New York lawyer with excellent family connections, suffered from no such inhibition, but he was not immediately attracted to Miss Ward. His sister, Margaret Stuyvesant Chanler Rutherfurd, wife of Lewis Morris Rutherfurd, the eminent astronomer, brought them together and employed her influence to predispose Maddie's grandparents to the match. Because of her Stuyvesant and Chanler connections, Margaret Rutherfurd's word carried weight; and in the autumn of 1861 the couple's betrothal was announced. The moment was propitious, inasmuch as Chanler was enjoying brief military glory as a member of New York's blue-blooded Seventh Regiment, and he hoped shortly to be elected to Congress.

Although he possessed no great wealth of his own, by birth, education, social heritage, and temperament, John Winthrop Chanler was a desirable consort for an Astor heiress. Personally charming, he was respectful of the conventions, upright, and affectionate. His family had originally spelled their name Chaloner, and were presumably Norman-French, settled in England. In

Cromwell's time three Chaloners had sat in the Long Parliament, according to family tradition, and at the trial of Charles I, one of the three had voted to acquit the king, one to behead him, and the third, sniffing danger on both sides, had walked out without voting. After the Restoration, the royalist was advanced in favor; the regicide disappeared; and the abstainer withdrew into prudent obscurity. As least, this was one version of the tradition handed down through generations of Chanlers, and it illustrated an abiding family trait—the capacity for disagreement among themselves, stemming from strong convictions.

The first Chanler to reach America was the Reverend Isaac Chanler, a Baptist divine. Born in Bristol, he sailed from Tenby, Wales, in 1710, and settled at Charleston, South Carolina. Made welcome there by the lordly planter aristocracy, he prospered, published theological works, and fathered a son, named Isaac also.

This son was sent to Europe for his education, and took a medical degree at the University of Edinburgh with a thesis bearing the not unprophetic title of "Hysteria, Its Causes and Aspects." He returned to South Carolina and during the Revolutionary War was a surgeon in the Continental Army. He had entered the communion of the Church of England while abroad, and his son, John White Chanler, became an Episcopal clergyman. A vestryman and intimate friend of this ecclesiastical Chanler was John C. Calhoun, and something of the statesman's grim implacability and fanatical dogmatism was reflected in the clergyman. Like Calhoun, John White Chanler was an alumnus of Yale College, where he had taken his divinity degree. A classmate, named Winthrop, had invited him to New York to spend the holidays, and there Chanler met his friend's sister, Elizabeth Shirreff Winthrop. The visit was fateful, for eventually they married, and Chanler, who was bred to the freer social customs of the South, drew down some reprobation on himself by boldly taking his bride to the theater. On her father's side Elizabeth Chanler traced to the Winthrops of Massachusetts, while her mother, born Judith Stuyvesant, was closely related to the Livingstons and Beekmans.

John Winthrop Chanler, this couple's only son, was born in New York City in 1826. Educated by tutors, he was graduated from Columbia College in 1847, and after a visit to Europe which included both travel and study at Heidelberg, he returned home and was admitted to the bar. Politics attracted him, and in 1858 and 1859 he was elected to the New York State Assembly from a Tammany district. In 1860 he was defeated in a bid for election to Congress, and upon the outbreak of the Civil War he had a taste of military service with the Seventh Regiment when it marched to the relief of Washington in the early weeks of the war. Upon the expiration of his three-months call-up, he returned home and in 1862 was to win election to Congress as Tammany's candidate in the Third Congressional District of New York City.

His betrothal to Margaret Astor Ward, therefore, came at the outset of what gave every indication of being a career of solid achievement if not of brilliance. The match was not a flighty one: Chanler was thirty-five and his fiancée was twenty-three.

Once the decision was made, the Astors unfroze. The setting for the wedding was their home on Lafayette Place, just after New Year's, 1862. In a honeymoon letter written from Rokeby to an Armstrong cousin shortly thereafter, the bride described the wedding minutely:

"You ask me to tell you about the ceremony, my dress, etc. The latter was a low neck white corded silk, covered with lace which Father had given me—in my hair was an exquisite lace shawl, put on in the Spanish fashion and wound in a wreath of beautiful white flowers. On my neck was Winthrop's wedding present, a locket studded with diamonds attached to a very pretty gold chain . . ."

The date of this letter was January 27, 1862, and it went on to profess loyally that the honeymooners found Rokeby in midwinter as delightful as it was in midsummer. The truth was that the bitter cold in a house without a furnace soon drove the bridal pair to Cuba.

The preparations for the forthcoming election recalled them to New York; and upon Chanler's victory, plans had to be made for a suitable residence in Washington. In March, 1863, the new congressman took his seat as a member of the Democratic minority, and thereafter dutifully fulfilled the role of a minor member, mindful of the interests of his constituents and his party. After a brief period when she rented the Dolly Madison house, Maddie purchased a residence closer to the Capitol, and there entertained decorously.

RIGHT Samuel Ward ("Uncle Sam"), grandfather of the Chanler children. Rare photograph dating from the period of Ward's greatest political influence in Washington, during the Andrew Johnson administration.

LOWER LEFT John Winthrop Chanler and Margaret Astor Ward Chanler, parents of the Chanler children, shortly after their marriage in 1862.

LOWER RIGHT John Armstrong Chanler (seated) and Winthrop Astor Chanler, the two eldest children, about 1870.

Although active in committee work, Chanler seldom participated in the debates of the House. His most notable speech was made in defense of the contention that "this is a white working man's government," reflecting the apprehensions of the Irish and German immigrants crowded into New York City that their jobs were to be taken over by an influx of freed Southern slaves.

Chanler was reelected in 1864 and 1866. Meanwhile, Maddie's children were arriving with almost calendar regularity. The first, John Armstrong Chanler, was born on October 10, 1862, and then followed Winthrop Astor Chanler, born a year later, and a daughter, named Emily for Maddie's mother, born in 1864. A second daughter, Elizabeth Winthrop Chanler, arrived in 1866, and William Astor Chanler, the third son, in 1867, at Newport, where the Chanlers maintained a summer home, Cliff Lawn. Two more children would be born during Chanler's congressional tenure—Marion Ward Chanler (named for the *respectable* Wards, not for his grandfather), in 1868, and Lewis Stuyvesant Chanler, also at Newport, in 1869, actually soon after the close of his father's legislative service.

Determined not to coddle her children, Maddie Chanler governed them with loving restraint. She saw that they were early introduced to the amenities of their world; the four eldest—Armstrong, Winthrop, Emily, and Elizabeth—making their bow in social life at the celebrated children's Christmas ball that President Andrew Johnson gave for his grandchildren at the White House on December 29, 1868. Winthrop Chanler would retain a memory of that children's ball all his life—a memory of terrifying moments when he and Armstrong became lost amid the forest of crinolines billowing around them, and were found in a corner, clutching hands, in tears.

The Chanlers' residence in Washington ended with the adjournment of the memorable Fortieth Congress in 1869. In the 1868 election Chanler had been renominated, but owing to his opposition to Tammany's corrupt boss, Tweed, he was defeated. This defeat terminated Chanler's office holding, although he would continue to be politically active, and after Tweed's overthrow would become a sachem of Tammany Hall and participate in its rehabilitation.

In the autumn of 1870 the Chanlers and their children moved into a home in New York City, a spacious brownstone at 192 Madison Avenue, between 34th and 35th streets (on the site of the present Altman's store); up to that time they had lived, when in town, with Maddie's grandparents on Lafayette Place. The Astors were reluctant to let their granddaughter go; but advancing age had made the presence of the children a strain on the older people, and the Chanlers had already suspended their summer visits to Rokeby for that reason. The Astors' interest in their great-grandchildren had not lessened, however, and little Willie Chanler, born at Newport in the summer of 1867, had been brought to Rokeby for his christening so that his great-grandfather might see him and stand as sponsor. The baptism was performed in Christ Episcopal Church in Red Hook, the other sponsor being Laura Astor Delano, the child's great-aunt. Christ Church had become the home church of Rokeby, being less than two miles distant from the estate.

The departure of the Chanlers from Lafayette Place saddened old Mrs. Astor. She told her sister-in-law, Mrs. Henry B. Armstrong, in March of 1871, that the next time big brother came into the city he ought to bring his daughter along, since it would be "her only chance of seeing Maddie's family assembled, for they are too numerous to move in a body any where except in her own house, and Henry will tell you that they are well worth coming to town to see. The dear little baby laughed aloud all the while we were looking at her, and all were friendly except Lewis Stuyvesant, who is very shy. . . ."

Lewis was not yet two, and the "baby" mentioned was Margaret Livingston Chanler, who had actually been born in the Madison Avenue house before the entire family had moved in. Although she would live at number 192 only until she was five years old, Margaret would remember the place as vast and gloomy, heavy with dark woods and cavernous rooms. The location of the house reflected the northward drift of fashion in the city; although the older aristocracy, the Fishes, Stuyvesants, Rutherfurds, and their offshoots, clung to lower Second Avenue, Stuyvesant Square, and Gramercy Park, already Fifth Avenue was being lined with the homes of the rich. The Chanler home had been erected on Astor property, as a matter of course; the family's holdings were scattered all over Manhattan, with a heavy concentration in midtown Manhattan. Three family brownstones occupied the whole block along Madison Avenue—the homes of the Chanlers, the Delanos, and the Careys. Thus Maddie's much loved Aunts Laura and Alida were her next-door neighbors.

The philoprogenitive Chanlers produced still another child, Robert Winthrop Chanler, on February 22, 1872; and later that year they suffered their first bereavement when Emily, the eldest daughter, died of scarlet fever before her eighth birthday. Maddie felt her loss poignantly; her children had been a joy to her; she insisted that there could never be too many. "God's brightest inspiration," she called them, and maternal responsibilities she accepted lightly, almost gaily. At a gathering of ladies she took out her knitting and announced cheerfully that she was starting on her winter quota of seventy-two pairs of children's stockings.

The year of Emily's death brought a second grief to Maddie when old Mrs. Astor died, cutting a link with a world that already was alien to the bustling, pushing, dollar-scrambling New York of 1872. Maddie attested her sorrow by every conventional token —mourning veils, black-bordered notepaper, and abstention from secular amusements. This last gave her more time for domestic concerns, which were onerous, and the arrival of a new daughter in June, 1873, partially eased the poignancy of Emily's loss. This new child was named Alida Beekman Chanler, Alida being a Livingston name and also that of her great-aunt Carey next door. A year later, in November, 1874, another boy was born, the Chanlers' eleventh child, and was given names taken from Southern branches of the family, Egerton White Chanler.

In one respect the Chanler household differed radically from the home of William B. Astor. There taciturnity was the rule, but the Chanlers all talked, and they were capable of all talking together. Chanler himself favored this; he excelled at conversation, and never excluded his children from discussions of business or politics or other grown-up concerns.

This free stating of one's mind sometimes led to embarrassments. The children had often heard their father speak with abhorrence of General Benjamin ("Spoons") Butler, expressing his disgust that such a villain could ever have belonged to the Democratic party. One day Chanler and one of his sons boarded a Broadway stage (horse-drawn omnibus) in which Butler was riding, and the general's walruslike figure was pointed out to the boy, with the result that when the general started to alight, he found himself tumbling into Broadway with a small boy clinging to his ankles.

"You always said you wished he was dead, so I thought I would kill him for you," was the boy's explanation. In direct-action ways of thinking and behaving, the Chanlers started young.

In 1875 a long chapter came to a close when, on the day before Thanksgiving, William B. Astor died, aged eighty-two. Since the death of his wife he had lived humorlessly, devoting all his time to business. Five days before his death, little Margaret Chanler had been taken to visit him in the Fifth Avenue house to which he had moved, unable to endure the emptiness of the Lafayette Place mansion. The child had found him sitting in an armchair, looking no different from any other time to her; and having been told that she might cheer him up, she proudly announced her latest accomplishment, picked up from the Irish servants:

"Grandfather, if you'll whistle 'St. Patrick's Day in the Morning,' I'll jig for you."

William B. Astor did not seem to know that tune; but the jig was performed anyway.

Margaret was not taken to the funeral; Maddie did not believe in "parading her children," and only Armstrong and Winthrop attended. The services were held in Grace Church, the stronghold of Gotham society, and afterward the long procession of carriages wound through rain-swept streets to Trinity Cemetery far uptown.

The newspapers estimated that William B. Astor had left an estate of more than $100,000,000, "even at the present depressed values of real estate." (The nation was in the grip of a severe depression and property values had shrunken greatly.) When the will was opened on December 7, therefore, the public craned to see what would become of the millions left by "old Midas"—the largest fortune in America.

The bulk of the estate, it developed, was left to Astor's three sons, John Jacob Astor III, William B. Astor, Jr., and Henry Astor, with John Jacob, the eldest, receiving the lion's share. After these three, the chief beneficiary was Maddie Chanler. (In the will she was identified as "Margaret Astor Chanler, only surviving child of my deceased daughter, Emily Ward"; even in his last gasp William B. Astor had refused to sully the record with the name of Maddie's father, the wastrel Samuel Ward.)

Altogether, Maddie was left property worth about $5,000,000, including the house at 192 Madison Avenue, and Rokeby and its contents. She received in addition improved property to the value of $175,000; the income from $375,000 held in trust; three houses and lots on Fifth Avenue at the corner of 34th Street; other improved property to the value of $40,000; $30,000 in cash; one-third of another sum of $50,000; and so forth, the list rolling on and on.

The acquisition of Rokeby delighted Maddie, for there she had spent the best-remembered days of her childhood, and she anticipated eagerly returning there in the spring. But for Margaret Chanler that spring never came. The long, tiring drive in her grandfather's funeral procession, in blustery, raw weather, had induced a chill, which speedily passed into pneumonia. Immediately after the funeral Sam Ward had called on his daughter and found her already ill. But he was shocked when a telegram reached him in Washington on December 13, stating that Maddie had died that morning. Only thirty-seven, she left a grief-distracted husband and ten children, ranging in age from thirteen to two.

The saga of the Chanler pride had begun.

Cast Adrift

When an Astor died, the talk was of mourning and money. As soon as Margaret Chanler had been decently buried the consuming topic of interest was how she had disposed of her fortune. Her will, entered for probate four days after her death, was proved on December 28, 1875; and though it dealt with a conglomeration of properties and investments, essentially its intent was simple: everything was left to her husband and ten surviving children. John Winthrop Chanler received $100,000 in cash and securities and additional real estate, while the entire general estate, which included Rokeby, was bequeathed to the children collectively, "share and share alike."

There were a few personal gifts, the largest being $6,000 left to "my faithful nurse, Nancy Richards," together with the income for life from a trust fund of $4,000. Nancy had been so shaken by the untimely death of the second of her charges (Emily Ward having been the first) that her reason was affected and she lived on in a state of apathy. Donations of a few hundred dollars each were left to approved charities; the mission school and chapel of St. Mark's-in-the-Bouwerie, the Chanler church in the city, received $500, and Christ Church, in Red Hook, the same sum.

There was some invidious talk about the will's sole mention of Maddie's father, under which Sam was left an annuity of $1,000, to be paid only on the condition that his creditors should not benefit by it. The wording of the bequest was offensive, and Sam expressed himself bitterly—not against his daughter, but against the Astors at this fresh evidence of their vindictiveness.

Margaret Chanler's funeral in St. Mark's was in accord with the best taste of the period. The coffin, covered with purple velvet, was carried by the most aristocratic of old-line New Yorkers. Then the route that her grandfather's hearse had traversed a few weeks previously was traced again to Trinity Cemetery, and Margaret Ward Chanler was laid in the family vault, while attention turned to the disposal of her children.

The death of their mother was felt by these with different degrees of intensity. The youngest were hardly aware of the calamity; those older dimly grasped its significance. While their mother lay dying, the younger children had been taken Christmas shopping, in order to get them out of the house, and upon their return were told that their mother was no more. Five-year-old Margaret felt no sorrow, but exclaimed, "She has gone to join dear Emily in heaven!" Armstrong and Winthrop, however, would retain a clear-cut impression of the mother they had lost; to them she would remain a tender, gentle figure, somewhat shadowy, sincere in her religion, and in the surroundings of the nursery revealing a surprising capability for gaiety at variance with her reserve in public. Elizabeth, who was nine at the time, felt that her mother's responsibilities had devolved upon her as the eldest daughter, and this role of quasi-authority her brothers and sisters deferred to.

Margaret Chanler had named her husband sole executor of her will and guardian of their children, and in order to devote himself wholly to these cares he retired from political activity. An early removal to Rokeby seemed desirable, since that would be their home henceforward; and an unmarried cousin from South Carolina, Miss Mary Marshall, consented to assume charge of the brood. She deemed it a duty to volunteer her services, and to Mary Marshall *duty* was a word of sacred obligation. The pivot upon which her life revolved was religion, a stern Calvinist religion of inflexible principles. Yet she was kind and endlessly patient, and was imbued with a profound sense of family loyalty.

The first necessity was to organize an adequate staff at Rokeby. Two months after his wife's death, Chanler applied to the court for an allotment of funds from the children's income to meet the

Miss Mary Marshall, South Carolina cousin who was called in to mother the Chanler orphans in 1875 when their own mother died.

costs of supporting and educating them. These he estimated at not less than $40,000 a year, the total including outlays for the upkeep of Rokeby, with servants, gardeners, and farmers; the salaries of a governess for the girls, and a tutor for the younger boys; boarding school for those who were older; a nurse or nurses for the babies; a housekeeper; food, fuel, lights, and medical and travel expenses. The domestic staff called for a cook, laundress, three maids, seamstress, and butler; the outside help comprised a coachman and three grooms, a gardener and three assistants, and a farmer and three helpers. Chanler called the court's attention to the children's property, valued at more than a million dollars, and to their "high social position and station in life," which made it desirable that their education "and manner of living during their minority should correspond to the position to which it is probable [they] will each occupy upon attaining his or her majority." The court concurred, and ordered that all necessary and proper expenses for the children's support be paid out of their income.

The education of the children was a pressing concern. Armstrong and Winthrop were at St. John's Military Academy at Sing Sing, conducted by Chanler's distant cousin, the Reverend J. Breckenridge Gibson; and while that was very well as a start, Chanler felt that his elder sons, at least, should have a more gentlemanly education, such as a first-rate English school could provide; and certainly Elizabeth, as eldest of the girls, should receive the benefit of European polish. A fortuitous chance allowed a separate provision for the boys who were too young for school: on a trip home, Winthrop and Armstrong had brought a nephew of Dr. Gibson, named E. B. Bostwick, who made so favorable an impression that he was engaged as tutor for the younger boys at a salary of seventy-five dollars a month, quite a handsome stipend for the time. Bostwick was pleasant, pliant, and mild of manner, and strictly upright in his conduct; and although his educational qualifications hardly extended beyond geometry and mediocre Latin, as "Mr. Bostwick" he would remain at Rokeby for years. This in spite of the subsequent irreverent chuckling of his pupils, who were really fond of him, that the only occupation at which he ever shone was the one he took up in his old age—raising pigs.

In 1877 John Winthrop Chanler sailed for England with Armstrong, Winthrop, and Elizabeth. He carried letters of endorsement from bankers and clergymen of the social eminence of the Reverend (later Bishop) Henry C. Potter, New York society's favorite divine, and hoped to enter Armstrong in Rugby, Winthrop in Eton, and Elizabeth in Miss Sewell's select school for young ladies on the Isle of Wight. Unexpected difficulties were encountered: Wintie had passed the age at which boys customarily were received at Eton, and Archie * failed in the entrance examinations at Rugby. But after negotiation, Winthrop's handicap was surmounted, and Armstrong, although denied enrollment in the "big school" at Rugby, was taken into Hillbrow, a preparatory school conducted by a Rugby master, J. W. Vecqueray. No difficulty arose in Elizabeth's case; and after seeing all three children

---

* William B. Astor had given his first great-grandchild, Armstrong Chanler, this affectionate diminutive, and it was used universally in the family.

satisfactorily bestowed, their father sailed for home by way of Paris. His mind was at ease regarding matters at Rokeby, for throughout the trip he had received weekly bulletins from the assiduous Mr. Bostwick, reporting on current events—the children well as usual—the boys busy with their rabbits, goats, and chickens—Margaret being taken into town by Miss Marshall to have her teeth straightened—crops thriving despite the bothersome drought—"potato bugs numerous, more so than ever." The picture was reassuring.

Reaching New York in the autumn, Chanler enrolled his third son, William, in St. John's, and proceeded on to Rokeby.

There, long serious letters were arriving almost diurnally from Armstrong, and short, merry ones from Winthrop. Archie's progress was disappointing: his teachers found him mentally quick, but undisciplined and neglectful. His conduct was generally good, his French "very good," and his Latin "bad," while in mathematics he was "very backward," standing next to last in his class of fourteen. Wintie was less conspicuously either good or bad, although he obviously spent his time more congenially with Tommy, the horse his father had bought him, than with his books. He told happily how he rode Tommy bareback, and at times went fox hunting nattily attired in knee breeches and gaiters. ("Now ain't I a swell?") His tutor, the Reverend G. Hale Wortham, with whom he boarded at Shepreth Vicarage, reported that he took fences rather too recklessly ("I give him perpetual warnings on this subject"), but Wintie laughed reprimands aside. Mrs. Wortham was completely won by his infectious smile. "He is a dear happy little fellow & we are very fond of him," she wrote indulgently.

A letter penned by Armstrong on September 29, 1877, enclosed another indifferent report card, but dwelt on his athletic progress—hare and hounds and football, Rugby style—"a splendid game a great deal different from the way we play it at home," he explained. "Our side had the best of it at first but as the other side had a master with them they beat."

Entrusted to the leisurely mails of that unhurried age, this letter reached Rokeby in mid-October, about simultaneously with a note from Willie Chanler at St. John's, requesting that Mr.

Bostwick be notified that the "pea jacket got here yesterday," and asking for home news: "How is the farm getting on and the goats? How is my little calf getting on? How is all the family?"

Five days after the date of this letter to "Dear Papa," John Winthrop Chanler was dead. He had been in perfect health, apparently, but caught a slight cold while playing croquet on wet grass. He had suggested breaking off the game, but his lady opponent had objected, and chivalrously he had continued. The cold led to pneumonia, and swiftly he died, aged fifty-five.

His funeral in St. Mark's-in-the-Bouwerie, which the Chanlers deemed their family church through their descent from Peter Stuyvesant, who is buried there, conformed to the highest standards of respectability and impressiveness. Smith Ely, mayor of New York, headed an official delegation, with former Secretary of State Hamilton Fish. Various Astors appeared among the mourners, and the pallbearers included several who had fulfilled the same office for Maddie Chanler a few months before. Then John Winthrop Chanler was borne to Trinity Cemetery and laid beside his wife in the family vault. *The New York Times,* commenting upon his passing, stated that "he was much respected by persons of all political tendencies."

How to convey the shattering news to the children abroad plunged the relatives into a quandary. Finally Winthrop cousins who happened to be in Paris were appealed to by cable. The response was recounted by fifteen-year-old Armstrong Chanler in a letter composed with self-conscious care, on black-bordered stationery, and addressed collectively to "Willie, Marion, Lewis, Margaret, Robert, Alida, and Pedge [Egerton]:

"My dear Brothers and Sisters: I am very well and am trying to bear up under this great affliction, which God has seen fit to send us, as well as I can. Dear Cousin Bob sent me a telegram last Wednesday saying that he would be at Rugby that day. So I went into Mr. Vecqueray's study and waited for him . . . until the dinner bell rang and then I went to dinner telling the servant to call me as soon as Cousin Bob came. After I had been at dinner for about a quarter of an hour he came and told me that somebody wanted to see me. So I went in and found Cousin Bob. He looked rather pale and asked me to sit down. Just then Mr.

Vecqueray came in and I introduced him to Cousin Bob. He
then left me to go to his dinner. Cousin Bob then began . . .
He first told me that he had some very [bad] news to tell me, and
I asked him what, and he said that dear Papa was dead. Of course
I was nearly knocked off my feet by the blow. But Cousin Bob
comforted me and told me that I must be the strongest as I was
the oldest, and bear up against it. So I went to Mr. Vecqueray and
asked him to come in, to speak to him a minute, so he came in
and Cousin Bob told him. He seemed very much touched by it
and was very kind to me, and we all agreed that the best thing
to do was to stay as I was and work hard. So Cousin Bob and I
went for a walk and talked it over, and he was awfully kind to
me and comforted me a great deal. . . . When I got back Mr.
Vecqueray was in his study and he took me by the hand and
told me that he was very sorry for me and wanted me to make as
much of a friend of him as possible. And Mrs. Vecqueray kissed
me and told me she was awfully sorry for me. The next morning
I went over and took breakfast with her. Cousin Bob went to
Shepreth on Thursday to tell Wintie but Mr. Wortham had already got a telegram so all Cousin Bob could do was to comfort
him. Bob then went to the Isle of Wight but she [Elizabeth] had
also been told by Miss Sewell who had received a telegram. . . .
I have just got a letter from Wintie yesterday and one from Mrs.
Wortham. Wintie is bearing up very well, and so is Bessie. . . .
We are all in perfect health, and are in as good spirits as we can
afford. Give my love to Mr. Bostwick and dear Bunk [Willie] and
let him read this letter as it is for him as well as for you and I
only send it to Rokeby as you are nearly all there. Write to me
soon. How are you all. Keep cheerful as possible. From your
loving Archie."

Wintie's letter of condolence was no less earnest, although
more lightly phrased. Addressing "all the children at Rokeby,"
he explained that "I have not time to write to each of you, and
as neither Dear Bob, Lallie [Alida] or Pedge could read them, I
will write to all and you 'great big ones' can read it to the little
ones." Starting with Willie, the eldest, and addressing him by the
nickname his brothers had given him, Winthrop sagely admon-
ished:

"Remember, my dear Bunk that you are the head of the house & what a responsibility you have, and so do your best . . . and stand well in school, and never do anything that you know papa would not like. . . . Did all of you go to dear papa's funeral? Do poor Edgie and Lallie seem to understand that they are Orphans? . . . Sister Bessie, Brother Archie and Wintie are coming to you all next summer, and then we will be together again like old times, except we will not have either dear Mamma or Papa but will talk about them and try to remember them just the same as if they were with us. . . ."

In this abrupt way an awareness was implanted in these motherless and fatherless Chanlers that they had become different from other children; and that because of that difference they must cling together to draw comfort from each other. Cast adrift, denied the certainties that sustained other children, what would become of the orphans?

A Curious Childhood

John Winthrop Chanler's will was designed both to protect and to unite his survivors. One problem that had much occupied him had been how to head off the remotest possibility of his father-in-law's obtaining any share in or control over the children's inheritance. Sam Ward had never dreamed of interfering, but Chanler had dreamed of little else for a long time. Sam was attached to his grandchildren, the more so for having lost his own sons, born of his second marriage. Only rarely was he permitted to see the grandchildren at all. The older ones would remember these almost clandestine calls at Cliff Lawn, in Newport, when Sam would line the children in front of him in order of age and size and study them intently, seeking family likenesses; then suddenly would break into a smile and begin pulling presents from his capacious pockets.

Chanler's solution of the problem had been to leave control of the children's upbringing, education, and material wealth in the hands of trustees and guardians, whom he named in the will, all of whom were as averse to Samuel Ward as he was himself. Nearly all these trustees and guardians were relatives. They included four Astors—John Jacob III and his son, William Waldorf (later Viscount Astor), Laura Astor Delano, and Alida Astor Carey; Rutherfurd Stuyvesant and his wife, Mary, and his sister, Margaret S. Rutherfurd ("Daisy," later Mrs. Henry White); and Mrs. William Preston Griffin, a cousin who was the widowed sister of Mrs. Hamilton Fish and was affectionately known to the Chanlers as Aunt Tiny, an abbreviation deriving from her name, Christine, and not from her size. Among the executors and trustees named were Lewis Morris Rutherfurd and Franklin Hughes Delano.

In general, the estate was left in trust to the children in equal shares. In addition, to Armstrong was left the land and buildings of St. Margaret's home for girls at Red Hook, together with $50,000 to maintain the institution as a memorial to his mother and great-grandmother. Armstrong also received a farm, Orelot or Ravenswood, lying south of Rokeby, which Chanler had held in his own name. The Chanler children owned Rokeby jointly already, but Archie, as the eldest son, was left the contents of the house and all the farm stock and equipment, together with $100,-000 with which to maintain the property, it having been the wish of the children's mother, the will explained, that eventually Armstrong should own it wholly and live there, to perpetuate the Chanler name on the river.

Winthrop Chanler received the contents of the Madison Avenue house, which was then rented unfurnished to others for the remainder of the Chanlers' minority, and eventually sold. Wintie also received farm property in the Catskill region of Delaware County, across the river from Rokeby, and Cliff Lawn, the family's summer home at Newport. Each of the other children received a separate lot at Newport for his or her own use. Various friends were left minor sums, and $1,000 was left to Columbia College to endow an annual prize for the best student paper on a historical subject (a prize that is still awarded at each Columbia commencement). Their mother's jewelry was divided among the three Chanler sisters, and the entire balance of the estate was placed in trust for the benefit of the children, share and share alike, with one significant exception, as follows:

The trustees were instructed to set aside $50,000 for each of the three Chanler daughters, Elizabeth, Margaret, and Alida. These funds were to be invested and the income reinvested until the girls either married or attained the age of twenty-one; thereupon the income was to be paid to them directly and unconditionally, free from control even by their husbands. Since the sisters' ages in 1877 were eleven, seven, and four, respectively, these legacies would accumulate into sizable fortunes; and upon reaching legal age, each daughter would be assured of an independent income exempt from male control in a manner rarely found among women of wealth at that time.

The men and women named as guardians of the Chanler children were of the highest respectability, but their notions of how to raise a brood of high-spirited youngsters were deficient. All were middle-aged or older, and some were childless. Nevertheless, on December 21, 1877, the entire group, with the exception of John Jacob Astor, legally accepted their responsibilities; John Jacob begged off because of pressure of business, but promised to lend his counsel whenever requested.

None of the guardians could face the prospect of taking all ten orphans into his or her home, and there was anguished debate as to how to dispose them. But the very thought of being separated appalled the children, and they begged to be allowed to stay at Rokeby. Finally this was agreed, after Mary Marshall consented to stay on as the household authority. Her decision required courage, for these Chanlers already were exhibiting more than ordinary energies, and the conditions under which they would live promised to intensify their spirit of independence. At Rokeby, knowing that they were on their own ground, and in the absence of normal parental guidance and discipline, they would be encouraged in the feeling that they were a special group, unique to themselves, different even from their closest relatives.

The isolation of Rokeby was moral as well as geographical. Old ideas, remnants of a previous century, permeated the house. The visitors who drove up in stately carriages to exchange polite courtesies were mainly old relatives; old retainers manned the grounds; old ways of living were the rule. The Chanlers, too, were attached to their home by influences and impulses of which they were only dimly aware. Rokeby was their feeding ground, their hunting demesne; three generations before them had called the place home; proprietorship of the land in which it was rooted extended back to the first European settlers. Every room had associations with some forebear—the westward-facing bedroom where a Charleston relation, old Mrs. Maynard Marshall, used to sit with the girls of the household through long, hot summer

afternoons, languidly reading antique romances—the room holding the enormous bed on which generations of infants had learned
to creep—the library stacked to its vaulted ceiling with the elegantly bound residue of decades of reading, including all the
eighteenth and early nineteenth century classics—the dining room
where the specter of General Armstrong hovered at the table—
these and a hundred other shadowy associations bound the Chanlers to Rokeby ineluctably.

The guardians ruled benignly, but from a distance. Once a
month they gathered in the parlor of "Tiny" Griffin, received
Miss Marshall's monthly report, audited her accounts (always
correct to the penny), laid down policy for the conduct of their
wards, and authorized the necessary outlays. Governesses were
engaged for the girls—three Frenchwomen in a row, and then a
cultured Englishwoman whose chief pride was in having beheld,
with her own eyes, Thomas Babington Macaulay. A mousy German piano teacher made trips periodically from Vassar College
in Poughkeepsie to instill familiarity with music, and Mr. Bostwick functioned as tutor for the boys, a schoolroom being fitted
up for them on an upper floor of the tower. Bills for the expenses
of the three children in England required checking, payments
had to be forwarded, and surplus income accruing from the
funds in trust must be judiciously reinvested—not always with
fortunate results, despite the prestigious advice available. The
children's income totalled about $80,000 annually, and the guar-
dians had sought permission to spend $70,000 of it; but the court
set a limit of $30,000 a year. In consequence, there was no luxury
at Rokeby, merely an abundance of plain fare and substantial
comfort.

This suited the frugal tastes of Mary Marshall. Her overriding
concern was to instill high moral principles in her charges; do
that, she believed, and conduct would take care of itself; but
her rules for social intercourse made slight impression upon her
hyperactive group. Voices resounded everywhere in the great
house, children talking on all floors, at all hours, and all at once.
Each child was prepared pugnaciously to challenge anything
said, and to back up the challenge with arguments. Since the
disputants seldom allowed an antagonist to finish a sentence, in

these noisy debates pro and con could be heard simultaneously. The participants enjoyed their verbal battles with sensual satisfaction. There were rules, one being that there should be no hitting ("take it out in words"), and another forbade "showing off." A third provided that "a bore must shut up."

Tutors and governesses were considered fair game. William developed a fiendish talent for tormenting a French governess by throwing out such seeming-innocent questions as "Charlemagne was really a German, wasn't he?" or "I understand that German champagne is preferable to the French stuff," or "Honestly, now, wasn't Napoleon just a second-rate general who happened to have all the luck?" These depth bombs could usually be counted upon to bring on a fit of hysterics, and the children would be dismissed. This would allow them to spend the lesson time with their pets, while their baited victim slowly calmed down.

The animals housed at Rokeby were almost numberless—dogs, cats, chickens, rabbits, birds, goats, and ponies, with an occasional raccoon or snake. Whenever the children went for a walk they were escorted by a pack of yelping hounds, bulldogs, setters, and crossbreeds. Puppies were carried cheerfully for miles. Whenever there was a sick dog, some Chanler would sit up with it. Just letting the animals in and out of the house kept small feet on the go, and there were always dogs underfoot. When children and grownups gathered in the "home parlor" to sing hymns and country songs, a certain note struck on the piano would send Willie's setter bitch into a howl, but it was never banished for that. Mealtimes were animated by dogs scuffling under the table and getting kicked by legs of various lengths. And when Robert introduced a goat, Miss Marshall fled in panic, and Mr. Bostwick froze in his chair until Billy was chased out by nipping dogs.

In their self-contained community the children tended to pair off in twinlike intimacies. Lewis and Margaret, a year apart in their ages, made such a pair, and Alida and Egerton another. Egerton, a sweet-tempered, lively boy, romped with Alida all over the grounds; together they fed the snowbirds in winter, and spotted the first snakes emerging from their torpor in the spring. Alida was not as sharp in her responses as her more aggressive brothers and sisters; she had been neglected by lazy nurses when a baby, and Margaret finally had taught her to walk when two and a half years old. But Alida was imaginative, as practical-minded Margaret was not.

Margaret and Lewis were inseparable from the time they shared their first nursery together. Lewis teased her, frightening her deliciously by saying there were bears under her bed. She would dash with pounding heart past a tall armoire that he called their lair. Both Lewis and Margaret took to books when very young. Reading, either alone or aloud in a group, was a principal diversion at Rokeby. It formed an important part of the children's education, for they were given the run of the library where the shelves were thick-packed with English and French classics. Starting with fairy tales, they read their way through Victorian children's stories, such as those by Miss Yonge and Mrs. Molesworth, *The Little Duke,* and Kingsley's *The Heroes,* and so on to Cooper, Scott, Dickens, and always Shakespeare and Plutarch. Willie reveled in Marryat, while the girls wept over Little Nell. The Bible was read daily and religiously, at morning and evening prayers.

Robert was a puzzling child, unlike the others. He was not attractive in appearance, and was difficult to control, seemed absolutely averse to learning, and at nine was found trying to read a book held upside down. He played with the farm children, was rough in manner, and passionately devoted to animals, which seemed to understand him. He broke a steer to harness to pull his sled when he was very small; Marion hitched a goat to his. Impulsive and undisciplined, Robert was constantly violating the rules, coming late to meals, neglecting lessons, disappearing at church time to hunt rabbits, failing to account for how he spent his time. His originality sometimes took startling forms. When his bulldog came to grips with Willie's setter on the parlor floor, Margaret ran to the kitchen for a pail of water to break up the fight, but Bob did it quicker by biting the dogs' tails.

Signs and portents were commonplace at Rokeby and were accepted without question; second sight was a frequent manifestation. One morning at breakfast Mary Marshall calmly reported that during the night a cousin had come and stood at the foot of her bed; and nobody was surprised when word arrived that during the night that cousin had died.

The servants were an important element in the world of Rokeby. Constantly thrown among them, imbibing their ideas, adapting to their example, the Chanlers found in their dependent household a partial substitute for the parental instruction and guidance they were denied; the servants, in fact, exerted a stronger influence than any Mary Marshall could bring to bear. Most of the domestic help were Irish, recent immigrants from class-conscious Europe, and imperceptibly they imparted to the children their concepts of caste. They had very pronounced ideas about their own position and duties, and correspondingly firm notions regarding the proper behavior for their employers. By daily contact they instilled in the Chanlers a sense of superiority and self-sufficiency that would make it impossible for the children ever to doubt their own social elevation, or to condescend to persons of an inferior rank. No matter how familiarly the children might run in and out of the kitchen, the laundry, or the stables, they were never unaware that a social gulf separated them from their employes; the employes required this attitude for their own mental comfort.

The house staff comprised many types. At the head was Hade, the coachman, who had been a trooper in McClellan's cavalry during the war; he would teach the Chanlers to ride and handle horses fearlessly. Of equal authority with Hade was Mary Meroney, the head nurse. Mary, with her "tread like an empress," ruled the servants hall by weight of dignity and force of character. She came of an English family said to have "lost caste by turning Methodist," and she had made the grand tour of Europe in the service of Governor and Mrs. Hamilton Fish; her room was filled with keepsakes from every country she had visited. Nurses, housemaids, governesses, cooks, and footmen might come and go; Mary Meroney was immovable. When the children had complaints, they took them to Mary; when they had crises, she was the one who listened and pointed the way out. It was to Mary that the weeping sisters ran when they encountered man's perfidy in the form of the butler, who had borrowed their mite-box savings and failed to repay them. (This tragic experience at the age of six would give Margaret a lifelong mistrust of male servants.)

On the third floor the housekeeper, Mrs. Redmond, lived in

silent melancholy, mourning for a brother who had gone to sea and was never heard of again. Dressed in black, she moved slowly through the house, mute and solemn. The only visitor she ever had was the Methodist minister from nearby Barrytown, who came periodically to inquire after her. At each of his calls, she would hurry down to the parlor, pathetically hoping that this time the caller was her brother. Her room was decorated with faded bouquets from the steamers of crepe that were hung on front doors to signify a death within. She would never accept a ride to church, but walked, in sun, snow, rain, or heat. The housemaids scorned her as a "spiritualist" and were disrespectful to her, but she did not complain. And she taught Margaret Chanler all she knew about housekeeping. Coming upon the child one day playing at cleaning the furniture, Mrs. Redmond patiently showed her the correct way to dust, polish, scrub floors, clean windows, and tidy a room.

There were two Katherines in the servants' hall—Katherine Wallace, the seamstress, and Katherine Madden, the laundress. The latter seemed to the children to live in a perpetual cloud of steam and billowy linen. She was never too busy, though, to help a child who preferred to wait in the laundry while her soiled dress was cleaned, rather than go upstairs dirty and endure the taunts of her brothers.

The one servant who could more or less handle the obstreperous Chanler boys was Jane Cross, a former slave whom Maddie Chanler had found working as a day laborer in the navy yard at Washington. Old Black Jane, she was called, and she served as the boys' nurse at Rokeby, continuing to serve and manage them long after they were grown men. Jane had an appreciation of good manners and a sense of the family's importance. When friction developed between a haughty French governess and the Irish kitchen help, it was Old Jane's tact that calmed the storm. And when Margaret Chanler was fifteen, Jane took her aside and said in sharp reprimand:

"You too old to poke your head forward when you walk. Better begin right now and hold it up like the rest of the family."

Margaret paid heed.

Jane could neither read nor write, and though the children in relays tried to teach her, she seemed incapable of learning. Into

LEFT Mary Meroney, originally the head nurse, who became a general facto-tum and power in the servants' hall at Rokeby. (*Courtesy of Chanler Arm-strong Chapman*)

RIGHT Jane Cross ("Old Black Jane"), nurse to the Chanler boys at Rokeby. (*Courtesy of Chanler Armstrong Chapman*)

old age Jane tidied and swept the boys' rooms, kept their cloth-ing in order, and scolded them when they departed from what she deemed propriety. Her death came eventually from what she called "falpulations of the heart," although really it was pneu-monia, contracted while sweeping the unheated billiard room in the tower. Her ghost remained attached to the house, and on the anniversary of her death whoever was occupying the room below the billiard room would hear Old Jane, sweeping, sweeping.

Irish wakes were held in the servants' hall at Rokeby, and the children attended them. The stark, the grisly, and the super-natural were not kept from them; they experienced a full quota of childhood's shivery terrors. In the White Room, which had been Maddie's when she was a girl and would always be assigned to a young girl in each generation, there was a mirror in a carved frame with figures of angels holding swords, and these angelic warriors, it was well known, came down and danced on the floor "in a terrible manner" unless the fire on the hearth remained aglow. Old Jane had a clock that ticked scarily when the light was turned off, and stopped as soon as the lamp was lit.

When the children moved into Rokeby in 1876, a hot-air furnace had been installed, but this did not heat the third floor of the house, where some of the servants slept. In winter the cold there was bitter. Mr. Bostwick slept on the top floor, and during cold snaps the children would politely ask at breakfast how thick the ice had been in his water jug that morning, and he would answer politely, one, two, or three inches; the phenomenon formed a sort of gauge by which the severity of the weather was judged.

Sedate and composed though she was, Mary Marshall would join in games with the children, and she saw to it that they mastered two accomplishments deemed essential by any gentlewoman of Southern birth and breeding—card playing and dancing. Whist she approved of as a good school for manners and a useful curb on tempers. When snowstorms raged, the household would absorb themselves in whist, and in summer they would sprawl on the floor absorbed in bezique. If an argument grew uproarious, Mr. Bostwick would rouse himself from his frequent silences to referee the dispute. There were times when it might have seemed to an outsider that Rokeby was occupied by stark savages, but the only wounds inflicted in these furious word battles were wounds of mortification at having been outshouted by an opponent. Chanler voices registered several decibels higher than those of other people; and when two or more came together, they could not only be heard above the ordinary conversational din, but they might be heard in chorus, for they thought nothing of all talking at once.

Quarrels among them might last for years and flare up again periodically, to the bewilderment of persons not in the know. There was Margaret's quarrel with Robert over the ownership of a goat. The goat was his, and Margaret begged to be given half-ownership. Bob refused, and bit by bit she scaled down her request, wheedling for ownership of just a piece of the goat— its head, one leg, and finally just the tail. Magnanimously Bob agreed to this; whereupon Margaret dashed to the kitchen and came back brandishing a knife, prepared to slice off her property then and there. Amid the ensuing uproar the goat was led away, tail intact; but it was characteristic of the Chanlers that this dispute would be revived between the two antagonists intermittently for years afterward. It was characteristic, too, that no rankling animosity was left over from these disputes; and while they raged they were thoroughly enjoyed.

Sundays at Rokeby were dedicated to religion in some of its most oppressive forms. Before breakfast Cousin Mary would hear each child in a short Bible reading, and then would hold family prayers. After breakfast came the ride to church; rented carriages would convey the servants to the churches of their choice. In the afternoon there was more Bible reading, singing of hymns, and prayers again at night. No child was allowed to pull a bell rope except for firewood, the servants being relieved of all but indispensable tasks. The children were told that Sundays belonged to poor people just as much as to the rich, but they did not really believe this. Nevertheless, they conformed, although the boys would sometimes relieve the tedium by taking their dogs out on the servants' porch and fighting them, urging them on with blood-curdling yells. Nothing could be done about this unseemly racket, for the authority of neither Mr. Bostwick nor Cousin Mary extended to the servants' quarters, and a predilection for full-blooded sports was looked upon by the Irish help as a proper trait in young gentlemen.

A feudal atmosphere enshrouded all the proprietary estates strung along the Hudson, a holdover from an earlier time. Each estate had its retainers—farmers, villagers, household staff—often serving from father to son. And each estate was self-centered, alive to its own interests and fairly indifferent to the interests of its neighbors. This peculiarity further contributed to the young Chanlers' sense of being unique—a band of privileged inheritors, but not quite like the others around them.

Their sense of individual importance also was cultivated by Miss Marshall, sometimes in bizarre ways. At one point she gravely sent the children one by one to a popular phrenologist to have their cranial bumps examined; and she was gratified but not surprised by the reports, which forecast a brilliant future for each and all: one boy bound to become a statesman, another a millionaire, a third a judge or a general, while all three girls would surely marry into the nobility. The children took these predictions skeptically; they knew that some of the bumps on their heads were more likely the result of falling off a horse or out of a tree than evidence of genius. Nevertheless, the pompously florid documents were preserved, to be laughed over tolerantly in later life.

The Education of Bess

and Other Matters

The three Chanlers marooned in Europe escaped such occult insights into their predestined fate. Thrown prematurely on their inner resources, they found that coping with the present kept them occupied enough. In their different ways, all three rebounded with the resiliency of youth from the numbing shock of their father's death. Although cast adrift in a very special sense, far from home and family, their crisis was eased by relatives who took them in during vacations and watched over their progress at school. The Henry Whites were especially helpful; White was secretary of the United States legation in London, and "Daisy," his wife, was a Rutherfurd and a Chanler guardian. A kindly Astor connection was the Countess de Steurs, who was the daughter of another guardian, Alida Carey, and was married to a Dutch diplomat stationed in Paris. But the children still were mainly forced to rely on their own resources of character, and in consequence they developed a precocious self-sufficiency; as the elders of the family, they rose to their position of leadership and readily assumed the prerogatives of their promotion. Two months after his father's death, Archie was writing to the tribe at Rokeby:

"I got your sweet round robin yesterday and I thank you and Cousin Mary for writing it. I am awfully glad to hear that you are all well and are in good spirits again. I am very glad that you are going to spend the winter at dear old Rokeby with Cousin

Mary. How I wish I could be there with you around the fire in the dear old library. But I hope to have a very pleasant winter with Mrs. Wortham and Wintie and Bessie. I go to Shepreth day after tomorrow and I am in high spirits at the thought of leaving school. I got a letter from Wintie and Bessie last week and they are both in excellent health and spirits. . . . Wintie is having a splendid time hunting, he hunts on Tommy and enjoys himself very much. Give my love to all the guardians [N.B. "children" here was crossed out and "guardians" substituted] and Mr. Bostwick and Cousin Mary and Aunt Betty and Aunt Margaret and give my love to dear old Hannah and to everybody that asks about me."

On this same day the ebullient Winthrop was writing to his brother Marion from Shepreth Vicarage, on mourning paper decorated with a fancifully drawn "Merry Christmas" inside a garland of holly:

"Dear Fat: Your very nice and well written [letter] arrived here to day and please allow me to congratulate you on having attained to that high honour of long trousers. I can well understand that you are feeling 'very big' (as Lewis or Munga [Margaret] said you did) for I know how I felt the first day that I wore long trousers! How Dear Papa took me down to Brooks & said that he did not see why I was not tall enough to wear long ones instead of knickerbockers. I was highly delighted & was looking at my legs all the way home! Hope that you are enjoying yourself tumbling about on that pond & that you have not succeeded in fracturing your skull, I remain, Ever your affec't Brother Winthrop A. Chanler.
"P.S. Did you receive my Xmas card? W.A.C."

Wintie already was remarkable for his light-hearted determination to extract enjoyment from each passing moment; regardless of risks or reprimands. Once he jumped through a glass door on a dare, and after being duly spanked for this, cheerfully jumped through the door again. Long, long afterward, his daughter would recall that he enjoyed only those pastimes that involved some risk to life and limb. With his grandfather Sam

Ward's disregard for consequences, Winthrop Chanler had inherited Sam's verbal facility, radiant charm, and social ease.

Armstrong was giving the guardians cause for anxiety by his
dull showing in school. A trait that he had inherited from Grandfather Ward was reluctance to apply himself to uncongenial
studies. His teachers' impression of their far from star pupil was
summed up by the headmaster in three words: "indifferent at
best."

Elizabeth Chanler consoled the guardians somewhat. Bessie
was growing into a beauty and promised to be a social belle later
on; already she won all around her by her poise and good nature.
But about a year after her father's death, she developed a disease
of the hip that radically altered her prospects. The cause of the
malady, and even its exact nature, were obscure; it might have
been a tubercular infection of the bone, or a mild form of polio-
myelitis; the doctors sought in vain an effective treatment. With
the guardians' consent, she was taken to London for examination
by a noted Harley Street surgeon, Sir James Paget; but his obvious bafflement was plain even to the thirteen-year-old invalid,
and the meaningless banalities he murmured as he departed
plunged the child into a deep depression.

Her gloom was intensified by the drab dowdiness of her surroundings in ultra respectable Brown's Hotel, where she was
lodged. Then suddenly the whole outlook changed, thanks to her
first real meeting with her Grandfather Ward, forbidden to her
heretofore. Unknown to her, Sam had arranged the consultation
in London; he had even tried to fee the surgeon, but had been
prevented by the jealous guardians. Sam was in funds just then
and in high favor in England, where he was the guest of Lord
Rosebery and had just come from participating in Gladstone's
famous Midlothian election campaign. Because of Elizabeth's
illness (the guardians secretly expected her to die), Sam had been
permitted to see his granddaughter, and the wonder of that brief
meeting would remain with Elizabeth all her life.

There was no tiresome conversation, no dwelling on symptoms,
but a succession of marvelous presents—a ruby ring, a grown-up
woman's ring, not a childish trinket—a sumptuous traveling case
lined with maroon-colored silk and fitted with cut-glass flasks

Elizabeth Winthrop Chanler, 1877, at the time of her father's death and the start of her long illness.

capped in gilt—a camel's hair traveling robe, rolled in its straps. After each enchanting present Sam would pop into the room to enjoy her amazement, his twinkling eyes the most brilliant Elizabeth would ever see. The whole occasion she was convinced was straight out of fairyland, and all her resentment and despondency were dispelled. The handsome traveling case came into immediate use when she traveled on to Paris to spend Christmas there. Wintie and Archie were on hand, and Wintie indicated that their grandfather's munificence had been general in a report of the visit which he sent to Mary Marshall on his return to Eton in January, 1880:

"Dear Cousin Mary: I have been back at Eton since Thursday night after having had delightful holiday days in Paris. We have had a good deal of snow in Paris & also some very good skating. I went to two parties. . . . Bess on account of her leg has not returned to Ashcliffe [school] & is staying with the Steurs where she is very comfortable & happy. We got a great many presents for Xmas. Bess got from Grandpa Ward a beautiful ring of 3 rubies surrounded by diamonds & a dressing case & a lot of books & ornaments for her room. . . . Some beautiful china from Aunt Alida & Maggie, & a brooch from Aunt Augusta & a bracelet from Aunt Laura. I got a beautiful sapphire ring from Grandpa Ward —and a scarf pin from Aunt Alida & a cane from Maggie, also a large book & a brass inkstand. So you see although we are a long way off we have not been neglected in the Xmas present way."

Elizabeth did not return to the Isle of Wight. The doctors in Paris resorted to heroic measures in an endeavor, they said, to prevent a threatened permanent curvature of the spine; and for two years Elizabeth would live strapped to a board, a complete invalid. The fortitude and dignity with which she bore this agonizing treatment earned her the family title of "Queen Bess"; and well might she have claimed some spiritual kinship with Elizabeth Tudor of England. Her character crystallized during this period into a patient inflexibility that would become her dominant trait. She never whined; self-pity was never allowed to intrude; and she tried to spread cheerfulness to those around her. In fact, she seemed at times to sustain those filled with pity for her more than they sustained her. In a revealing letter written to her sister Margaret from Trouville-sur-Mer in August of 1880, her refusal to give way to despair under affliction was strikingly conveyed:

"My dearest Margaret—I hope you know the reason why you have not heard from me in so long a time. For the last two months & more I have been strapped down in a machine flat on my back & have not been allowed to write—but you will see me soon now for I am going to sail for home with Uncle John [Jacob Astor], Cousin Stuyve & Winty on the 26th of this month. I will probably go to Newport very soon after arrival. I must thank you, Cousin Mary & the boys for all your nice letters which have given me great pleasure. I have been down here a week all but one day. Of course I do not drive, but I am out on the porch all day when fine & am carried down on the lawn to look at Harry & Julian play lawn tennis. Already I sleep better & have a better appetite.

LEFT Egerton White Chanler, youngest of the children, who died in 1882.

RIGHT Marion Ward Chanler, the handsomest of the children, who died at St. Paul's School two and a half months after Egerton.

In order that I should not be jolted in the train coming here from Paris, I was put into a hammock which was slung with elastic ropes from the ceiling of the carriage. There was quite a procession down at the station to meet me, and to drive up to this house. I had a wagonette all to myself which I quite filled up with my long machine. Cousin Stuyve stayed here two or three days & then left for England but he is coming back in about 10 days to help Harry take me to England. We expect Winty tomorrow from Paris, where he has been staying with Uncle John since Eton broke up. The family here is very large & the house is full. We are eleven people in all so I am never alone. Old Mr. White is very devoted to me, he reads the newspaper aloud to me & sits with me a great deal every day. My best love to Cousin Mary & all

LEFT The young patrician and glass of fashion, John Armstrong Chanler, on his return from Rugby to enter Columbia College. (*Courtesy of University of Virginia Library*)

RIGHT Alida Beekman Chanler, left, and Margaret Livingston Chanler, about 1880.

of you. Hoping to see you before long I am your most affec'te sister, Bessie."

Elizabeth would return to New York that autumn, and while lying strapped in her apparatus at the Brevoort House she would see again briefly her "fairy grandfather," Sam Ward, and enjoy again a magical rain of presents. Thereafter their paths would diverge; but to the end of her life he would remain in her memory as someone outside the bounds of ordinary human living. That Rokeby should harbor a resident fairy did not seem impossible or even strange to Elizabeth Chanler; she had psychic intimations of her own. By 1882 her recovery had so far progressed that she could walk with crutches, and gradually she dispensed even with these, although periodically she would be forced to use a cane, and she was never strong.

Cousin Mary Marshall had fortified Elizabeth's bent toward self-abnegation by inculcating resignation to God's will. Of course she could never marry, Elizabeth was told, and Cousin Mary sadly stressed that she must never entertain even the thought of such a step. So completely was this fact accepted by the family, any suggestion to the contrary would have come as a disagreeable shock.

The year that brought Elizabeth release from total invalidism was, however, one of grief, for Egerton Chanler died that year of a brain tumor. He was only eight. Alida, his special playmate, was so affected that for a while she seemed destined to follow her brother. During her slow return to health she formed a habit that she kept a secret. In her loneliness she would steal upstairs to one of the guest rooms, ordinarily forbidden to the children, and from a westward-facing bedroom that looked out over the Hudson and far away to the Catskills she would watch the gorgeous colors of sunset, the clouds and hills, and would weave romantic imaginings about them.

Mysteriously, during this same critical period, Armstrong Chanler became ill and the family desponded of his recovery. Armstrong had returned from England and was attending Columbia College in New York, where suddenly he had become studious. Rokeby was kept in a state of tension for weeks, until the crisis of his unexplained illness passed and he slowly regained his vigor. Then, in February 1883, the family was stricken anew when Marion Chanler, the handsomest of the boys, died suddenly at St. Paul's School in New Hampshire. He had had a contest with another boy to determine which could eat the most "Turkish delight." Marion won, but became deathly sick and rolled about all night vomiting in the bitter cold dormitory, thereby contracting pneumonia. Wintie, who by then was at Harvard, had hastened to his brother's bedside at the first alarm and found him apparently past danger; but Marion died twenty-four hours later. He was only fourteen.

Because of his bearing the name of their famous Revolutionary ancestor, General Francis Marion, the South Carolina relatives attended Marion's funeral, and the calm faith of Mary Marshall helped to carry the surviving eight Chanlers through this melancholy period. By 1884 they were back on even keel, when word came that Grandfather Ward had died in Italy. With him at the end had been a well-loved nephew and niece, F. Marion Crawford and Margaret ("Daisy") Terry, whom the Chanlers had met at Newport some time before.

Archie, by this time being restored to health, was doing well at Columbia, working hard with his tutor, a brilliant fellow student named Michael Pupin. The keen intelligence of young Pupin had aroused the admiration of Lewis Morris Rutherfurd, Archie's uncle, and upon Pupin's graduation Rutherfurd and Armstrong would jointly finance Pupin's postgraduate studies abroad, first at Cambridge University in England and then in Germany.

These formative years the Chanler girls spent mainly in the city, attending classes under select tutors—French class, dancing class, and so forth. To their socially eminent aunts they seemed "dreadfully countrified," and these matrons united in the campaign to teach their nieces how to dress, walk, entertain, and comport themselves in the society in which they were destined to move. Their Aunt Lina (Caroline Schermerhorn Astor, wife of William B. Astor, Jr.) was the undisputed ruler of New York's "Four Hundred," by her fiat making and unmaking reputations ruthlessly. To her generation she was *the* Mrs. Astor, without qualification, and she saw to it that her Chanler nieces should be a credit to her imperious court. Assisting in the process were three other Astor matrons, Aunt Alida Carey, Aunt Laura Delano, and Aunt Augusta Astor, the wife of John Jacob III. The girls struggled through it all and by force of personality were not submerged.

Idyll in Rome

Bestrewn though it be with risks and wreckage, the institution of marriage is the culmination of romance, and Wintie Chanler was the first of the family to plunge into its hazards. This he did with the same cheerful abandon with which he had jumped through a glass door. The reverberations at Rokeby were correspondingly shattering.

Wintie had given ample notice of his intention, and the family had done its best to deflect him from it; in their eyes the step he contemplated could only lead to remorse and disunion. But opposition was the wrong way to influence Winthrop Chanler; naturally headstrong, he was in love, and love has a logic of its own.

The genesis of the affair dated back to 1879, although at that time nobody had guessed what impended. The prime mover, it turned out, was again that mysterious Grandfather Ward. In the spring of that year, Sam had contrived a surprise for his sister, Julia Ward Howe, on her sixtieth birthday, by arranging a reunion of the three Ward sisters, the first in many years, bringing Annie Ward Mailliard to Boston from California, and Louisa Ward Terry from Rome. With Louisa came her seventeen-year-old daughter, Margaret Terry, universally called Daisy. At Newport, during the summer of 1880, Daisy had met her cousins the Chanlers. Armstrong and Winthrop were preparing to enter Columbia and Harvard, respectively, and Daisy thought Wintie quite the nicest young man she had ever encountered. Then the Terrys had returned to Rome, and Wintie put in four years of desultory industry at Harvard, while Daisy continued her music studies at home. As a pianist she was giving evidence of considerable ability and certainly of great determination to excel.

In college Wintie set his own pace, principally as a social cock-of-the-walk. Another freshman in that class of 1885 was socially eligible Amos Tuck French; he was quite mesmerized by young Chanler's jaunty man-of-the-worldliness, his English accent, his London clothes, his nonchalance, and his sparkling wit. Upper classmen might resent Wintie's "infernal cheek" in doing such things as gaily joining in the steeplechase races at the Brookline Country Club (no sport for a "cub," it was thought), but such daring and good humor won Wintie popularity; he was chosen for the "First Ten" of the Dicky (D.K.E.) and was elected to the most exclusive of Harvard clubs, the Porcellian. As for studying, he was not above paying impoverished students to prepare papers for him, and although he piled up "conditions" recklessly, he managed, by charm and adroitness, to keep just short of a flunk-out. Wintie was perfectly aware of the privileges his social position and wealth gave him, and he availed himself of them without apology. Over an expensive cigar he once told French, with youthful impudence:

"The Chanlers were a very respectable lot of people in Charleston until the yellow splotch of the Astors stained their escutcheon." Then with a twinkle he added: "But you never would have heard of the Chanlers if it hadn't been for that yaller stain."

There were some aspects of his friend's character and family relationships that eluded French. During vacations Wintie frequently stayed in New York with his guardian Rutherfurd Stuyvesant. One evening French was taken to the house, and found Armstrong Chanler there. French was astonished when the brothers, ignoring him, immediately started ragging each other, and then had a regular wrestling match all over the floor of the billiard room. French was embarrassed and mystified; he did not know that other signs of sibling rivalry between the brothers were not lacking. Wintie seemed to resent his subordination to the older brother; he would have loved to be the head of the family, and he felt that Archie at times was deficient in that role. Archie's better showing in college also irritated Wintie, as did

Winthrop Astor Chanler, student at Harvard, about 1884. (*Courtesy of William Astor Chanler, Jr.*)

Armstrong's greater height and his impressive patrician stance; Winthrop was short, slight in build, and nervously quick in movement.

Winthrop's cavalier disdain of academic punctilio led to embarrassment when, at the commencement of 1885, the university authorities withheld his degree because of deficiencies in his record. Wintie denounced the injustice of the procedure, carrying it off with a high hand in a letter to his sister Bessie, written from New York while laid up with a minor illness:

"The chief excitement I have is a heated controversy between me and the authorities at Harvard, carried on through the agency of the U.S. mails. It is about my degree, which I rightfully & lawfully got, but which sundry blunders of the authorities at Cambridge prevented my getting at Commencement. I passed all my examinations & have a clear record of work at college, so that they must give it to me now. As soon as I am well enough I shall run on to Cambridge & beard the lions in their dens."

Winthrop seemed to be developing a somewhat martinetlike tendency, but it was not pronounced as yet. Certainly nothing of such an attitude had been visible a year previously, when he visited Rome during the summer vacation and again met his cousin Daisy Terry. (The degree of their cousinship was somewhat puzzling, since Wintie was Sam Ward's grandson, and Daisy was Sam Ward's niece.)

Louisa Ward, Daisy Terry's mother, in youth had been married to the Irish-American sculptor, Thomas Crawford, whose heroic statue of Armed Freedom tops the dome of the Capitol in Washington. Three children had been born of this marriage, the youngest being F. Marion Crawford, the future novelist. After Thomas Crawford's untimely death from cancer, Louisa was married to Luther Terry, an American painter who had traveled to Rome from Connecticut in 1833 and had never returned except for sporadic, unsatisfactory visits. Two children had come of this union, Margaret and Arthur Terry.

Luther Terry possessed a talent sufficient to bring him commissions, mainly for portraits of Americans passing through Rome; to have one's likeness taken in Rome was the stylish thing. Louisa, heiress to a comfortable fortune, had been the financial prop of the family, elegantly established in the faded splendor of the Odescalchi Palace, on the Piazza dei SS. Apostoli. The panic of the 1870s in the United States swept away most of Louisa's wealth, and the family was forced to move into a cramped apartment in the Palazzo Altemps.

This comedown made a deep impression on teen-age Daisy Terry. She recalled resentfully the elaborate trousseaus provided for her two half-sisters, chestfuls of dainty lingerie that contrasted painfully with the plain cotton underthings she was condemned to wear. As a small child, seeing her mother harassed by the importunities of the throng of lame ducks whom she supported and whose constant complaints she patiently endured, Daisy had promised herself to exclude from *her* life, as far as possible, everything that was ugly and repellent and poor. And what could be uglier than poverty? The beggars of Rome daily taught her that fact of life.

The Crawfords and Terrys, although nominally American, were solidly Italianized. The children, born and reared in Rome, speaking Italian from infancy, had little in common with their parents' homeland. Yet they were not truly Italian either, but existed in a condition of rootlessness, at ease in, yet slightly foreign to, both civilizations. Daisy Terry, steeped in European culture, had always lived in the midst of art and artists, and considered them quite as normal, useful, and unexceptional as senators or priests. This point of view, of course, was incomprehensible to most Americans of the time.

In the spring of 1884 Louisa Terry noticed in a newspaper that Winthrop Chanler was in London, and she wrote inviting him to Rome. In June he came. He was just short of twenty-one years old, abounding in vitality, carefree and anxious to please, and in a trice he rejuvenated the staid Terry household. Only a few weeks previous to Wintie's appearance Grandfather Ward had died at Pegli, near Genoa, and the family was in mourning. But Wintie Chanler was not equipped to mourn long, and his effect upon Daisy was instantaneous.

"Hazel eyes full of a merry light, irrepressibly curly brown hair, an air of great good breeding and courage in his handsome face, with a constant ripple of fun playing over it"—that was how Daisy saw her cousin. The tip of his nose had a way of wrinkling whenever a joke came into his head, which was often, and in old, old Rome he seemed incredibly boyish. He did not mind any of the drawbacks of summer in the city, neither the heat nor the fleas. In search of a little coolness the family took him to Tivoli for nights of "moonlight on the cypresses, nightingales in the laurels, soft summer wind blowing the spray of waterfalls on our faces . . . days of being utterly happy in the moment—young and lazy—the sweet, warm sense of being alive." So Daisy wrote in her enraptured diary.

Wintie, too, felt the magic. (How far this from the rustic hamlet of Tivoli beside the Hudson!) And gaily he prolonged the holiday by renting a villa at Rimini, on the Adriatic coast, and whisking them all there for a solid month. There Daisy, more matured by her education and environment than her American cousin, began to feel that she was "preparing to bid farewell to youth," as she phrased it—in plain speech, thoughts of marriage to an enchanting young man whose middle name was Astor. Had she not banished from all plans for her future the possibility of ugliness? And what was more ugly than poverty? The beggars of Rome again arose in her mind.

Wintie was simply having a wonderful time; he never looked for complications. A month of fun and off he dashed to visit relatives in Germany, then hastened back to Harvard for his final year, while Daisy waited for letters that did not come.

Two years passed before Wintie returned; but in the summer of 1886 he went abroad again, traveling with added jauntiness because he had come of age and was now himself a guardian exercising authority over his younger brothers and sisters. Their father's will had provided that each of the five elder Chanler brothers upon reaching legal age should automatically become a guardian and executor and trustee; Archie had been installed in that position for some time. From Vienna, on July 23, Wintie set down his contentment in a long letter to Mary Marshall, writing:

"As you can see from the heading of this I am still in Vienna, but my time here is drawing to a close. I shall be off to Italy in a week. The Terrys are at a place called Vallambrosa near Florence. It is in the mountains & according to their account very pleasant. . . . You will be glad to hear that I have got my degree without further trouble, which is satisfactory. Parson Lambert [rector of Christ Church in Red Hook] wrote me the other day informing me of my election as a trustee of Red Hook Meeting House. I accepted of course, for I think the closer corporation we make it the better. . . . Had a letter from Daisy the other day. All are well. . . ."

And just after this Wintie did drop down on the Terrys at Vallombrosa, in the mountains, and the way of a maid with a man, and vice versa, was resumed.

Armstrong Chanler was with his brother. Both young men were doing Europe as persons of independent means, out for a good time and having it. In a gesture of bravado befitting their years, they had stopped at Genoa on their way and had driven out to Pegli to inspect the grave of Grandfather Ward. Taking along a bottle of the best wine they could buy, they stood beside the grave, each took a sip from the bottle, and emptied the remainder on the grass.

At Vallombrosa there were no intrusive tourists, just a few old acquaintances of the Terrys' rusticating in the country hotel. Life moved placidly, time drifting by, and Archie himself seemed on the point of yielding to the romantic spell of the place and his cousin; but at the close of summer it was to Winthrop that Daisy became engaged.

The news was flashed to Rokeby by means swifter than a letter, and it was September 15 before Wintie sat down to write dutifully to Mary Marshall; he and Daisy were then staying with the Marion Crawfords at Sant' Agnello di Sorrento, across the bay from Naples:

"My dear Cousin Mary: You will have heard the news . . . so there is no need of my dwelling on it. . . . I hope you are pleased & even if you are not now, I know you will be as soon as you see & know Daisy. What a lucky man I am! . . . I wish America were only round the corner so that you could all see her. As it is now we shall not be home before May or June. I want her to see Rokeby first in the spring & early summer, for she is not used to the cold. We intend to be married on New Year's day if possible & then spend the rest of the winter in the south of Spain. That is all I can write now for I have so many letters to write. Love to all the kids & give us your blessing. . . . By the way, you may be surprised that it is me & not Archie who is going to marry Daisy. The reason is easily explained. Archie made a mistake in his own feelings. I know I have not."

But there was a difficulty; and although Wintie dodged alluding to the obstacle, he knew what it was. And he was determined to surmount it. The obstacle had to do with religion: Daisy Terry was a Roman Catholic. And to compound her undesirability at Rokeby, she was a communicant of the Roman Church not by reason of birth, and hence absolved of personal predilection for gross error, but by her own choice, fervently expressed. This had come about naturally, in view of her Roman birth and Italian upbringing. Her parents had remained rooted in their Protestantism; but the cold fervor of the Anglican ritual, the plain

Margaret Terry ("Daisy," afterward Mrs. Winthrop Chanler) at seventeen, when she first met "Wintie."

hymns and generally lackluster setting of the English church outside Rome where the Terrys complacently worshipped, left their children cold. Daisy Terry had grown up hearing the bells of Rome ring in the year-round cycle of religious pomp and drama, and it was natural that she should find fulfillment in that church. Her mother had been distressed by her conversion, and one of Sam Ward's last kindnesses had been to comfort his sister in her grief and prevent any breach between mother and daughter.

At Rokeby, however, Winthrop's announced intention to marry a Catholic created a shudder of revulsion. Catholics were tolerated in the kitchen; nobody oppressed them, of course; one just pitied their ignorance and misfortune; but in the front of the house they were *déclassé*, definitely out of place. Wintie knew the storm his choice would raise, and he punctiliously fulfilled every family obligation in an attempt to lighten the blow. Coming home specially to mollify the Rokebyites, he found the family sorrowful and immovable; not only did they reprehend his choice, they feared his own eventual contamination. Not that there was any real danger: the Chanlers were Episcopalians traditionally and that settled the question for Winthrop personally; he took religious questions as lightly as he took most of life's concerns. Nevertheless, when he headed back to Rome the family loaded him down with tracts bearing titles like *Plain Reasons Against Joining the Church of Rome;* these he never bothered to read, but he had a good laugh over them with Daisy.

She had made her own overtures to the relatives at Rokeby during Wintie's absence; but her letters, while well meant, were stiff and self-conscious. The equally reserved reaction did not alter her determination to marry Winthrop Chanler quickly. Wintie was as eager as she.

Three dispensations were required to achieve the speedy marriage the young couple desired: first, because marriages were not customarily celebrated during Advent; second, because of their consanguinity; and third, because Chanler declined to agree that all children of the union be reared in the faith of their mother. Family pride, descent, and inheritance all were involved in his attitude, and a compromise was arrived at whereby the daughters should be reared as Catholics, and the sons as Protestants. Wintie's charm and Daisy's determination succeeded in overcoming the other two obstacles, and on December 16, 1886, they were married in the French church of St. Louis in Rome.

The honeymoon was spent in Algiers, a place which after a few days they voted a bore. Escaping by steamer to Marseilles, they met Archie there (he reported to his sisters that both looked "as well as I've ever seen them, Wintie as rosy & fresh as a girl, looks younger than ever"); dashed across to Italy to spend some time with the Terrys and Crawfords at Sorrento; and then by way of Paris and England sailed for home at the end of May. In June they reached Rokeby, and were accorded a decidedly chilly welcome.

Mary Marshall was narrowly religious, even bigoted in her Calvinism (although she would have been shocked by the word); but she was conscientious, and she was resolved to do injustice to no one. Rather than countenance any ill-speaking, she laid down the rule that Daisy must not be mentioned by the children among themselves. Daisy herself stood up to the ordeal of meeting her husband's embattled relatives courageously, supported by the poise which her more extensive experience of the world gave her.

Her first impression of Rokeby and its occupants was one of dismay. To her the Chanlers seemed a race of barbarians laboring under a strange delusion as to their importance in the scheme of things. The cultural influences that had shaped and enriched her character were unknown to them; their manners were countrified; the girls dressed like dowdies; and the boys were rude and bumptious, more taken up with their barnyard pets than with things of the intellect or gracious living. To a musician with Daisy's training, the Rokeby repertory of one hundred and twenty-six songs and hymns known by heart and sung in rotation was pathetically ludicrous, while their ignorance of contemporary political, artistic, literary, or scientific trends was appalling. Their vigor of speech shocked one unaccustomed to such liberty of expression. When, for instance, at dinner Robert burst out that hairs from the English governess's wig were falling into his soup, Daisy squirmed, but nobody else paid any heed.

It was all bewildering to Daisy, but she coped with it loyally. Her own training had been so different that the constricted values of Rokeby frustrated her; it was all so dry, so meager, so provincial. Only gradually did she come to understand that she had married into a family of essential primitives, who lived by standards not only of another civilization but, in part, of another age. And only gradually and painfully would she come to comprehend the toughness of the personalities comprising her husband's furiously individualistic family.

On the point of religion Daisy encountered frigid opposition. Miss Marshall bore her presence in prim silence; the boys paid the matter less regard; young Alida was secretly thrilled, without daring to say so; Elizabeth was smoothly polite but inwardly disapproving; and Margaret was irreconcilable. Margaret was not introspective; she was practical and expressed herself best by action; and for her the barrier between herself—between all Rokeby, for that matter—and the superstitions of Rome was not to be explained away or talked out of existence; no sophistry could justify so gross and perverse a departure from truth.

The appearance of Rokeby itself irritated Daisy Chanler almost as much as its occupants. The heavy, tasteless furniture was

ABOVE Rokeby, front entrance hall. Photograph taken by the staff of Stanford White when he was planning renovations in 1894.

LEFT Robert Winthrop Chanler, about 1885; unruly, boisterous, sensitive.

clumsily placed, and the finest room in the house, the drawing room, with tall windows opening ontó the lawn and the magnificent river view, was never used except for funerals. During August, while the family was at Lake George, Daisy carried out a rearrangement more to her own taste. She opened up the drawing room, brought in her piano, added flowers and book stands, and converted it into a pleasant sitting and music room. When the family returned, she was in possession; and after getting over their shock, they generally approved the change. Not so the implacable Margaret. To her the drawing room had been sacred to the memory of her parents; her mother had ranged the chairs in rows along the walls, and Daisy's innovations were a desecration. When the family gathered there of an evening for music and cards, Margaret would withdraw into the "home parlor" across the hall, and sulk there in silent reproach. From time to time one of the others would join her, trying to cheer her up, but she would not be cajoled.

Wintie Chanler took both his wife's irritation and his sister's obstinacy light-heartedly. Riding, shooting, tennis, or swimming kept him occupied while he and Daisy awaited the birth of their first child. Julia Ward Howe came from Boston for the event, and under her auspices the baby arrived on September 30, 1887, and was promptly christened Laura in honor of the Chanlers' Aunt Laura Delano. But when the christening was performed by a Catholic priest, Margaret was horrified, and she told her brother Lewis that it would have been kinder to have "smothered the little creature in its innocence at birth." She refused to remain in the same room with the child, and if it were brought in, she would walk out. Yet in her heart affection struggled with principle, and she confessed to Elizabeth that she loved Laura more than anything in the world, but couldn't show it. At night she would steal into the nursery and kiss the baby as it slept.

One uncensorious friend Daisy did find at Rokeby, and that was fifteen-year-old Bob Chanler. Bob, with his erratic ways, his refusal to learn, his obliviousness of rules, had become something of a family problem; he seemed to be lacking in the traits expected in a Chanler. He shared the schoolroom in the tower with Lewis, and was stubbornly unamenable to Mr. Bostwick's most earnest efforts to instill some formal learning. Bob just didn't seem to fit in, and he was full of surprises. Left alone in the tower one day, under orders to write a certain number of lines as a penalty for inattention, he drew instead a well-proportioned horse on the blackboard. When Mr. Bostwick returned, he asked who had drawn the figure. Bob, fearful of incurring a fresh penalty (for his lines were not written), mumbled something about Woods, the butler. Woods was summoned and denied all responsibility. Just then Wintie happened in, and to settle the question he suggested that Bob draw another horse. Bob did so, drew the figure well, and the mystery was solved—with another punishment for Robert, but no comprehension by anyone that he was giving expression to an unguessed talent.

Another surprise provided by Bob was the enjoyment he derived from Daisy Chanler's piano playing. He would listen in rapture to Bach fugues as she played them over and over. When she tried to find out what fascinated him in this intricate music, which was not relished by his brothers, she drew out, in stammering phrases, that it revealed to him a world of beauty; and by beauty, she gathered he meant a rhythmic pattern—constant change recurring within a fixed frame. A Bach fugue meant colors to him, he said; it made him think of things he had never thought of before. Then he would dash off to hunt rabbits or romp with the farm lads, unwilling or unable to tell her any more.

At the approach of winter, a milder climate than Rokeby's was recommended for Daisy and little Laura, and in November the Winties moved to Washington, to sample the social and intellectual atmosphere prevailing along the Potomac. For Winthrop the location promised to be ideal—cosmopolitan society in town, and plenty of riding and fox hunting in the nearby Virginia hills. But in those hills was a developing drama that would involve him deeply. Of that, however, neither he nor any member of the family was yet aware.

The World Beckons, and

Goodbye to Cousin Mary

The saga of Armstrong Chanler entered upon a more vital and brilliant phase (he hoped) when, after taking his M.A. at Columbia in 1884, and being admitted to the New York bar a year later, he set sail for Europe as a man of independent means in May of 1885. The idea of practicing law bored him, and he embarked upon the grand tour as the proper finishing education for a gentleman of the beau monde. Being already an original, he had improvised a variation on the classic theme by postponing Europe for a while, and heading west, where for several months he stalked the elusive Apache chief Geronimo with the troops of General George Crook. Then wheeling about, John Armstrong Chanler left New York for London, amply provided with introductions, fortified by awareness that he was young, rich, and privileged (his annual income ran well into five figures), and attended by a valet to look after the luggage and take care of other "beastly details."

His stateroom on the liner *Adriatic,* he cheerily told his sister Elizabeth, was a modern marvel—"a perfect luxury, no smells, no stuffy air, & electric light which I can turn on or off at pleasure which burns all night. Its light is soft & as good as gas." Until further notice his address, he reminded, "is & will be c/o Junius Morgan & Co., 22 Old Broad St. E.C. London."

In England the doors of the great world swung open for this overseas visitor at the touch of well-placed relatives. Also, the influence of his lately deceased Grandfather Ward was still potent.

With the nonchalance proper to his age Archie informed his brother Willie, stuck at home:

"I took some letters I had from Mr. Mailliard to Lord Rosebery. He was a great friend of Grandpa Ward's. Ld R wrote me a very nice note & I found him to be, as far as I could judge from first sight, a very pleasant & clever man. Lady R was a Miss Rothschild, enormously rich & enormously fat."

The second time he was the earl's guest was at luncheon. He met Lord Houghton, "a very nice old gentleman & asked me for my card & address. He knew Grandpa Ward very well. He is a little man with large blue eyes & a fringe of gray hair running from his cheeks to his chin and around it."

To be sought out by the elegant, fashionable, and fastidious Earl of Rosebery, dandy, dilettante, future prime minister, was a compliment falling to few transatlantic travelers, and Armstrong did his best to live up to the distinction. He attended a reception at the Foreign Office given by Lord Granville, and saw the Prince and Princess of Wales—he a "good natured looking fat rascal & wore a gorgeous uniform. The Princess is very handsome & looks very nice."

The turnout affected by the diplomat in whose carriage he arrived aroused Archie's envious admiration—"shiny boots, gloves & well tied tie. I notice he is treated with great respect by all the swells that are presented to him." The girls caught his young man's eye, and he conceded that they had lovely figures, but thought they could not compare with American girls in style or looks. Their coiffure he did not like. "They are doing their hair in the most unbecoming way. It looks like a coil of overgrown angle worms at the back of their head."

Willie Chanler was regaled with a report on Archie's run up to Cambridge to see his protégé, Michael Pupin:

"He nearly fainted on seeing me. He didn't know I was in England. He is looking very well & has grown a black pointed beard which improves him. I stayed with him until this morning. He has very nice quarters & is very happy there. . . . Pupin spends the summer studying at Edinburgh & Glasgow & goes to

Berlin in the winter. You needn't say anything about this to anyone outside the family. He is getting on very well."

Day after day of delectable entertainments filled June and July as young Chanler savored the lingering charm of that mellow afternoon of Victoria's reign. Then he sped to Paris by the night train, tormented by fleas ("the most uncomfortable journey for its length I have ever made"), and after paying homage to the Louvre and Napoleon's tomb, explored the Bois in a rented carriage, voting it a "very pretty place but don't equal the Central Park."

The summer was topped off by a visit to the Terrys at Sorrento, swimming, sailing, and lazying in the sun; the "clear metallic look" of the air reminded him of "a cool clear day at Newport."

Feeling the tug of home, in September he went back, only to take off again on a voyage to the West Indies and South America. In the party were Winthrop Chanler (his marriage still in the future), young Oliver Hazard Perry Belmont, and two chums. Stops were made at St. Thomas and Martinique (that island Archie was amazed to find as green in February "as Rokeby in June"), and they sampled the exotic foods of the tropics, including yams and bread fruit. The results were disappointing.

"A yam cooked looks like a potato and tastes like castile soap," was Archie's verdict, while bread fruit tasted "exactly like the mash of ground corn soaked in water which we feed chickens. We didn't order any more bread fruit."

Two months were spent unsatisfactorily in Mexico, Wintie assuring Cousin Mary that that country, although the very "garden of the Lord," was defiled by its inhabitants. Then at Caracas the group separated, Winthrop and one companion, who had had "quite enough of the tropics & South America for the present," taking off for Europe, while the other three moved on to Panama. There the heat and primitive discomforts were too much for Belmont and his chum, and they sailed north to San Francisco, leaving Armstrong to press on indomitably to Ecuador. Landing at Guayaquil, he made the hazardous trip inland to Quito, across mountains, through rain jungles and past the forbidding peaks of Chimborazo and Cotopaxi. Quito was good for a stay of several weeks; the hotel was clean and comfortable, and the food excellent and amazingly cheap.

Then Europe and the serious business of life beckoned, and a few months later Archie was settled in Paris, attending lectures at the Sorbonne and embarked upon an ambitious attempt to bring his baritone voice up to concert pitch. But several months of strenuous endeavor convinced him that the latter task was futile, inasmuch as nature had not provided him with a vocal organ capable of the refinement he aimed at. He abandoned the experiment, and advised his sister Margaret, who was off on the same quest, to do the same.

Returning to the United States, he dropped by Newport and Rokeby—put in a season enjoying the conviviality of his numerous New York clubs, of which he had joined half a dozen (the Union, Century, Democratic, Manhattan, Tennis & Racquet, and that most exclusive assemblage of bloods, where family standing took precedence over other qualifications, the Knickerbocker Club). He took a turn at athletic sports, showing marked proficiency as an amateur boxer; then, a well-turned-out clubman, traveler, and man-about-town, in 1887 he drifted toward Washington, where the Winthrop Chanlers were establishing themselves in a house at 1347 Connecticut Avenue. There was visiting in the countryside, and Archie was invited to spend Christmas at Castle Hill, the ancestral seat of the Rives family, in the fashionable horse country near Charlottesville.

Armstrong had met the eldest Rives daughter, Amélie, at Newport during the previous summer. It had been her first season, and she had attracted much comment by her extraordinary beauty and reportedly extraordinary ways. Amélie Rives had artistic and literary talents; she had had a poem published when she was fifteen, and she was already at work on a novel; Armstrong was told that he would figure as the model for the hero. Wintie heard the rumor and was amused by the prospect of "Brog," as the family called Archie, making his bow as the beau ideal of a young girl's moonings.

Wintie was experiencing mundane annoyances, including the financial pangs produced by wedlock. "Hard up as Blazes," he confided to his Harvard chum, Amos Tuck French, at Tuxedo Park. "Marriage & house furnishing play merry Helbore with one's nice bachelor income, as you probably know." But his gaiety did not forsake him; it was not in Winthrop Chanler to worry for long; and by that Christmas he was saluting the members of the clan gathered at Rokeby (not overlooking the dogs, Gex and Shot), with no trace of anxiety:

"Dear Family: You must be satisfied with the compliments of the season this year for I can't do any better by you. For the first time since I came of age I find myself very poor as far as the ready money goes. However, you dear boys, I know will be *quite* content with my blessing. As for the girls, I believe there is something for them. . . . The baby & Daisy are very well indeed & send love & Merry Xmas to you all. The baby was not as coherent in expressing the wish as I could have wished, but still her meaning was pretty plain. Give my best love to Gex & kick Shot all round for me."

Shortly after Christmas, Armstrong headed back to Paris, to resume attendance at the Sorbonne, while Wintie and Daisy Chanler settled into the social life of Washington. Righteously determined to reform his desultory habits, Winthrop applied himself to a course of serious reading. The taste for good literature inculcated at Rokeby would never leave Wintie, but now he proposed to introduce some system into his reading. As a help toward this he commenced keeping a diary, carefully endorsed "Strictly Private." The first entry was made on February 4, 1888; it set forth praiseworthy intentions:

"*Incipit* . . . This is the hundredth time—more or less—that I have begun to keep a diary. Never have I gone longer than a month & rarely so long. This time, however, I shall start upon a different principle. My own private affairs shall be mixed up with those of others. Probably the affairs of others will predominate, for my own are, as a rule, far from interesting."

He then recorded his own first "private affair":

"Today made inquiries about a horse at Burne's the feed man. He says I ought to get one for $200."

Acquiring horses (and all too frequently making a bad bargain) would be a recurrent theme in Winthrop Chanler's life.

On February 8 Daisy and he entertained, and he recorded:

"Our first dinner of any importance. Went off very well thanks
to the chap from the Russian Legation . . . The guests:
    "Mr. & Mrs. Cabot Lodge
    "Mr. & Mrs. Lloyd Bryce
    "M. de Ströve, the German minister
    "Miss Tuckerman
    "Miss Hobson."

Appended was a comment concerning Henry Cabot Lodge,
who, although serving only his first term in the House of Representatives, was already being spoken of as a rising figure in Republican circles. Wrote Chanler:
    "I think I like C.L. less every time I see him & Mrs. L. more."
Wintie could not foresee that Cabot Lodge would become one
of his most intimate lifelong friends.
    And so the time passed, with dinners, dances, and parties, all
"very jolly." On February 18 there was another note about Lodge:
"He improves very much on acquaintance."
    Then on March 8 an entry spelled "finis" to a long chapter in
the Chanler family chronicle:

"Cousin Mary Marshall died on Wednesday Feb 29th after an
operation for gall stone. I went to New York on Thursday the
first. Found the girls [Margaret and Alida] very brave, but looking pretty well worn out. Funeral on Saturday . . . On Tuesday
night left New York with the two girls. We are going to keep
them with us for a week or two. . . ."

Elizabeth Chanler, visiting with the Crawfords at Sorrento, and
Armstrong, in Paris, were notified by cable. All the Chanlers were
keenly sensible of their loss. The example of calm perseverance
in the performance of duty, of devotion to principles, and of
patient piety set by Mary Marshall would remain with her charges
for life; unfortunately, her removal also removed one restraint on
their tempestuous temperaments. Now that she was gone they
realized in greater or less measure how lonely her life had been,
and it seemed in keeping that she should have died on the lone-
liest day in the calendar.

The period of mourning prescribed for his cousin enabled Winthrop to devote more time to that promised serious reading. For a starter he had taken up Horace, and found a reading companion in a secretary at the British legation, Cecil Spring-Rice.

Spring-Rice was young, witty (too witty for a diplomat, as time would show), and he proved entirely sympathetic to the Chanlers.

Margaret and Alida, meanwhile, adhered rigidly to the etiquette of mourning, confining their outings to church-going. Wintie escorted them happily enough, and usually slept through the sermons. What to do with fifteen-year-old Alida, who was sentimental, and eighteen-year-old Margaret, who was practical and opinionated, posed a problem for the guardians, Winthrop included. Rokeby without the presence of a chaperone was unsuitable. Temporarily the girls were placed in the care of the Rutherfurd Stuyvesants in New York, and Wintie was released to go on with his reading. He took time out to entertain his admired great-aunt, Julia Ward Howe, when she came to Washington to lecture on Greek literature; and he sweated out one hectic weekend when Willie Chanler came down from Harvard with two chums, one of whom "spent Sat night in jail for simple drunk," while the other was "bounced from Kernans theater," and Willie was "slugged by the barkeeper for calling him Gustave." Winthrop set down the events in his diary, adding in laconic relief: "Willie left this afternoon."

Throughout all this he pursued his search for a good saddle horse, and finally was able to state, on April 16: "Bought a bay gelding . . . this A.M. for $190"; only to amend this three days later: "The new horse has corns & contract hoof but goes sound. Still think he'll do." The seller had refused to take the mount back.

This acquisition had been made in preparation for a riding trip through western Virginia to the Caves of Luray in the Shenandoah Valley. A party of congenial young people had been made up, including Spring-Rice, and a feature of the trip was to be a stopover at Castle Hill to meet the now suddenly celebrated Amélie Rives. The novelette on which she had been working had just been published in *Lippincott's Magazine,* and it was creating a furor. Not for years had a book so shocked, scandalized, and enthralled the reading public; its sales soared. And the point that interested the Chanlers most was that Archie really had been the model chosen by the "fair authoress" for her hero.

Wintie of course had lost no time in reading the book, titled provocatively *The Quick or the Dead?*, and he recorded his impressions in his diary with "strictly private" candor. On March 23 he noted:

"Read the first chapter of Amélie Rives' 'The Quick or the Dead?' Very well written & bids fair to be interesting." But regarding a portrait of Amélie and an interview with her at her home that appeared with the story in the magazine, he fairly snorted:

"Beastly portrait of her . . . & also vulgar article called 'Some Days With Amélie Rives' by a fellow named Hurrell. Describes her bed and bedroom. Horrid!"

At this point Wintie's eyes gave way temporarily ("too much use at night by candlelight") and he did not get back to the book until five days later. When he did so, a decided entry was made in the diary:

"Finished Amélie Rives' 'Quick or Dead.' A most sensual bit of rot. Presumably a love story but not a decent bit of love making in it. Distinctly horrid, & when one thinks it is written by a young girl it fairly makes one sick. Brog is the hero—very well drawn. Wrote & told him my opinion of the book but reserved my opinion of the authoress . . ."

Disapproving but doubly curious, Wintie and Daisy and their merry companions set out in May to meet the purveyor of this bit of "sensual rot."

PART TWO

Pursuit of Happiness

Of the Perils That Lurk
in Virginia Hills

If Winthrop Astor Chanler was never wholly oblivious of his patrician origins, Amélie Rives could match him ancestor for ancestor. The Rives were allied with the most of the Old Dominion's proudest families. Amélie's grandfather, William Cabell Rives, had studied law under Thomas Jefferson and had been a United States senator and twice minister to France. His son, Alfred Landon Rives, Amélie's father, had been born in Paris, and Lafayette was his godfather. Marie-Amélie, Louis-Philippe's queen, had stood godmother to Amélie's aunt. During the Civil War, Alfred Landon Rives had served as chief of engineers in the Virginia forces, retiring with the rank of colonel. Since the war he had been active in engineering projects abroad, and in 1887 and 1888 he was in Panama supervising railroad construction.

Amélie had been born in Richmond in the midst of the war. She was fortunate in *her* godparents, her godfather being Robert E. Lee and her godmother that aunt who bore the name of the Queen of the French, and passed it along to her niece. Amélie had been reared in Mobile, Alabama, and at Castle Hill, the family's country seat in Virginia's Albemarle County near Charlottesville. Her education had been erratic, under a governess who taught little but encouraged reading. At a precocious age Amélie became a devourer of books, and early showed a facility for phrase-making. She had a quick intelligence and great sensitivity, and had been humored in the indulgence of whims sometimes fanciful, sometimes morbid. She would shut herself in her room for days and pour out a stream of poems and stories, some of which found their way into print; and in 1887 a book of her tales, *A Brother to Dragons,* was published, drawing some critical acclaim. Public curiosity was piqued by the rumors of her bewitching beauty as well as her odd ways. As a small child, it was said, she had been given to strange imaginings that frightened her playmates. Once, wandering in the woods with another little girl at twilight, she had asked wistfully, "Do you think if I drank a whole cupful of warm, bubbly blood, I would see a real fairy?" Her playmate fled. Then there had been the period during which she suffered anguish over the thought that Satan was banished from Paradise *forever;* she had prayed with tears that ultimately he might be pardoned and readmitted to celestial bliss. Weaving such fantasies had led to her writing fiction of a moody, intense, passionate sort.

Armstrong Chanler had been decidedly attracted to Miss Rives at Newport in the summer of 1887, and that autumn one object of his visit to Virginia had been the hope of seeing her again. The hospitable Rives had invited him to Castle Hill, and the acquaintance had ripened until Archie sailed back to Paris. Then in April of 1888 Amélie's novel, *The Quick or the Dead?,* had appeared, and overnight she became a celebrity.

Her book was indubitably scandalous—so scandalous that it sold three hundred thousand copies, an enormous sale for the day. Situations and subjects that were taboo in current society she dealt with either boldly or by innuendo. The plot concerned the emotional writhings of a hysterical young widow (remarkably resemblant to the authoress) who was torn between orgiastic craving for the embraces of her deceased husband and carnal attraction to his flesh-and-blood cousin and physical double. The heroine swung from whimpering submission to "pantherish" paroxysms of passion in the privacy of her bedroom, while wavering between the living and the dead wooer. The setting of the story was recognizably Castle Hill, and the model for the dual hero (real and spectral) was recognizably John Armstrong Chanler.

The mood of the tale was set in the opening lines—"There was a soughing rain asweep that night, with no wind to drive it, yet it ceased and fell, sighed and was hushed incessantly, as by some

LEFT   Violet-eyed Amélie Rives at the time of her marriage to Chanler.

RIGHT   John Armstrong Chanler, 1888, at the time of his marriage.

changing gale." And the impassioned tone held to the very end, when the heroine dismissed her living lover in spite of his plea to "think of my kisses—of the way you have clung to me—of the way you have kissed my hair, my eyes, my throat—as I kiss you now!"

Such hyperbolical fervor raised an outcry among moralists, and *The Quick or the Dead?* was denounced in countless letters to newspapers, while the publicity flowered and bore fruit. And equally naturally, the idea of having the Chanler name associated with such frenetic frothings was distasteful to Winthrop Astor Chanler.

Anybody could perceive that the model for the suggestively divided lover in the book was plainly Archie, the description of his appearance being precise, although poeticized: "curling brown hair above a square, strongly modeled forehead; eyes the color of autumn pools in sunlight; the determined yet delicate jut of the nose; the pleasing unevenness in the crowded teeth, and the fine jaw which had that curve from ear to tip like the prow of a cutter" —it was Archie to the life. Wintie Chanler hardly relished having his brother's teeth flaunted publicly, and his irritation was not lessened by the qualified charm which the author assigned to her dichotomous hero—"delightful in manner, abrupt, frank, original, and a trifle egotistical."

It was with a well-settled prejudice, therefore, that Wintie and his cavalcade cantered up to the stately columns of Castle Hill to meet in person the perpetrator of all this "sensual rot."

The visitors were received hospitably, with simple good breeding, and the effect produced by Amélie was described by Daisy Chanler as "dazzling." Especially the effect produced upon the men. According to Winthrop Chanler's wife, the lovely authoress had "the largest dark blue-grey eyes; the longest black lashes; the most wonderful halo of loosely curled ash-blonde hair; very regular features, and a shapely, well-curved mouth." The only defect that Daisy could detect was a slight lack of height, but this shortcoming was artfully concealed by the "romantic white tea gown that draped and flowed from her shoulders in the most becoming fashion." The poised young lady (Amélie Rives was twenty-five) seemed "full of life," and spoke with a "slight Southern drawl that was attractive," and Daisy readily paid the bewitching creature the tribute of calling her "a siren, a goddess, perhaps a genius . . ."

The party rode away in a daze—especially the men.

The Bride Wore White

and the Family Saw Red

In the Astor connection there was one name that was never spoken. That name was Henry Astor. Henry was the third son of William B. Astor. His elder brothers, John Jacob Astor III and William, Jr., had assumed the responsibilities expected of them in the business and social world; but Henry, who detested society and loathed business, had rebelled. A great hulking fellow, given to flying into ungovernable rages, he liked the country and uncouth ways. For years he had lived in a gardener's cottage on the Rokeby grounds, despised by his brothers, despaired of by his parents, and avoided by his sisters, but acclaimed as a good fellow in every alehouse for miles around. There were those in the family who thought that Henry was not "all there," and anyway he was a disgrace.

Henry fell in love with Malvina Dinehart, the buxom daughter of a farmer in Rondout, across the river from Rokeby, and suddenly, without notifying his family, he married her. His brother William raced up from the city to prevent the marriage but arrived too late, so that to the ignominy of the match was added the mortification that Malvina had retained her dower rights—the only woman who ever married an Astor in the direct line and kept them. The practice was to settle a handsome sum on the Astor men's brides in exchange for waiving their dower rights in the Astor estate; thereby control of the Astor wealth was kept firmly in Astor hands. Henry's action was considered as worse than folly, as a kind of criminal defiance, by his family, and old William B. in anger had revoked a $350,000 bequest he had written into his will for Henry and cut him down to a paltry $30,000. Not that Henry was in any way impoverished; his grandfather, the founder of the fortune, had left him a quarter interest in the Eden farm, which John Jacob had purchased for $25,000 and in less than a century would be valued at $20,000,000. (The farm took in the area between Broadway and the Hudson River, from West 42nd Street to West 53rd. Just north of this tract, running from West 53rd Street to West 57th and also west to the river, was the Cosine farm, another Astor property that John Jacob had obtained at distress prices.)

Henry Astor and his wife were cut off from all recognition by his immediate family. His formidable income was remitted without comment from the Astor estate office every quarter, and he would deposit the checks whenever he got around to going to the bank, which was not often. Malvina and he settled on a farm east of Rokeby, where he cultivated his tastes—hobnobbing with the farmers, wrestling the young men and fighting their elders in and out of court while simultaneously paying their debts. He liked to preach sermons in his parlor, the floor of which was inlaid with $20 gold pieces, and he would announce the oncoming of one of these homilies by smiting a large gong. The country people liked him, though they suspected that he was crazy. Once or twice the Chanler children had been taken to gaze upon their mythical great-uncle, but the acquaintance went no further. But whenever some marriage occurred without due formality and previous family discussion, the specter of "Henry the Forgotten" would arise to haunt the entire connection, near and remote. Marriage ceremonies and marriage settlements were Astor rites, and in that tradition the Chanlers had been educated.

Shortly after returning from the Virginia riding trip, Winthrop and Daisy Chanler moved to Rokeby for the summer; the upkeep of their Washington establishment was draining their income, and they were thinking of returning to Italy to economize.

At about the same time Armstrong Chanler returned from Paris, and again he was entertained at Castle Hill. Wintie began to hear rumors that his brother was seriously enamored of the siren of Virginia, and the furtiveness of these rumors was displeasing. The truth, though Winthrop did not know it, was that Archie had proposed several times to Amélie and had been turned down; but now at last they were engaged and were debating how to break the news and avoid the rash of publicity that probably would follow. The press had been describing the temperament of the bride-to-be as akin to molten lava, and word of her intended marriage would be sure to be seized upon as an excuse to print "a lot of stuff" from the thought of which Archie recoiled.

Late in May, 1888, he wrote to his sister Margaret, who was at Rokeby, hinting at some mystery and saying that he wished to consult her on "an important matter"; he asked her to meet him in New York in a few days.

"Don't show this [letter] to anyone," he cautioned; "just quietly come to town. Tell Lewis I want him to bring you. Don't tell Alida, she isn't needed. . . . Don't get scared there's nothing serious. Just say to the Winties & Alida (if they question you closely) that I wanted to see you in town & Lewis can bring you down."

Needless to say, Margaret answered this mysterious summons with alacrity, proud that at seventeen she should be taken into her brother's confidence. After meeting him in New York, she continued on with him to Castle Hill. And there she incontinently fell under the spell of Amélie Rives.

The sequel unfolded in swift order through the public press.

On June 1 a brief announcement appeared in a Richmond newspaper, which was picked up by a newspaper in Baltimore, and thence reproduced in *The New York Times* on June 3, under the headline:

MISS AMÉLIE RIVES TO MARRY.

Her fiancé was identified as "Mr. Archie Chandler, grandson of John Jacob Astor." It was added that "Mr. Chandler lives in Paris."

If there was one thing that would cause a Chanler to shudder, it was misspelling the name with a "d." Wintie was outraged; especially when the *Times* still had not got the name correctly in a fuller account carried two days later. This report said that news of the engagement had been received in Richmond social circles "with some surprise"; the wedding, it added, would take place in the autumn.

Meanwhile, no word from Archie arrived at Rokeby, and speculation grew feverish. A week went by, and then an undercurrent of gossip surfaced in the *Times,* in a column of society chatter, to this effect:

"The engagement of Mr. Armstrong Chanler [thank heaven! at last!] and Miss Amélie Rives has excited no end of gossip. The simultaneous announcement of Miss Rives' engagement to Mr. Coolidge of Boston was rather confusing, but those persons who know Miss Rives would not have been surprised at the announcement of her engagement to six men, for it has been hard to decide which of the small army with whose individual members the fair authoress, it is understood, has carried on a more or less desperate flirtation for some years, she would finally choose. . . . Mr. Chanler [ah!] is something of an athlete, and was educated in England. Through his mother he inherited a handsome fortune. . . . Miss Rives by this marriage will become a member of the Astor family. She has always been an extraordinary young woman. As a young girl she was fond of shutting herself up in her room for some days at a time, subsisting on strong tea and bread and writing epics on the Deluge and kindred subjects. She is an accomplished horsewoman and is in the saddle most of the day when at home in Virginia."

A notorious and desperate flirt about to be grafted onto the family tree! This was not the sort of thing the Chanlers could face with equanimity, and Brog's mysterious silence seemed to them insulting. To make matters worse, Armstrong unwisely consented to be interviewed by a reporter for the *New York Herald,* while snubbing other papers. This of course produced exactly the effect Archie had hoped to circumvent—a rash of highly fanciful, vulgar publicity.

The unseemliness of the whole affair raised the hackles of Wintie Chanler. He was not even mollified by the *Herald*'s spelling the family name correctly (without a "d"), thanks to Margaret's prompting the interviewer.

The temperature at Rokeby was shooting up toward the boiling point when another laconic dispatch published in *The New York Times* stated that a marriage license had been issued at Charlottesville on that day to "Amélie Rives, authoress, and Mr. John A. Chandler [that damned 'd' again!] of New York." The date was June 13, and the county clerk had been sworn to secrecy, with predictable results. And the very next day, June 14, 1888—without a word of notification to any Chanler, Astor, Winthrop, Stuyvesant, Rutherfurd, White, or any other blood relative of the bridegroom—the wedding was celebrated at Castle Hill.

Wintie fairly erupted when he read the newspaper accounts. These made no attempt to disguise the surprise which the hurry-up wedding had occasioned in Virginia, inasmuch as "some weeks ago it was authoritatively announced that the marriage would take place in the fall." The attributed reason for the change of plans was that "the sensational stories of newspapers determined Mr. Chanler [correct at last!] and his lady upon an immediate and strictly private marriage."

The ceremony had taken place at two o'clock in the afternoon in the drawing room at Castle Hill.

"The only persons present," the *Times* reported, "were Mrs. Rives, the mother of the fair writer of weird stories; Misses Gertrude and Dalay, her sisters; an uncle, Mr. William Cabell Rives of Boston, who gave the bride away; Miss Lou Pleasants, and several cousins. The bride's gown was of white silk cut high in the neck, with long sleeves. She wore diamond ornaments. The sisters also wore white, and the mother wore black."

To the bridegroom ("a rather handsome man, with a decided English accent") was attributed a desire to correct the statement that he was a millionaire.

"I have some money," he was quoted as saying, "but I am not a millionaire by any means."

In only one newspaper was there mention of any member of the Chanler family being at the wedding, and even in that "Miss Margaret Livingston Chanler," without further identification, was listed simply as among those present. The bride's father was in Panama and could not attend, it was explained, but he had been informed of the wedding in a "fully descriptive cable." To the Chanlers no message had been sent.

The family was humiliated, and Winthrop was too angry to

trust himself to write to Archie immediately. He fumed for five days, and then wrote to Margaret, in response to a naively rapturous letter from her:

"If ever two people deserved a good spanking, those two are Brog and you. Of course, you were but as putty in his hands, and backed him up in his absurd mysteries—but still your own commonsense, if no other feeling, should have told you that he was quite wrong in what he did. . . . You could write to Mr. Morris [the family lawyer] and tell him to be sure the 'd' was left out of the name, etc., etc.—and yet you could not send one line or word to any member of your family so that we could drink the bride's health. . . . All of us at Rokeby heard it from an outsider & the daily papers. Of course Brog, like Sir Andrew Aguecheek, will have fifty 'exquisite reasons' for it all. He always has. It won't make much difference now what he says. It is all over the country that not a single member of his family knew he was going to be married so soon. That don't look well does it? I am glad he is where he is so appreciated, for his stock is below par up here. I cabled the news to Bess [at Sorrento] lest she too should hear it through the newspapers. Alida [visiting in New Jersey] wrote me a piteous letter today asking for news—What news can I give her? That you will leave Va. in a week? Another little point for you & Brog to digest at your leisure is this. The outcome of his sublime and fatuous predilection for mystery is that as your name was only in one paper the great majority for whom he poses think that no member of his family was present at his wedding. You can draw your own inferences. This is all I am going to say on the subject except that it is useless to tell Amélie anything about it. She has nothing to do with it, and need not be made uncomfortable."

Of course Wintie did say more—pages of it. On receipt of a pitiful letter of exculpation from Margaret he scolded her again:

"Your reasons for not letting us know are precisely what we all supposed them to have been. Of course we all knew perfectly well that you wanted to send us word & that Archie would not let you. . . . It was your business to fight any such proceeding on his part with all your might. . . . The Rives had a perfect right to wait till after the wedding before cabling the Col. if they so wished. They had plenty of relatives in the house to back them up in anything they chose to do. Besides, there were half a dozen ways in which Brog could have let us know the day before if he had wished. He could have written or telegraphed in French. . . . The whole trouble is that he apparently looked upon the family in the same light as the public—with a strong preference for the public. I am not going to discuss the matter further as regards the disagreeable position he has seen fit to put us all in and its result in the eyes of the world of whom he seems to stand in such dread. Nor am I going to discuss the utter fizzle of his attempt at secrecy. I will simply say that he has done the very thing of all others he should have not done under the circumstances & that he has hurt the feelings of his entire connection on this side of the water in a way that though they may say nothing yet will make them show it for a long time to come. In the most important epoch of his life he has made a fool of himself and hurt his wife in the eyes of the public. . . . I will write to him as soon as I can talk of something else."

Hoping to calm the strife, Daisy Chanler took a hand, congratulating Archie on his and Amélie's happiness, but pointing out that "you do not seem to realize in the least how very keenly we all felt your treating us as if we were mere outsiders to be classed with reporters and other noxious and inquisitive bipeds. The news of your marriage was known to hundreds of people before it reached us. Aunt Caroline Astor was here . . . and said: 'Well, I hear Archie is being married.' We naturally poohpoohed the thing as a newspaper story. The next day the 'Herald,' 'Times,' etc., confirmed the fait accompli, not until Monday did we get any news from Virginia and in the meantime we had a stream of visitors who could none of them fail to be surprised at our being left so totally in the dark.

"Poor Bunch [Alida] has cried her eyes out several times feeling that you do not care for her. The boys are all vexed and affronted. Wintie and I try to make the best of the matter, but for several days we could not trust ourselves to speak of it. Your announcement that you will stay in Virginia all summer, read aloud at table last night, reopened the wound, poor Bunch's tears rolled down her cheeks into her strawberries. . . . Mr. Bostwick has just returned from Baltimore, quite worn out with dodging questions as to why none of the family were present, and he told Wintie last night that you really ought to know how the farmers and people here are talking. . . ."

There was just one way to save the situation, Daisy advised, and that was for Archie and Amélie to put in an appearance at Rokeby quickly, and in this way counteract the talk of a family division.

"You have got yourself into this false position," Daisy put it frankly, "and you owe it to the family to get yourself out of it."

When at length Wintie did write to Archie, he was bitingly sarcastic:

"Dear Brog: Just a line from an outsider to disturb the bliss of Armida's garden. Ask for and read the two letters I have written to Margaret in the name of the Rokebyites and use your own judgment about repeating the contents. Love to Armida. We don't want any cuttings from the Herald or any other of your friends the journalists.

"P.S.—The weather here is very warm, 93 in the shade today. I wonder if you wouldn't find it cool in spite of the thermometer."

To which Armstrong instantly replied:

"Dear Wintie: I have just received your note of June 21st, and I shall want an apology from you in writing before anything further can pass between us."

The diversionary dogfight of a Rokeby Sunday afternoon had reached a satisfactory yapping stage.

A Dubious Conquest

The honeymooners put off their visit to Rokeby for several weeks, not because of any reluctance on Armstrong's part to face the family's frown; it was Amélie who begged off. Margaret Chanler had left Castle Hill aglow with heroine worship of her glamorous sister-in-law, and Amélie had posted letter after letter to her, counting her as the one ally she could be sure of in the strangers' camp. Taken literally, these letters would have seemed to indicate that Amélie viewed her induction into married life as a prelude to tragedy; but it was not alone in fiction that Amélie's flawless penmanship would flow in torrid, torrential phrases.

Writing from Castle Hill on the 30th of June, after two weeks of connubiality, she poured out her mood to her "dear, *dear* Sister":

"Yesterday I was so tired and worn out body and soul, that I simply curled up in bed all day and my mother read to me. You will never know my Margaret, the comfort your little note brought me. It was like a kiss on a bare and aching heart, and the tears came into my eyes and stayed there as I read it. God has given you to me Margaret—has given us to each other, and you do not know how humbly thankful I feel to him, or how I think of you with almost every breath I draw. No matter what happens, no matter how life may widen or contract for us both, we have each other, and so much sweetest and best of all—love each other

with all our hearts. God has let you save me from the very pit of
gloom, and grief, and terror. I will remember it all my life with
thanksgiving. . . ."

And so on and on this fortnight's bride continued, in a deluge
of words covering ten, fifteen, two dozen pages of exquisite paper
engraved with Amélie's cipher (an "A" and a "C" interlaced,
which was Archie's cipher, too), the paper having "just arrived
from Tiffany," she noted parenthetically. Strewn throughout were
forebodings—premonitions of some desperate ordeal, "some terrific
blow," that they all were going to be called upon to undergo
soon. "I think my mother and Archie feel it too, and something
tells me that you did. . . . Darling, darling Margaret—I wish your
dear strong arms were tight about me. . . . Everybody misses you
so—you do not imagine—even the servants—while your name is on
my mother's lips from hour to hour. . . ."

Two days later came another anguished appeal from Castle Hill
("Oh! Margaret, pray for me!"); and by the middle of July Margaret, who meanwhile had sailed for Europe with Alida, was being
pursued by such expressions of mingled fear and endearment as
"My darling Sister of Charity—(which means Love)"; and "Archie
brought your dear, loving letters, and the precious and touching
mementos of your dear ones and the Rokeby they lived in. Oh!
Margaret—How I wish you or someone who loves me could be
there when I first go. . . . I *dread* Daisy. I am not afraid of anyone, but I *am* afraid of treachery, oh! so tremblingly afraid. . . .
Archie and I are going to Rokeby about the middle of August
and then to Portsmouth to stop with Arthur Carey. . . . I never
had anything quite so distasteful to do in my life, but duties
aren't to be shirked, are they dear? . . . Please write whenever
you can dearest, & *not* on thin paper. It hurts my poor old eyes
so dreadfully. . . ."

If anyone had intimated to John Armstrong Chanler that his
bride was hysterical, he might have met with tacit agreement, although Archie would never say so. Amélie was bound by no such
reticence, however, and the letters she continued to pour out to
Margaret, especially, were filled with insinuations that she had
given herself in thrall to a madman. But an acute observer, on the
scene, might have noticed also that no matter how she agonized

with pen in hand, Amélie's physical hardihood seemed in no way affected. Her grasp on the reins when she put her stallion Usurper over a five-barred gate was firm and emphatic; yet in her letters she was a poor thing, a madonna of sorrows, sobbing for love and pity:

"Margaret, tell me as though you were my own sister as well as Archie's, have you ever thought in the bottom of your soul, that Archie's mind was not quite right? He laughs at me in such a dreadful way at times, until I am crying & trembling with terror. And the more I cry & beg him to stop or to tell me what is the matter, the more he laughs. Oh! Margaret, Margaret, write to me darling. Pray for me."

There had indeed been scenes between these two high-strung, sensitive, imaginative personalities. Archie's mockery at times had driven his own sisters to tears, and Amélie was not attuned to the violent horseplay of Rokeby. She had been all her life the star of a never ending drama, supported and encouraged by her adoring relatives, and the adjustments required by marriage she was unwilling or unable to make. Both she and Archie were strong-willed, and neither had practiced self-discipline. After each turbulent falling-out, Amélie would dash off a harrowing account of the indignity to Margaret, full of hyperbole ("Margaret, what I have suffered no earthly power can describe!"), set down in flawless calligraphy:

"Margaret, you know how I love you. Oh! pray for me for Christ's sake, that I may be guided to do what is right. Pray for poor Archie too. . . . Don't tell anyone of this my darling. Alida of course is too young, & Bessie does not know me. . . . My little sister of Love, Good Night!"

A change came in August, when Amélie laid aside her timorousness and with Archie descended upon Newport. Immediately she basked in a blaze of social homage. Amid the glitter of society and the adulation of people of warranted wealth and position, she was exhilarated. Young, beautiful, and a best seller—it was a heady wine that was poured out for her, and she responded brilliantly. Archie was proud of her.

The ordeal of Rokeby still lay ahead, and it was fortunate that

Amélie knew nothing about the sarcastic quips that Winthrop Chanler was passing to his chum Tuck French in anticipation of her arrival. Wrote Wintie:

"My brother J. Armstrong Amélie Rives Chanler and his consort are expected up here for a few days, and I am reading 'Titus Andronicus,' 'The Curse of Kehama,' and 'Ten Nights in a Bar Room' so as to have a little ready conversation of a literary turn."

Amélie was at her histrionic best when, about October 1, she and Armstrong reached Rokeby, and the siren spell produced its usual effect: Rokeby was conquered. Wintie was still nursing his grudge against Archie, but he was too instinctive a gentleman and far too well bred to be other than gracious to his brother's wife, and the visit passed off famously. Far from proving a "dragon," Daisy Chanler got along excellently with her sister-in-law; both were intellectual, both were widely read, with similar cultural interests; both loved worldly society. As for the Chanler boys, Willie and Lewis were bowled over by the sweeping eyelashes and the melting gaze, while sixteen-year-old Bob wrote to his sisters abroad, his spelling shaky but his sentiment solid:

"Amélie has arrived. She was not feeling very well & did not come to dinner; I know that I have not seen anybody that can hold a candell to her in the way of looks, & besides she being very religius, I do not know what more we can want in the way of a sister in law."

Lewis reported similarly, although with more restraint, as became a nineteen-year-old budding barrister enrolled in Columbia's school of law. He had met the bridal couple in New York on their way to Rokeby, and had dined with them, Wintie, and Willie at Delmonico's. Amélie, Archie, and Willie then went on to Rokeby, while Lewis was detained in the city for another day, and he told Margaret:

"I got to R. [the next] night but Amélie was not well & was not down nor did she appear until next day at lunch. After lunch until six she was receiving the 'county families.' I had to leave in the midst of dinner to go to Barrytown & did not see her again until lunch on Sunday & I left for N.Y. Sunday evening so you see I have hardly seen her at all & have had no chance to talk with her to speak of. But it would be impossible for me to like any one, after so short an acquaintance, better than I do her; nor is there any one whom I am more anxious to get to know—not because she is Archie's wife but because she is so thoroughly unaffected & charming."

Archie's report to those overseas was jubilant:

"All goes well. Amélie has had success wherever she has been. We got to Newport Sept. first and . . . went everywhere, to dances, dinners, and luncheons. The papers were full of Amélie & all complimentary. They couldn't have been anything else about her looks. After ten days or rather two weeks we went to Arthur Carey's near Portsmouth, N.H. It was cold and wet up there & Amélie was anxious to get here so we left. . . . *Every*thing is all right. . . . Lewis & Willie & all were here & every one of the boys likes Amélie. She likes them all & Daisy & she are close friends. . . . You don't know how delighted I am to be able to say that Amélie is a success with all here. It is the greatest relief to her & to me."

When the couple departed for Castle Hill, taking Daisy and Wintie with them for a week's stay, Bob reported glumly:

"Rokeby is looking quite desolate, all the leaves have fallen off & everyone has gone away."

But for the conjugal pair the Indian summer of harmony did not last. Wintie's eyebrows very soon had cause to shoot up with an I-knew-it expression of smugness, and the anxieties of the absent sisters were rekindled when word came that Archie and his wife had decided to spend the winter apart. Although they both insisted that the separation would be temporary only, the tension it bespoke was apparent. Margaret got the first word, from Amélie, who wrote on November 15 from Castle Hill:

"My dearest, sweet Margaret: I am so glad to be able to tell you, that the worst is over, for the present at least. Archie agrees fully with me that for the present it is much best for him to go abroad without me. I am not going to write of him any more after this letter, because I want to be perfectly loyal to him. I *had* to tell you, so that you would not think me shirking my duty. Think of how he has made Bessie cry, & then know how I have been tortured. Oh! Margaret, no one but Christ, our blessed Saviour, knows the unutterable tortures that I have endured."

The dike having been breached, the pellucid penmanship flowed on:

"You know of course that life is ruined for me. My chains cut and gall me at every turn. I am to be a prisoner (God knows a willing one!) in my old home. I have promised Archie to sign a paper to the effect that I will not go away from Castle Hill for two years, also to sign one giving him permission to remain abroad two years.

"Since then however he has spoken of returning in the spring. He has been *very* sweet & kind this last week, but perhaps you know he turns in a minute. Oh! Margaret what awful, cruel, insulting things he can say.

"Never let him dream that I have told you this Margaret. Just accept his statement that I am staying here to write a book this winter for which I have been offered $25,000. It is true, but of course only part of the truth.

"Oh! Margaret, Margaret—give me of your strong love, and sympathy, and help. I am in such despair and anguish . . . I do not believe that things will ever come right between me & Archie. I hope sometimes, but no sooner is the hope born than it dies miserably. . . . Good-bye, good-bye. Oh! My heart aches so. Pray for me. Pray for poor

"Amélie."

The pledge not to write further on the subject held good for three days. Then the freshet broke out of bounds again, and Margaret was informed:

"I know that it will rejoice your heart to know that Archie and I are 'perfect friends' again, understand one another absolutely, and both entirely agree that to be separated for a while, is the best thing for us.

"He is like a different man—like the old Archie I used to know. He says that he thinks he must have been possessed of a devil to behave as he did. I think so too—honestly. His face didn't look like his own. It was frightful—so malignant and half smiling. Oh! it is such blessed peace now. The parting will of course be very sad, but we are both *convinced* that it is best, and I have not yet quite recovered from my terror—(not of *this* Archie but of the Archie I have seen at times)."

Armstrong put the matter more straightforwardly to his sisters. He wrote from Castle Hill on the eve of his sailing that "it is undoubtedly best for Amélie to stop here this winter both on account of the rest it will be to her nerves, which have been on a tremendous strain for over twelve months, & for her writing. I ought to, and want to, see you all, so I go abroad. The rest to my nerves will be most refreshing after the strain I have been on since I first set eyes on Amélie. . . . People will of course talk and say 'separation' & prophecy trouble. What people say is a matter of infinite indifference to both of us. Other people can misunderstand us until they are tired of it or begin to get some sense. . . . It is an affair between us & no advice or talk can be of the least use. So cheer up. Everything is all right."

Then he tossed his sisters the budget of news from home:

"Willie Chanler is here [at Castle Hill] now. Has been here several days . . . away tomorrow, I the day after. We go to Rokeby soon and sail he & I in the Bretagne next Saturday for Havre. We spend a few days in Paris and then run on to you. Won't it be jolly. A regular family party. The rest are all well & are at Rokeby. Wintie & Daisy rent their house in Washington & go to Italy in February, stay at Rokeby until then. Lewis is getting on well in law. Bob & Mr. B. leave Rokeby when Daisy does, what the two will do then I don't know, it has not been decided. Amélie joins me in love to you. . . . Yr loving bro J.A.C."

Of course unsought advice *was* showered upon the disagreeing newlyweds, and Amélie's letters took on a tinge of asperity when she assured her "sister in Love" that although the latter, true to her principles, had spoken "from the heart" in recoiling from the notion of a separation:

"But, my dear one, I have learned much in the past few weeks, and this first of all, namely, that it is disastrous and impossible for anyone, no matter how true and loving, to advise a woman in regard to her husband, or a man in regard to his wife. . . . Archie and I understand each other *absolutely*. You can leave our future to God and to us."

The firm hand on the reins spoke there.

Willie and Some Home Thoughts

William Astor Chanler had emerged from the chrysalis stage of growing up endowed with more energy and drive than most of his energetic clan. Left far behind were such juvenilia as this 1880 appeal to Cousin Mary Marshall from St. John's Academy:

"I have not had a letter for a whole week and I have been looking for one every day; why don't you write? Please send a dollar for the speculum as soon as possible. . . . The bicycle has not come but I expect it tomorrow. McClelan's father [the general] was up here last Thursday and admired our picture of Hancock very much. [General Winfield Scott Hancock was the Democratic candidate for President that year.] The picture cost 10¢ and the banner 25¢ but as I did not pay for any of them it did not make any difference to me. Have you heard the bad news from Ohio & Indiana [states voting early—and Republican]? But New York [he hoped] is still democratic."

George Brinton McClellan, Jr., was Willie's roommate and shared his tastes. "There is a book coming out in monthly parts that might interest you," he alerted Willie from the McClellan home in New Jersey—"Pugilistica, or the History of British Boxing!" Such communications crossed others of sedater import from Willie's female kinfolk, solicitous for his spiritual welfare and social guidance. From Newport ten-year-old Margaret would write doggedly: "Today is Sunday & we have just come from church.

Their was an ordanation and the first thing we had was the sermon bishop clark preached. Afterwards their was communion
& Cousin Mary staid." And guardian Alida Carey would add her
gentle caution: "About going with other boys' parents who may
invite you, it depends entirely on who they are, so I want you
to ask Dr. Gibson's permission each time & tell him that I would
be very pleased for you to go *if* he approves of it."

Five years later, at restless eighteen, Willie was posing prob-
lems for his older brothers, by then guardians themselves and
youthfully aware of their grave responsibility. Winthrop did his
utmost to keep Willie in the path of virtue—so deftly avoided by
Wintie himself at the same age. When Willie rebelled at a summer of cramming at Newport for the Phillips Exeter examinations, and agitated for an increase in his allowance, Winthrop
lectured him roundly:

"As for the argument my having $1750 at your age it does not
hold water, for I lived at New Port & New York on $600 with
greater expenses than yours are now. . . . You are put at New
Port not because it has a Casino where you can meet boys your
own age—not because it is a fashionable watering place—but
solely because [the tutor] is there. So the sooner you make up
your mind to bury yourself in your books for the next 6 or 7
weeks and shew us that you *can* work, the better it will be for
you. . . . Make friends with Virgil, Homer, and Chauvenet for
the next few weeks and try a little self-denial."

While Wintie went off to watch the America's Cup match that
year (the English challenger *Genesta* being defeated by the American defender *Puritan*), Willie did apply himself—just enough to
pass his tests, to Wintie's surprise. But a few weeks at Exeter
demonstrated that the place was not for William Astor Chanler,
and in the spring of 1886 he hied south to hunt in the Florida
Everglades. The rigors of wilderness life he found entirely to his
liking. Certainly it was a far cry from the placidity of Rokeby.
From there sister Elizabeth reported such amenities as "the excitement of this week has been a fair in Mrs. Aspinwall's Sunday
school house. They have some pretty things for sail & the prices,
wonderful to say, are very reasonable. . . . This is a very untidy
letter but Bob is struggling over his Collect next me and It is

rather disturbing. We are reading Mansfield Park by Miss Austen & like it as much as her best. It is, I am sorry to say, the last of her novels that we have not read. We are reading aloud with Alida Hawthorne's Tanglewood Tales. They are so prettily told."

In the Everglades, Willie wrestled alligators and longed for bigger game.

That autumn Willie passed the Harvard entrance examinations and matriculated at Cambridge, and the guardians voted to give him the same allowance in college that Wintie had received, $1,600, plus money to furnish his rooms and pay a tutor "if necessary."

When Willie set off for Harvard, he took with him a fourteen-year-old lad named George E. Galvin, the son of the gardener at Steen Valetje, the Delano estate near Rokeby. George was a product of the feudal society of the region. One day his father gave him the simple command:

"You go with Willie Chanler and do everything he says."

Thereupon that became young Galvin's program for living. He turned his hand to whatever was required; he slept in Willie's rooms, ran errands for him, shared in his escapades, and filled the roles of valet, secretary, confidant, and factotum with remarkable adaptability and address—a perfect Figaro. But in many ways Willie Chanler himself was an eighteenth-century man.

At Harvard Willie proved a desultory student, reading for his own enjoyment and taking nothing too seriously, unless it was his developing passion for horses. He was elected to his brother Wintie's club, the Porcellian, and his collegiate ambition became to play on the college polo team, but the expense of providing horses was an obstacle. In the summer of 1887, however, he circumvented that handicap by making a trip to Arizona with his brother Archie and rounding up a carload of wild mustangs and shipping them to Boston. There they were broken to saddle, and enough were sold profitably to pay expenses.

Throughout his days at Harvard, Willie looked forward to the time when he would become twenty-one and gain his freedom of action. That release came on June 11, 1888 (three days before Amélie and Archie were married), when he was in his sophomore year; and without ado he bade Harvard goodbye. He was out for adventure, and in December of that year he sailed for England on the quest for danger and excitement that he would never abandon. With him he took George Galvin.

For the Chanlers, 1888 was proving to be the year of dispersal. With the removal of Mary Marshall, the guardians had been confronted by the problem of how best to dispose of the four remaining minor children—Lewis, Margaret, Robert, and Alida. Elizabeth, having come of age in 1887, was on her own, accountable to nobody for the use she made of her considerable income. This was intensifying her natural self-reliance, as it would also in the case of her sisters. That Margaret and Alida should remain at Rokeby the guardians thought inadvisable. Nor was New York felt to be the proper milieu for them yet. After "much thought and deliberation" (so recorded in the minutes), the watchdogs of the girls' well-being decided that they had better be entered in Miss Sewell's school at Bonchurch, on the Isle of Wight, the same that Elizabeth had attended.

Archie, about to sail for Europe, volunteered to see his sisters safely bestowed, and in a burst of generosity the guardians allotted both girls special allowances to pay for "gloves and ribbons" and suchlike fripperies. Margaret was granted seventy dollars a month for this purpose, and Alida twenty dollars; but then, Margaret was expected to share.

(Lewis Chanler, studying law at Columbia, at this time was allowed seventy dollars a month for "clothes, amusements & traveling expenses," while Robert, at home, was forced to content himself with fifty dollars.)

It was partly to discharge his responsibility toward his sisters that Armstrong sailed in December of the breakup year, the sisters having preceded him to pay a visit first to the Henry Whites, at the embassy in London. With Archie went Willie Chanler, not as a dependent and subordinate, but embarking upon his manhood. In London the brothers rejoined Margaret and Alida; Elizabeth, meanwhile, had come on from Sorrento, and there was a grand family reunion abroad that Christmas.

Christmas had always been a high festival at Rokeby, but that year the outlook was rather bleak, with five members of the family absent. Daisy and Winthrop were at the estate, marking time until they should return to Rome in the spring, and Robert and Mr. Bostwick were with them. Lewis came up from the city on the weekends, for he loved Rokeby and its countryside and spent only such time in New York as was unavoidable. But despite the depleted family, it was the set wish of those on hand to celebrate Christmas as it always had been celebrated there. The ritual was feudal and traditional, and to share it with those absent Wintie started a Christmas letter to the "dear girls" on December 17:

"All the compliments of the season to you! May you have a merry Xmas & a happy New Year!" Then he listed the holiday preparations under way at Rokeby. "The baby is to have a small Xmas tree to which all the children on the place are to be invited. They will receive sundry presents & their parents will drink a glass of champagne, munch a slice of cake & pocket $5.00 with my blessings. . . . D[aisy] & Robert are upstairs playing billiards. Mr. B. also above reading the New York Times & trying to find out why Harrison was elected [President]. . . . Tomorrow is a guardians meeting which I attend. Jex has the mange and has been banished until cured. . . . Robert goes to church every Sunday & Lewis ditto when here. All are well & send love & greeting. Affectionately, W."

And Rokeby was merry on Christmas Day, although everyone felt that something was lacking: there was no Cousin Mary, and thoughts would reach out toward London with a pang, remembering the Christmases when they had all been together.

As the winter progressed, Winthrop grew restless. To occupy the time, he reopened his diary, which, in spite of good intentions, he had neglected since the previous April. On New Year's Day, 1889, he made a fresh start, setting down the eventful year's many happenings:

"The house in Washington is to let for 5 months. . . . We are living at Rokeby with Robert & Mr. B. The girls are in the Isle of Wight under Miss Sewell's wing. Archie & Willie are also abroad. Amélie is at Castle Hill. We, that is D[aisy] & I, go abroad in Feb. or Mar. for several months. . . . I am reading Pepys Diary which D. gave me for Xmas & have finished the first Volume. As old Pepys would say, 'It is very well writ & as good as anything ever I read in my life.'"

Decidedly, country life was not gay. On January 12 Winthrop wrote:

"Got up at 9:30 as usual. I must contrive to rise earlier, as this late lying abed does hurt my health and makes me stupid all day. I intended to ride the roan in the morning but did not because he had another attack of colic. . . . Walked with D. a while & then wrote [a letter] about Cliff Lawn, which does badly, not paying expenses even. . . . After luncheon walked to Red Hook & saw Parson Lambert about the girl from the Home [St. Margaret's orphanage] & told him how inefficient & ill taught she is. He told me the shoe man has intrigued with —— the banker's daughter —he is a married man—& that one followed them & found them at it in his (Parson L.'s) garden within 10 yards of his study window. Got home by 5 o'clock much refreshed by my 6 mile walk across country.

"After tea with D. Robert came in & talked about his studies with Mr. B. which are in a very bad way through no fault of Mr. B.'s. Told him he must improve for his own sake in spelling & arithmetic. Read Pepys till 6 & then finished Anthony & Cleopatra with D. . . . After D. had gone to bed . . . read Pepys with great delight in the library. Finished the 3d vol. Then wrote out today's doings & so to bed after a pipe & a hot rum punch. . . ."

Feeling himself stultified by the stagnant life, Wintie at length definitely booked passage for Europe, to sail on March 30. Robert was to go with him, Daisy, and little Laura, nominally in the care of Mr. Bostwick, to continue his education abroad.

Not only Bob's studies were causing his elders anxiety. Robert was seventeen, big and virile. He had romped with the village and farm children all his life, and his popularity, especially with the girls, had caused comment. There had been whispers, quickly squelched, connecting him with one of the farmers' daughters who had been married off with suspicious suddenness, and with the same suddenness had produced a child. The family was uneasy: there must be no more misalliances between Astors and farm women; Henry Astor's horrid example was in many minds. How widely the uneasiness had spread was reflected cryptically in Winthrop's diary. After relating that he had gone into the city to attend to business, Wintie set down:

"Drove uptown with Uncle John [John Jacob Astor III]. He looks well & seems in good spirits. Told me we must be very careful with Robert lest he should 'do something devilish like Henry Astor.' This is the only time I have ever heard him allude to Henry."

It was time to get Bob Chanler away.

After making the pertinent entry, Wintie hunted for a place of safekeeping for the diary, to prevent its being read by unauthorized persons. He finally lighted upon a secret drawer in a writing case that stood at the foot of his bed, and there he locked the book with its personal allusions, promising himself to keep the key always in his possession. And there the diary would be discovered three-quarters of a century later, undisturbed since the date of its last entry—January 15, 1889.

"Rose-Red July,"

and Willie Finds His Way

The scattering of the family did not prevent their keeping in close touch with each other. Margaret and Alida were at Bonchurch, while Bessie (whom people were beginning to address more maturely as Elizabeth) stayed with the Henry Whites in London. Through White, Elizabeth was presented to Queen Victoria at one of the queen's last drawing rooms, and her "very American" disregard of etiquette made a minor stir in diplomatic circles. The rules provided that each debutante, as she was named, should step forward from the waiting line, curtsey to the queen, and pass across to the other side of the room. Elizabeth intensely disliked to be jostled or touched, possibly an effect of her long invalidism when she had necessarily been handled much. The presentation line was moving slowly, and when her turn came a court functionary nudged her and hissed, "Hurry!" Instantly Elizabeth froze, and forgetting all she had rehearsed so painstakingly, she strode across the room, omitting the curtsey. The egregious blunder ordinarily would have been the subject of an international explanation, but the deities of chance often favored Chanlers. At the moment when Elizabeth stepped forward, Victoria's veil became disarranged, exposing her little pigtail, and her ladies moved to screen her while repairs were made, and the courtiers glanced aside. Thus the American girl's omission either passed unnoticed, or was put down to consummate tact.

Elizabeth Chanler in court presentation dress, London, 1893.

The story brightened diplomatic gossip and even reached Rokeby, where Lewis wrote excitedly, "Just think, I heard it was in *Town Topics!*"

Archie, meanwhile, having settled his sisters at Bonchurch, took off for Paris, but shortly headed back to the United States. At Castle Hill he found all calm, the heat generated by clashing temperaments having dissipated. Amélie conveyed her sense of relief to Margaret, writing in February, 1889:

"O Margaret, I can scarcely believe it all. I look at Archie and think that he must be part of a dream, not the real Archie, not the man who has given me such unspeakable anguish during the past seven months. He is so gentle, so quiet, so considerate, so tender, so loving—I cannot write half my darling—but you will understand. . . . I am so dazed by it all that I cannot quite recollect things in order . . . it is such anguish to me to think of the past even now. O how God has blessed and comforted me! He has bound up my broken heart. . . . We will now surely come abroad in April, God willing. All and more than my old trust in Archie has come back. . . ."

It all sounded as though Amélie had won her point and would not be condemned to "voluntary" isolation in her country home, cut off from social pleasures. And at the start of April she and Armstrong sailed for England.

From the moment of their landing, they were caught up in a whirl of social activity. Amélie was the sensation of the season, the brightest literary, political, and artistic lights competing for her smiles. The author of *The Quick or the Dead?* was praised by Meredith, Hardy, James, and Oscar Wilde. Hardy took her aside to congratulate her personally on her new novelette, *Virginia of Virginia,* just on the stands, and Meredith declared that her eyes, of a blue so deep as to suggest purple, exactly resembled those of the young Swinburne; he called her "the poet's sister."

There were some carpers, of course, as there always are, and the *Saturday Review* made mincemeat of *The Quick or the Dead?*, terming it "housemaid romance—the old, old passionate business . . . the arms, the shoulders, the lips, the kisses, the straining, clinging embraces, the wild, weird, tear-fraught eyes, the romping and the rest of it, all cut after the ancient pattern." But such dissent was drowned out by a chorus of adulation. Hostesses showered invitations, and Meredith was positively fascinated by Amélie's quaint originality in bringing along her Negro mammy as her personal maid. Meredith begged to be introduced, and a private tea was arranged. Amélie left the two chatting amiably, and half an hour later returned to find Meredith affectionately patting the colored woman's hand and wheedling earnestly:

"Now, my dear soul, you must surely have a sister or a niece who is like you. Do promise to send her over to my housekeeper at Box Hill, and I'll pay her passage and give her good wages and make her happy—I promise you that!"

Oscar Wilde was infatuated by the fair Virginian and gave her a copy of *The Happy Prince* inscribed:

"London—a rose-red July, '89."

The incense being burned in honor of his wife sometimes irritated the nostrils of Armstrong Chanler; he deemed it in excessively bad taste. Week after week he found himself at dinners and receptions, all but ignored, while Amélie was the center of attention. The contrast wounded his self-conceit; after all, it was he who had opened the doors of international society to this country damsel from Virginia. She dazzled, that he conceded; but collaterally he felt that a Chanler did not need to dazzle: the name vouched for him. When Henry James urged Amélie to settle in England, where her talent would be better recognized and rewarded, she was inclined to agree, but Archie objected; he would not live abroad permanently, he said, and he meant it. There were scenes in private, and by the end of the London season both husband and wife were ready for a rest cure at Bad Kissingen, in Bavaria. Amélie wrote from there to Margaret Chanler, who was taking treatments at Schwalbach, in Austria, that she had developed a "chronic trouble of the throat, to which the doctor says my frightful headaches are owing. Won't it be a blessing if they are cured? Do pray that it will be so, dearest. . . . Archie and I are getting on splendidly. He gets better and better as to his nerves, & is very nice and considerate. He has written a sweet letter to Wintie which I am *sure* will dispel all past clouds. Tell dear Bessie, I am sure it will please her so."

Archie himself wrote only that Amélie seemed to be improving under the cure; otherwise he had no news to convey. Shortly afterward the two left for Algiers, where a new cause of friction developed. Armstrong wished Amélie to devote herself to painting, for which he believed she had a natural gift superior to her literary talent. He engaged an instructor to give her systematic training; but she treated the experiment lightly, confiding to Margaret that "between you and me and Queen Bess & the gate post," it was of no use. "I'll tell Bessie & you all about it when I come back, & in the meantime, dearest, don't breathe a word to anyone but Bessie." She sent her love to "pretty Alida, gadding about in her sweet, thoughtless way."

And soon Amélie was writing again about Armstrong's "coldness. . . . He is like that with everyone. . . . It is his nature to be indifferent & silent and I don't think it will ever change."

Archie made no allusion to the tense situation in his letters.

And all this while, Willie Chanler had been blazing his own trail. Strikingly handsome, with bold, arrogant features, hypnotic eyes, and perfect self-assurance, Willie made friends at every social level and felt that nothing lay beyond his powers. He escorted his sisters on a sightseeing tour of Scotland, and was disgusted by the ban on smoking cigarettes enforced in Scottish inns. Taking off with sister Bess for bandit-ridden Sicily, he lingered there several weeks in hope of meeting some outlaws, and when the hope proved vain, he talked the hotelkeeper at Palermo into letting him and Bess depart without settling their bill in full, having run short of cash. This would occur frequently with Willie. Nonchalantly he informed sister Margaret that she could settle the account when she reached Sicily shortly, and "at Taormina, under the frowning peaks of Aetna, in the Greek theater, a satisfactory settling will take place and Queen Peg shall come into her own."

But civilized travel failed to satisfy Willie Chanler's robust appetite for adventure. For more than a year he had been talking about hunting big game in Africa, though the family had not taken his talk seriously. Lewis Chanler had openly scoffed at the notion, telling his sisters not to worry about Willie, because "in the first place he cant get into Africa & if he could he has too much sense to go very far."

Willie, however, was determined. To get into the hinterland of East Africa, where he proposed to hunt, was not easy for an American; the rival colonial powers there were jealous of their secrets and suspicious of foreigners generally. But going to Berlin, Willie succeeded in obtaining a lieutenant's commission in the German East African Ivory Patrol that would at least procure him entrance into the backcountry. Hastening to Brindisi, he embarked for Port Said, Aden, and Zanzibar, taking with him George Galvin, who was not yet sixteen. During the voyage he revised his plans and decided to hunt independently through the lion and elephant country around Mount Kilimanjaro.

At Zanzibar he found himself in an atmosphere of conspiracy, intrigue, risk, and danger that exactly suited him. From the Criterion Hotel (a barrackslike establishment boasting a few rudimentary conveniences) he wrote to "Dear Peg" on March 20, 1889:

"My voyage from Brindisi was uneventful but pleasant & after

ABOVE Elizabeth, Willie, and Margaret Chanler in Sicily, 1892. Willie hoped to meet bandits, was disappointed.

RIGHT Mr. and Mrs. Winthrop Chanler with their first children, John Winthrop Chanler II (who died very young) and, right, Laura, 1890.

18 days voyage (a remarkably quick passage) I arrived here. The troubles here add to the amusements of the place somewhat, for if we were not hearing every now and then of fights with the natives I don't know what we'd do. Zanzibar itself is an island at least 20 miles from the coast and as all the fights are on the mainland you need not be alarmed for my safety. However, it seems like war when you can see the smoke of the cannon (through a glass) and when the wind is from the right quarter hear the boom of the guns. The rascally Germans are making all the trouble and doing nearly all the fighting. The English are simply putting down the slave trade with as little bloodshed as possible, while the Wadashi as the Germans are called are trying to capture territory.

"I am stopping at a very comfortable English hotel," he fibbed, "kept by a man named Cable who says he used to keep the Commercial Hotel at Ventnor [New Jersey]. There is an English club here and a lot of jolly Englishmen whom I see a great deal of. Our consul is not half a bad fellow but his wife is a typical nasal twanged Yankee of the strictest New England type. I dine at the English Consul General's tonight and expect a good dinner as I hear he has a French chef. . . . You see I am not in such an uncivilized spot after all. I am learning the language (Swahili) and do not find it hard. The climate is not so deadly after all, but I suffer very much from an exaggerated sort of prickly heat. I think I shall start for Kilimanjaro about the end of May. I shall settle on the sides of the mountain and shoot only about there keeping away from the dangerous part of the country. That is of course taking it for granted that I succeed in forming my expedition. I am having a great deal of difficulty in getting my men together but think I shall succeed."

Breaking off this letter "in time to dress for dinner," Willie resumed a week later:

"I got a letter from Wintie & one from Daisy a short time ago. By this time they are at home in Rome I suppose. It is now some months since Bessie was presented [at court] & she has had time to drop a little of her regal swagger I suppose. When she first got back she had the presence of Queen Kahliolani."

Luck favored the young adventurer, and on April 2 he wrote that his expedition was "getting on finely. I have already 60 men and two headmen or lieutenants both of which are men of experience and discretion." And in May the expedition, numbering 120 men and captained by Willie, with George Galvin as second in command, embarked by dhow for Mombasa, and from there headed inland.

They followed the old Uganda trail westward to Tsavo, in the heart of the lion country, then turned southwest and made for Taveta, the headquarters of the Arab slave traders. From Taveta, turning westward again, the safari reached the lower slopes of Kilimanjaro, and finding at a place called Nkiri Nkubwa a well-built "boma," or permanent camp (with the grave of the Englishman who had built it and had been killed by a buffalo nearby), they settled there for an extended stay. Game was plentiful, the buffalo were vicious and aggressive, and the rhinoceros the same. One night two rhinos charged right through the boma, smashing everything but luckily injuring nobody. There were other narrow escapes, and a constant lookout had to be maintained against the hostile Masai, whose territory lay to the north.

Although the region had been fairly well explored, portions were still unknown, and Chanler was the first American to hunt there. He loved the life, although he exasperated a German explorer, Dr. Hans Meyer, whom he encountered in the bush, by light-heartedly explaining that his only motive was to "have fun." Meyer's expedition was sponsored by three geographical societies, a trading company, and the emperor of Germany; Willie's was sponsored by himself. The cool daring of this twenty-three-year-old sportsman, roaming country that the great Stanley had called unsafe to enter "even with a thousand rifles," seconded only by a sixteen-year-old boy, perturbed the serious-minded German.

At home, Willie's sisters were both proud and anxious. The newspapers carried occasional reports of his progress, and Wintie reassured the girls that there was little or no fever in the uplands around Kilimanjaro where their brother was rampaging. But when Willie at length emerged from the interior, safe and sound, Wintie relayed the news with some surprise to Amos Tuck French:

"He says he had fine sport, though he doesn't mention what

kind. He pretends to like the life and says he is not coming home for a year or two. I fancy he can't raise bail enough to satisfy the Court of his African Potentate. He has his Irish groom with him and says he is a great success. I can't imagine at what."

Winthrop was a little envious of Willie's freedom to go shooting where he listed; and when his brother returned to Europe around Christmas time and failed to pass through Rome and render a first-hand account of his adventures, Wintie was nettled.

"So the mighty Nimrod has returned," he grumbled to his sisters. "Sings Masai war songs, does he? Frightens his sisters by imitating the Negro minstrel of Central Africa? Well, we are glad to get him back at any cost."

Wintie was bored during that spring in Rome; he did nothing, it seemed to him, but laze away the days. (Once he summed up his inherent nomadism in the phrase: "Somehow or other I manage to be at home wherever I find my hat.") And he confessed to French, not altogether mockingly, "Mere luxuries don't please me at all—oh, no—I must have excitement." Without, of course, forfeiting the crowning luxury of an intelligent and affectionate wife, who wisely let him have scope to ramble now and then.

Wintie believed that leisure was given to mortals to enjoy. To extract contentment from the passing moment, to be good-humored, jolly, well-mannered, and witty—that was the thing. He was not formed to muck and moil, but to pass his time merrily, within the limits of good form. Friends might choose to work—Amos French was in a bank, commuting between Wall Street and Tuxedo Park—Wintie refused to be ensnared by any dull grind. He was under no compulsion to do anything especially; he had no profession, and if hard up today, tomorrow would bring another check; one need never worry about money for long. If a bill could not be paid, why, send it to the family lawyer to settle. Wintie's eye would gleam as he pictured the discomfiture of that often harassed retainer upon receiving an account demanding immediate settlement. "This will make him sit up!" he would gloat. It was a Chanler prerogative to indulge one's own strongly accented tastes, and Winthrop Chanler lived in a world tailored to his desires, and no summons to work was going to dispossess him of it.

True, Wintie was capable of interspersing the aimless drift of his life with bursts of activity, but these were short-lived and usually led to nothing further. Hunting and horses bound the horizon of his serious interests outside the family; the social life provided by his wife he adorned with style, but he would leave it to hunt moufflon in Sardinia or chamois in the Alps with perfect tranquillity. He was aware of his shortcomings. That summer he visited a remote, picturesque monastery, difficult of access, and enjoyed the trip, but afterward confided to Daisy:

"I don't like Saints alive or dead nearly as much as I do sinners, and I am sure I was never intended for a monastic life."

Toward autumn he told his friend "Amoi" (French):

"I have bought a horse, on whose back I propose to follow the fleeting pack of hounds which the Eternal City supports. The country is grand, foxes aplenty, and if the weather permits, hunting is good. I have managed to get a little quail shooting, and hope for wild boar and moufflon, with woodcock & snipe in the winter. . . ."

This was shortly after the birth to the Winthrop Chanlers of a second child, a son, who was christened John Winthrop Chanler for his grandfather. To French, Wintie boasted that "like his namesake Falstaff," the boy in the future would be known as "Jack to his familiars, John to his brothers & sisters, and Sir John to all Europe." French was enjoined to repair to "Del's [Delmonico's] or the Knickerbocker at my expense and drink two bottles of phiz" to the health of the child.

Soon after this Wintie found himself hankering for his "ain countree," and by autumn Daisy was packing for Newport, and from there for a return to their winter residence in Washington.

From Lewis to Archie to Teddy

While his sisters and brothers were scattering about Europe, Lewis Stuyvesant Chanler shuttled between Rokeby and New York, where he was completing his law studies at Columbia. Lewis was especially attached to the homestead, in this respect resembling his "twin" of nursery days, Margaret Chanler. In both appearance and temperament he was decidedly different from his elder brothers; he had shot up to six feet four inches in height, and like Robert he was dark, in contrast to the fair complexions of Archie, Wintie, and William. His features were engagingly open, frank, and boyish, and the extreme elegance of his dress moved his brothers to protest that he overdressed. His nature was gentler, more sensitive (Willie disgustedly called him the "cry baby" of the family), and more altruistic than theirs; and what was striking in one so young was his air of good breeding and urbanity. Significantly, there was no "Astor" in his name.

A born lawyer, he had drummed up mock lawsuits when a boy, summoning brothers or sisters to the court of Mr. Bostwick to answer charges of failure to repay a loan of twenty-five cents, or infringing upon the plaintiff's right to occupancy of a rabbit hutch, all in strict legal form. He was also a born speechmaker, impressed by the sound of his own voice. When his unenthusiastic family drove him out of the house, he would roam Rokeby woods and frighten the crows by emulations of Demosthenes.

It was inevitable that Lewis should eye political life at an early

Lewis Stuyvesant Chanler, about 1887,
preparing to enter Columbia.

age; he took the family tradition of Democratic leadership very
seriously. At nineteen he reported exuberantly to Margaret from
Rokeby:

"Tonight I made my maiden speech at Barrytown. Everybody
turned out to see what I would do and there must have been fifty
or sixty at least there; it was the first regular meeting of the
[Democratic] Club & of course I presided; it was altogether a
success as far as the meeting went. As for my speech I say nothing
except that it lasted 25 minutes & they did not seem to be tired
when I stopped. They wanted to call it the Chanler Club but I
asked them not to."

The hold that Rokeby held upon his affections appeared repeatedly in Lewis's letters to those abroad.

"I had no idea when I decided to go to Law School how hard
it would be to know that I was only 3 hours from Rokeby & yet
as far away as though I were at Cambridge," he told "Mung-
wump" (one of his pet names for Margaret); and this theme he

varied throughout his correspondence that year. Margaret had sent him her latest photograph, and he promised to forward one of himself soon, "as I need no longer wait for my mustache which has been removed as not being professional." The Democratic defeat in the national elections of 1888 filled him with foreboding for the nation: "I shudder to think of the awful risk it runs, mark my words! Some awful catastrophe will occur that will shake it to its foundations!"

But the country puttered along, and a more cheerful prospect opened for the disappointed Democrat in June of 1889, when Lewis sailed for a vacation in England. The guardians had granted permission and had voted him three hundred dollars extra to pay for the trip.

Lewis had become increasingly irked by his subordinate position in the family. His three older brothers, Armstrong, Winthrop, and William, had become guardians on reaching their majority, and he chafed under their supervision. Longing for the day when he would come of age, he pushed his law studies and practiced his patrician flair at such establishments as Delmonico's and Tiffany's, where the cautious guardians sanctioned the maintenance of modest charge accounts.

(The scapegrace Chanlers, during their minority, sometimes turned the Delmonico's account into a source of much needed cash by ordering dinners that were not served, but were billed to the guardians, the corresponding sum in ready money being turned over to the lads by the complaisance of the management. Sam Ward's grandsons could command almost anything at Del's; friends of the family said that all their lives the Chanler men, when faced with a crisis, would settle it by proposing, "Let's have dinner at Del's.")

In June of 1890 Lewis sailed again for England, and while in London shocked the family into realization that he had really grown up by announcing his engagement to be married; his twenty-first birthday was only three months away.

Lewis's courtship had been quiet, and he made clear that he preferred to keep the wedding equally simple. The bride-to-be was well known to the Chanlers. She was Alice Remington Chamberlain, a former Dutchess County neighbor; her parents had occupied Maizeland, a fine Federalist mansion in Red Hook. Alice had played with the Chanlers as a child. Her father, a Vermonter, was deceased; he had been a railroad financier. There was a shy younger daughter, Julia, and both daughters had been taken to Europe by their strong-willed mother for their education, and had grown up there.

Lewis was self-conscious about springing his surprise on the family without prior consultation; but the match was suitable on both sides and he was finished with explaining his actions to his guardian-brothers. From the Century Club in London he dashed off an apologetic note to sister Margaret, saying:

"I enclose a letter to Alida telling her of my engagement. Everybody *in* the family know now so there is no reason why she shouldn't."

The family regarded Alida as too flighty to be entrusted with serious matters.

The relatives could hardly help but approve the match, but Amélie was uncertain just how to take it; the Chanlers as a clan were still something of an enigma to Amélie. From Fontainebleau, where she and Elizabeth were painting industriously, she reached for Margaret's reaction:

"What *did* you think of Lewis' engagement? I guessed who it was. *Well,* I hope & pray that he will be happy. I suppose those that we love very rarely marry as we wish them to."

Wintie and Willie got the news upon their return to New York from a hunting trip to Colorado with two sporting parsons—the Reverend Dr. Nevin, pastor of the American Episcopal Church in Rome and a colonel of Pennsylvania cavalry in the Civil War, and the Reverend William S. Rainsford, of fashionable St. George's Church in New York's Stuyvesant Square.

The expedition had been improvised with the happy nonchalance inseparable from Wintie Chanler. On their passage from Rome back to Newport, he and Daisy, with their babies, paused in London, where by chance he encountered Nevin. The "Reverendo," as Wintie gaily called the parson, mentioned that he was on his way to hunt in the Rockies, and casually invited Chanler to "come along." Just as casually Chanler accepted the invitation, and without ado sailed, leaving wife and children stranded in

England, where she knew no one and where the cold and fog chilled her Roman blood. Disconsolately she beat a retreat to Italy, where during succeeding weeks she extracted what comfort she could from the rollicking letters that her gadabout husband rained back home.

In New York, Wintie recruited his brother Willie and the latter's clerical friend, Rainsford, and arranging to rendezvous in Colorado, set out joyously with Nevin. Winthrop Chanler had the knack of his grandfather, Sam Ward, for penning a racy, conversational letter, and his adaptability to every sort of condition, surroundings, or companionship (barring only bores, from whom he fled) was another trait for which he was indebted to Sam. From Glenwood Springs, Colorado, the jumping-off point for the trek into the real wilderness in pursuit of game, he sent a vivid account of the stalling of their train high in the Rockies and passing most of the night in the open.

"What a journey!" he exulted. "Half an hour out of Leadville the train came to a standstill at a telegraph station. It seems that there was a train wrecked lower down on the road & that we must wait till it was cleared away. . . . Well, we stayed there until nearly 10 o'clock. The passengers built a huge bonfire & sang hymns at first & then more appropriate songs. . . . There was a man with a guitar & a man who through long years of trading with the Indians had learnt their ways. He was at last persuaded to perform a war dance wrapped in a woman's shawl which he did with great effect. I never saw a better-natured crowd in my life. There we were in the middle of a howling wilderness, most of us supperless, yet no grumbling & all as jolly as sand boys. . . .

"It would have amused you to have been present at that scene round the bonfire. A circle of nondescript people, some well dressed and others of the cowboy, miner class, all fraternizing & trying to pass the time pleasantly. No vulgarity & all good nature. The *Reverendo* in his straw-colored suit & gray helmet, an empty belly under his waist-coat but a merry heart in his ribs, sang & at times bellowed his bass to the old war songs. The air was so cold & clear (imagine what it is at over 10,000 ft.) & the fire so bright & warm that we were all half drunk & did not care whether the train stayed there all night or not. Overhead the stars were like gems on dark velvet & a little new moon smiled coyly down on us. Altogether it was a scene never to be forgotten. It was so purely American and Far Western in its character. There is good in this country, if one knows how to look for it. Fancy an English crowd on a Scotch moorland under the same circumstances. Part grumbling, part swearing, and the other half stonily silent or boisterously vulgar. Or an Italian party. Scared to death, huddled together, & thinking that their last hour had come."

The tender note was never long absent from Wintie's letters to the girl he so often left behind.

"Did I tell you that at Tuxedo I found among Amos' books your dear old 'Tennyson' in which we used to read together?" he rambled on. " 'Margaret Terry' on the fly leaf . . . I have it with me & it brings back the old Altemps & Rimini & the days when our Dan Cupid was very wee & small. Dear Dan! He has grown apace & waxed lusty & fair favored since, has he not? . . ."

Roam as he would, Wintie would never be far in spirit from his wife; and she, clever woman that she was, understood his restlessness and seldom held him back from his dashes after excitement.

Wintie received the news about Lewis's marriage "not disagreeably," and shortly after that Willie was writing to Margaret from the sedate surroundings of the Union Club that not only was Daisy Chanler due to arrive from Rome the next day, but that "Lewis should lead his blushing bride down the gangplank of the Aurania on Sunday. I smell speech making in the near future. Ah me! The air will be redolent with platitudes!"

He himself, he added mischievously, was "advertising for a wife, but unfortunately the requirements for that august position are difficult to fulfill & as yet the numerous applicants I have received with a cold dismissal. There are many with money, some with good looks, but alack! few with brains."

The Colorado trip had provided not only exhilaration but good shooting. Willie had not taken to Nevin—"a purely artificial product & comes near a poseur," he confided. But Rainsford, big, athletic, jolly, a clergyman who boldly preached social justice to his millionaire parishioners, Willie admired—"a really large man, broad and humanitarian in his views of life; strong and eager for good. We had good sport," the report went on, "and as no theological discussions took place, no jar marred the peace of the laity. Yes, the parsons cheerfully laid aside their stoles & surplices and in their Nimrod garb acted in quite the proper manner.

"Write and it shall be answered," he concluded. "Induce Bessie to put pen to paper again & whisper the same counsel to Alida. . . . I suppose Archie is dreaming dreams, pulling down old plans to build up new ones, drinking beer & water; in fact the same as usual."

And indeed Archie was dreaming dreams, in a practical way. His marriage was not going well, friction continuing over his view of where Amélie's real talent lay. He charged her with indolence, asserting she would rather sit and write than stand and paint; she spurned the accusation, and to demonstrate her energy buried herself in furious reading—"up to my eyes in Flaubert, Joubert, Stendhal, Gautier, and a few others," she bragged virtuously to Margaret.

But the basic cause of the couple's growing antipathy lay deeper. Fundamentally uncongenial, both were prone to excitability and were readily gripped by nervous tensions. In his calmer moments, Armstrong Chanler might have stepped from a novel by Jane Austen; somewhat old-fashioned in his social attitudes, serious-minded and conscientious, with the air and manners of a gentleman. Amélie, on the other hand, preened herself upon being "advanced" and "enlightened"—without, of course, becoming either a "frump" or "outré." Between husband and wife there were sunny interludes, but their incompatibility, aggravated by Amélie's celebrity, daily became more severe. Fame and adulation were dear to Amélie, and Archie could not help being jealous.

The Chanler sisters, who lived with their brother and his wife in Paris through two winters, were aware of the growing conflict. As homemaker, housekeeper, or hostess, Amélie was incompetent. The doors of society that had swung open to them, mainly through Armstrong's connections, gradually closed again. At the Dutch legation, the De Steurs paved the way for Amélie to enter the diplomatic circle; but when she failed repeatedly to appear after having accepted invitations, hostesses dropped her name from their lists. Nor could Archie depend on her to discharge the reciprocal obligations of entertaining those who had entertained them; domestic arrangements mystified Amélie; she insisted she could never understand them. Yet when her health and moods were favorable, she could be witty and responsive, charming all who came near her. During her "good spells" the household took on life; but when she lay prostrated by migraine, locked in her room, withdrawn from everyone except her female relatives, the house was intolerable. Margaret Chanler guessed that Amélie really wanted only to live surrounded by these relatives, idolized and pampered; and that she had used her husband to gain entry to a luxurious social circle, and had never loved him at all. The deductions of Margaret were rarely sentimental. Amélie's mother, sisters, and women cousins were much in the Paris house, and Armstrong was often excluded. His temper became uneven; he brooded and began to exhibit oddities of behavior; but he never spoke a derogatory word about his wife.

None of the Chanlers suspected, at that time, that with or without medical sanction, Amélie was experimenting with morphine. The drug may have been prescribed to relieve her excruciating headaches, but it had become an addiction. There were days when she remained in her bedroom, invisible to everyone except her mother, supposedly ill but really under the influence of the drug. A novel she wrote in Paris, titled, perhaps significantly, *According to St. John,* recounted the heroine's suicide by an injection of morphine, and preceding chapters dealt in clinical detail with the sensations produced by the drug.

Meanwhile, rumors drifted back to New York about dissension in Archie's household, and these were given a fillip by publication of a report that Amélie's beauty had driven a young Parisian artist to kill himself after she had "jilted him while they were studying together." Such a story, whether baseless or not, was not the sort of thing that was printed about "decent" wives in 1890, and the Chanlers were deeply offended.

During his years abroad, Armstrong had been struck by the need for some method of practical assistance to promising American artists who were too poor to complete their art education in the Old World. He had met not a few artists of pronounced ability who lived in direst poverty, enduring bitter hardships, as they struggled to continue their professional studies under competent masters. In the United States there were few art schools, few instructors of merit, so that an ambitious American painter or sculptor was forced to seek instruction abroad. Interested in the arts, Armstrong Chanler evolved a plan to meet this situation, at least in part, and he hoped that the example might inspire others to do more, and thus elevate the artistic standards prevalent in America.

At the start of 1890, therefore, Archie returned to New York to promote his scheme of raising an endowment fund to provide scholarships for gifted Americans aiming at careers in the visual arts. Amélie did not come with him. He proposed to award five-year grants, through selective competition, to support artists in reasonable comfort in Paris or some other European art center; the only return required being a pledge on the part of each scholarship winner to give a portion of his time to teaching upon his return to the United States. In this way Archie hoped that eventually a reservoir of teaching talent might be built up that would make it unnecessary for Americans to go abroad for their schooling.

The proposal was in advance of its time, although the newspapers gave it generous support, praising both Chanler's initiative and his plan of organization. There would be two juries; one, composed of artists, to select the winners of the awards on the basis of merit, and the second, of business men and bankers, to handle the money and make the payments. Neither board could interfere with the other. At first the scheme would be confined to New York City, but Archie hoped that in time there would be similar funds, raised and operating along the same lines, in other major cities.

He first approached his relatives and rich acquaintances, but met with skepticism. Several cousins flatly refused to donate a nickel to "support some young riffraff in Paris for five years doing nothing." But Archie persisted, priming the pump with a first contribution of $13,500 from his own pocket. His Aunt Laura Delano gave $1,000, and Elizabeth Chanler the same amount. Harry Carey in Boston was more open-handed, giving $5,000;

Uncle William Astor followed with $2,500. Gradually the fund grew, and one evening at dinner at the Somerset Club in Boston, Armstrong made his cousin Carey a sporting proposition.

"Harry," said he, "you have been very generous to the Paris Prize plan; you have given more to it than anyone else—twice as much in fact. Now, do one thing more. You are a millionaire and a bachelor. We are both of us in the prime of life and healthy, and you are younger than I. Now, whichever one of us dies first leaves $25,000 to the Prize fund."

"Done," assented Carey; and on his death two years later, the $25,000, although not expressly provided for in the will, was paid by his heir and brother. And in 1891 the Paris Art Fund was launched with an initial endowment of more than $50,000. Two artist friends of Archie's, Stanford White, the architect, and Augustus St. Gaudens, the sculptor, were active in support of the innovation, and the first winner was soon selected and sent to Paris for five years with a guaranteed income of $900 a year, an ample allowance for that day. And from that time to the present, the fund has continued to assist American artists and American art.

The plan having been securely launched, Archie returned to Europe, and a few weeks later was back, this time with Amélie, whose obscure derangements were growing worse. They went directly to Castle Hill, and there the hectic, unreal, dreamlike pattern of her turbulent adolescence was revived, with fresh implications of some fundamental illness which the doctors seemed unable to alleviate. The Winthrop Chanlers were staying in New York, in a rented house on 34th Street, Wintie's three sisters being with them; and reports of affairs at Castle Hill became so contradictory that it was deemed advisable to send an observer. Elizabeth volunteered to go, and the report she sent back painted a grotesque picture indeed.

Castle Hill was swarming with visitors and cousins, although in one darkened room the lady of the house lay apparently near death. Elizabeth reported her sister-in-law "much weaker . . . altogether worn to a thread of endurance . . . a shadow of her former self. Her hands have great hollows along their backs & her face is long and dragged. But she is tranquil & at peace &

Archie is very dear & sweet & though there are endless outside complications . . . there is perfect calm & peace in her soul."

The attendant household (to Elizabeth every one of them seemed to be a relative) was "divided into drawing-room & bedroom detachments," one being always on duty in the sick room. Meanwhile, elsewhere in the house social life went on uninhibited. One evening Armstrong precipitated an argument over the relative merits of Greek and modern literature, stating his opinion that "English poets could 'give more ideas to the square inch' than Greek ones," Elizabeth recounted; whereupon "we spent a delightful hour round the dining-room table comparing pages of Paradise Lost with pages of the Agamemnon & Virgil. . . . Of course it was a perfectly inadequate & childish form of comparison, but it was great fun. . . . We screamed and gesticulated to our entire satisfaction." The scene was Rokeby transported to Virginia.

Armstrong did everything in his power to halt his wife's wasting away, without success. She could not bear daylight, and kept the blinds of her room closed at all times. Sometimes she wished to be read to, but for hours she would lie inert, pallid, undoubtedly in pain yet consciously self-dramatizing.

As a last resort the doctors suggested that she be placed in the clinic for nervous diseases maintained by Dr. S. Weir Mitchell, the noted neurologist, in Philadelphia. Mitchell was pioneering in the diagnosis and treatment of mental and psychosomatic ills. After anxious debate, Amélie was taken to Philadelphia and placed under the direct care of Mitchell's chief of clinic, Dr. J. Madison Taylor. Her commitment was kept a secret from all except her family and the Chanlers, and the latter were discreet. Winthrop fended off inquiries with such vague allusions as this in a letter:

"Archie arrives today from the Unknown. He disappears & goes to Phila. every few days. There all trace is lost & suddenly out of Space he bounces."

The weekly visits to Philadelphia brought Armstrong into close association with Dr. Taylor, and a personal intimacy developed between them. Several times the doctor was a guest at Castle Hill, where he came to enjoy Archie's peculiarities, such as his adoption of a semivegetarian diet. Archie felt that his health had improved since he gave up eating red meats, and the subject of diet interested him greatly. Dr. Taylor predicted that Chanler would go further in his dietary scruples.

During this interim, Archie was engaged in a maze of business promotions. Although he declined to practice himself, he set up a law firm with two partners, W. G. Maxwell and Harry Van Ness Philip, and told Winthrop with immense pride that the firm had earned $10,000 in fees during its first eight months.

Then Archie turned to the promotion of patented inventions, including a self-threading needle for sewing machines. Elated by the success of his Paris Art Prize, he had in mind founding bigger and better philanthropies in neglected fields, schemes that would require large endowments, and he counted on his business ventures to bring in the money needed. Wintie took a hand in several of these projects, investing and acting as salesman for the products among his wealthy friends, especially pushing a fire-resistant paint which he urged they use on their horse barns. He used it himself. To a Chanler, exposing a horse to an unnecessary risk of fire was like exposing a human.

Wintie and Daisy had moved back to Washington, where in February, 1891, Daisy was stricken with measles. Consequently she was unable to attend the wedding of Winthrop's cousin (her own cousin more remotely), John Jacob Astor IV, the son and heir of Uncle William and Aunt Caroline Astor, to Ava Lowle Willing, of Philadelphia. Wintie had looked forward to the wedding with keen interest and Daisy insisted that he go along without her. He had been regaling his sisters with advance gossip about how "poor Jack," who "had not a friend in the wide world," had "at last found a young lady who is willing to marry him"—thanks entirely to his mother, *the* Mrs. Astor.

"It is amusing to see how Aunt Caroline has managed the whole affair," he wrote to Margaret. "It may be that Aunt C. went to some society caterer and gave him *carte blanche*. At all events, the friendless Jack goes to the altar . . . A day or two before the wedding he is to give a farewell (it is his first as well as his last) bachelor supper to his *friends* at the Knickerbocker.

Delicious, isn't it? Not one of the men would cross the street to shake hands with him for his own sake. But the mother is such a social power & has done so much for them that they are only too glad of the chance. I shall give you an account of the wedding when I get back from Phila."

Which he did, with a shrewdness and gusto that would have evoked the envy of a young chum of Willie Chanler, a reporter named Richard Harding Davis; for this wedding, one of the great social events of the era, was staged with appropriate lavishness in what was agreed to be the best taste of the period.

The "Golden Caliban" was what they were calling Jack Astor in Philadelphia, said Wintie as he launched into his narrative:

"Well! Jack has got his Jill at last! Let us hope there will be no 'vinegar & brown paper' required for some time to come. The wedding was really beautiful. The bride is a lovely girl. Tall, dark, clear white skin with well coloured cheeks. Beautiful expressive eyes & charming change of expression & play of features. Perfect manner. Self-possessed & ready of wit. If she does not make something of Jack nobody can. Poor girl! They tell me in Philadelphia that she has been perfectly desperate about the whole business. Has left a puddle of tears on every parlour floor in the town. Her family, which is very rich & quite the *fine fleur* of Phil, has forced her into it. Up to the last moment her friends feared that she would rebel & break loose—but she did not. They seldom do!

"The wedding took place in the Willing house. About 150 people were asked for the ceremony & about 50000 for the reception afterwards. You of course know from the papers who the ushers & bridesmaids were, so I shan't stop to tell them off. The maids were all in *couleur de rose* & were the prettiest lot of girls I have ever seen at such a ceremony. Just before the time came for the service I went up stairs to see Jack & cheer him up. He was up stairs surrounded by his ushers & best man. To my surprise he was not a bit scared or (apparently) nervous. He asked for a Prayer Book just to see 'what he had to say.' I told him it did not matter a single dam what he said now, for the Parson would only & could only understand him in one way. That seemed to brace him up. Then I went down stairs & squeezed myself in among the family at the right of the altar, just behind Uncle William. Best place in

the room where I could see everything. The music started up &
in they all came. First the ushers & bridesmaids; then Jack & Stew-
art [the best man]. Jack wagged (he *can't* bow) his head at the
Parson, who was a huge, unctuous man with a blonde beard.
Then came the bride (first time I had even seen her except once
across the house at the Opera in N.Y.) on her father's arm. She
looked like death, trembling & in a state of seemingly hopeless
despair. They stood under a sort of sounding-board of lilies &
greens in a bow window opening on the street. Then the service
began. After each sentence that fell from the Parson's lips, by
some curious coincidence, the crowd of people outside in the
street hoorayed & bawled. Just as if the thing was being done in
the open air. Of course the window was shut & the blinds down
but the mob yelled as if they were in the room. The effect was
ludicrous in the extreme.

"Jack answered up like a man. The girl whispered her responses below her breath. She trembled & cried a little, so that I
felt as if I were attending a sale in a slave market. Aunt Caroline
& Uncle W were both nervous. We all cried, as did all the members (female) of the Willing clan. The end soon came & we made
our congratulations.

"Jack never appeared as well. For the first time in his life he
did not behave like a fool. In spite of his ridiculous appearance &
manners, he was really dignified & at his ease. Had a word for
everyone, looked happy & self-possessed. She also braced up, like
one who has had a long dreaded cold douche & is delighted & surprised to find it not half so bad as it was supposed to be.

"Then came the breakfast. All the bridesmaids, ushers, bride
& groom were at a big round table beautifully decorated with
flowers. The effect was charming. Jack & his Ava were opposite
one another & not side by side. There was only one other table in
the room at which the fathers, mothers, Parsons & aged aunts sat.
The rest of us were fed in various troughs in different rooms. I
sat with the sisters & brothers in front of Jack & we had a very
jolly time. I have a very nice box of cake, which I shall send you.
The bride wore very few jewels. A beautiful diamond love knot
with a huge brilliant as pendant. Given by Uncle W. Said to have
belonged to Mazarin. A jewel in diamonds (I think a tiara—*fleur
de lis*) from Jack and that's all. It was all over by 4 o'clock. At
4.41 my train left & here I am. Yrs. W."

So ended Winthrop Chanler's blithe account of the start of one of the most fashionable, unhappy, and in the end ill-fated marriages of that social era.

A long-standing friendship, dating back to Harvard days, had existed between Winthrop Chanler and Theodore Roosevelt, and over the years this had ripened into intimacy. The two had similar tastes, adored the outdoor life, and Roosevelt was charmed by Wintie's liveliness and debonair wit. They were fellow Porcellians and fellow members of the Boone & Crockett Club, a group of sportsmen, big game hunters, founded in 1887 by Roosevelt and George Bird Grinnell. Both Winthrop and William Chanler had met the qualification for membership (bagging at least three specimens of American big game) and both took part in the club's summer camping trips and the annual banquet.

A tight circle of congenial spirits clustered around Roosevelt and Wintie Chanler. It included Owen Wister, who had not yet produced *The Virginian,* but was infatuated with the West; the Cabot Lodges; Cecil Spring-Rice; and, later, Henry Adams, who, although older, was in sympathy with the enthusiasms of the younger set. Wister had known Wintie at Harvard, and another link between them was the close friendship that had subsisted between Daisy Chanler's parents, the Terrys, in Rome, and Wister's awesome grandmother, the majestic Fanny Kemble. Fanny Kemble once coached Daisy in a children's play, instructing her how to "walk like a queen."

Wherever this coterie of wits foregathered, there was sparkling talk, uproarious debate, and much laughter, in which Winthrop Chanler effortlessly took the lead. After a rousing three-day celebration of the Porcellian Club's centennial, Wintie limped back from Cambridge with a superb hangover, and amused Daisy by his grave commendation of the industry of cousin Arthur Carey, who had actually gone to work, as a teacher at Harvard. "A great thing for him," Wintie sagely approved. Wintie was always swift to approve industry displayed by anybody but himself.

The annual reunion of Boone & Crockett Club members—men who had roamed the West and who also were accomplished tellers of tall tales—engaged Roosevelt's earnest attention. But one year, being detained in Washington by his work as civil service commissioner, he reluctantly entrusted the arrangements to Wintie Chanler. The date drew near, and Roosevelt became nervous over Chanler's apparent neglect of the job—even hinting that he might not show up at the affair himself. Teddy dashed off a peremptory note to his lackadaisical deputy:

"Dear Winty,

"You unsatisfactory cuss, what do you mean by saying that you may not be at the dinner, and that is all there is about it? More than that, I can't make out from your letter if you have engaged or will engage, the rooms at the Knickerbocker Club. Please attend to this at once, as I don't want to have a hungry crowd of hunters gathered and no fare for them.

"Give my love to your wife, and answer this in the affirmative at once. Cordially yours,

"THEODORE ROOSEVELT."

To which Wintie replied with lines scratched out in the office of Archie's law firm:

The Worm Turneth

Keep your shirt on little Teddy
And don't get in a stew.
The dinner will be ready,
The room is ordered too.
But *I* must know how many
Can be counted on to dine,
Ere I venture upon any-
Thing concerning food or wine.
I am willing & I'm able
To do my level best,
To arrange & set the table,
Kick the waiters & the rest.
You enumerate the Crocketts,
I'll their appetites indulge,
Till their eyeballs from their sockets
Do incontinently bulge.
And when the matter's ended
And laid upon the shelf,
You may know that I intended
From the first to come myself.

That Maverick Bob

Willie Chanler's experience of the West, acquired during undis-
guised adventure hunts, embraced a familiarity with its lawless,
rowdy aspects that his brother Winthrop would never achieve.
Willie at various times had scouted the plains with outlaws; he
had fraternized with members of the "Hole in the Wall" gang
of bank robbers in Wyoming, and he and Butch Cassidy would
meet surreptitiously again in New York. Willie had explored
San Francisco's Barbary Coast, and among his western friendships
one particularly close was that with Jack Follansbee, a cousin of
William Randolph, who managed the vast Hearst ranches in
California and Mexico. And Willie and young Hearst had played
uproarious and sometimes disorderly practical jokes together and
on each other. Willie knew the West.

Lewis Chanler was introduced to the region in a different way,
and for him it held no attraction whatever. His marriage had
started propitiously. Alice supported him loyally in his determination to practice law and provided the sort of smooth-running
domestic setting that he craved. He had chosen to specialize in
criminal practice, a branch of the profession then disdained by
attorneys with genteel backgrounds.

In the nineties, the criminal courts of New York City were the
haunts of legal tricksters who preyed on the unfortunates caught
in the meshes of the law. Lewis created a stir by taking cases that

he deemed meritorious, and whether the client was able to pay a fee or not, defending them with vigor and skillfulness. Most of his clients were too poor to afford counsel, but that did not deter Lewis; he paid all costs out of his own pocket, as a form of private philanthropy. He employed two clerks who attended each reading of the calendar, and whenever no defense counsel appeared, informed the court that the defense would be assumed by Lewis Chanler. Lewis had a strong sense of *noblesse oblige;* he was aware that the scales of justice were weighted heavily against the poor and ignorant, and he contributed his talents toward righting them. In addition, he greatly enjoyed the practice.

His appearance in the Tombs, coming to confer with his dubious clients, lent an unaccustomed air to those damp, sinister corridors. He was always immaculately dressed, erect and superbly gentlemanly, but never condescending; conscious of his own rectitude but not censorious. Once he accepted a case, he prosecuted it with zeal, and frequently won. His opponents, although baffled by his motives, came to respect his ability. His clients found him not only a skillful counselor, but a sympathetic friend. For a while a "Chanler Club," composed mostly of murderers, flourished in the Tombs, and was provided with a turkey at Thanksgiving and Christmas, along with tobacco and other small comforts, by its counsel.

The family approved of Lewis's ambition, although not always of his way of expressing it. Wintie confided to his friend Tuck French that he hoped his brother would "stick to it for the next two or three years." But Lewis's pompous earnestness his family found grating, and he was often subjected to fraternal scorn. At Rokeby one day, around the luncheon table, Winthrop, Willie, and Bob opened an attack on Lewis, ridiculing him as a self-important windbag, a "professional man," who actually worked in an office and vastly overrated his public services, and was incapable of ever smiling at himself. The attack went on for more than an hour, in language so violent that Wintie's daughter, Laura, a child, was shocked. The explosion had been set off by no special remark or incident, but erupted from the general conversation without warning. Lewis took the chiding meekly, made no effort to defend himself, and when eventually the storm subsided, all was easy and friendly again. Such were the tempests of Rokeby, enjoyed by all hands.

But Lewis's auspicious legal start was cut short by Alice Chanler's illness. A son had been born, who was christened Lewis Stuyvesant Chanler, Jr., although he would be known in the family as Stuyve. But Alice failed to recuperate. Her lungs were believed to be affected, and then a persistent fever led the doctors to suspect typhoid. Upon receiving this diagnosis, Lewis promptly closed his office, rented the handsome house he had taken in Riverdale, and moved with Alice and the baby to Colorado Springs. There they lived in virtual quarantine for weeks.

Disliking to be idle, Lewis opened an office and handled a little legal business—"probably hired a gent for one dollar to shoot another gent and then paid gent No. 2 a dollar for the privilege of acting as his counsel," Wintie scoffed. "Oh, these rising young lawyers!"

Slowly Alice won back her health, and then back to New York they all moved, and Lewis resumed his interrupted career along the same humanitarian lines.

He found his sisters established in a house on Murray Hill that they rented jointly, where they entertained and were entertained in turn as full-fledged members of the rarefied society presided over by Aunt Caroline Astor. All three were now mistresses of their persons and their fortunes, answerable for their actions only to themselves. The youngest, Alida, had emerged from guardian control two years after Margaret had turned twenty-one.

Independence exactly suited Margaret; she wrote to brother Willie that their first season had been an "idyl—we three quite on our own feet socially. 200 people eat with us in 4 months. . . . Alida was the belle at dances & came home covered with favors like a Xmas tree. We kept well & happy. I pray God next year may be as peaceful, but of course not one of us is by way of getting married. Oh, no!"

Alone among these family transformations, Robert Chanler was the maverick whose strangeness was causing misgivings. There were, it seemed, two sets of Chanlers—the fair and the dark—contrasting both in appearance and in temperament. Armstrong, Winthrop, William, and Margaret were rather fair in coloring, of medium height, with features suggestive of English country types; they were quick in thought and movement, and temperamentally restless, practical, and authoritarian. Their view of life was intellectual rather than emotional.

Lewis and Robert, by contrast, and Alida and Elizabeth to a minor degree, were dark. Both Lewis and Robert were over six feet tall, loose-limbed and graceful in movement, and by temperament moody and sentimental, gentler and more sympathetic. Their responses to life were basically emotional, proceeding from impulses that they did not feel any need to rationalize. In social intercourse they were both easier and harder to get along with, depending upon the balance that existed at the moment between their aspirations and their limitations. Yet though different in their characters, both groups of Chanlers together formed a distinct unit or group, readily recognizable and comprehended by themselves as much as by others. They shared in common typical family traits and attributes, one of which was the well-known "Chanler voice." All their voices possessed a unique timbre, clear and penetrating, capable of being heard above other voices without being unduly raised.

Bob Chanler, six feet three inches tall, was not handsome as a boy and very young man. His features had a sulky expression; yet he was fumblingly appealing. He craved affection and was unsure of himself, and under the inept tutoring of Mr. Bostwick, had managed to dodge learning, until in some ways he seemed hardly educated at all. At sixteen, he was capable of writing from Rokeby to his sister Margaret in Europe, with bland disregard for spelling and grammar:

"I am very sorry that I am not able to send you a birthday gift but funds are low, so instead will write to you in turn once a week, which I think ought to satisfy you. . . . Jex is well & sleeps with me every night. Tell Alida that Bum prospers & Warren rides him. I think everyone of you ought to write home more. You know the proverb, that charity begins at hom & as I am at hom & open to all kinds of charity, I think this would be the best. When you write to Lewis it is not writing to me. . . . When you write to me dont tell me about your friends how I can know them is a misterry to me. I want to know what you are doing, how many times you fall off in a week & things like that. Thank Bessie for her charming letter, & as I was feeling rather blue it was doubly Wellcomed. I have got to work now so will let down anchor in regards to this letter. . . ."

It was evidence like this—reinforced by Uncle John Jacob Astor's advice to watch out lest Bob do "something devilish like Henry Astor"—that convinced Wintie that his youngest brother would benefit by a sojourn abroad. Perhaps there his relatives could make something of him; certainly he gave no promise of being much credit to the family name. Daisy Chanler agreed that Robert should live for a while in Europe, but her reasons were different from those of her husband: she sensed in the ungainly adolescent qualities that set him apart from his brothers, which it might be worthwhile to cultivate in a friendlier atmosphere than the rusticity of the Hudson River valley.

In February, 1889, therefore, after the guardians had given their consent, Robert Chanler was packed off to Europe in tow of the Winties. The estimable Mr. Bostwick went along as equerry, theoretically assigned to the duty of holding Bob in line. The program laid out by the guardians called for travel and language study; but far from mastering any foreign tongue, Robert's facility in English seemed to deteriorate during the next year or two. His correspondence, sentimental, affectionate, and erratic, gave evidence of his inner turmoil—the nameless reaching-out of a sensitive nature toward something faintly glimpsed, yet felt to be imminent. Especially he seemed to be at variance with the social pattern in which he had been reared. From Wiesbaden he wrote to "Dearest Peg":

"I have not written to you my dear Peg for months but blow it all surely you would rather hear from me when I want to write than purely from duty. . . ."

Then from Paris, where he had gone to stay with Amélie and Archie:

"Amélie & Archie are as nice as they can be to me—I am just beginning to feel as if I knew her. Archie is quite talkative, not in the least like he was last autumn. . . . Tomorrow Archie is going to take me to Madame Galadvaize, she is the wife of the gentilman we are going to be with at Blois: she does not speak any English so I will have to whip up my French. . . . Archie took Mr. B. & I to the Louvre, & showed us the Venus of Milo, it is very beautiful, after you have seen one or two like it, the modern marbles are horrible, at least that is the way it affects me. . . . I had a long letter from Timpson [a Red Hook neighbor] yesterday and he picked some violets at Rokeby & sent them to me, was it not sweet of him. I have put them in my Bible, it made me so homesick, that I had to go and ask Amélie for a book to read. . . . I went to church on Sunday, it was what they call an American Chapple—I got there late, & what was my astonishment when I saw to [sic] men in the pulpit all in black. I looked & found it was a kind of Methodist affair, but I did not care & lissend to the sermon which was very long & pretty good. . . . Tonight I go to Romio, by Gounhou, I have not the least idea how to spell his name but knowing you to be a kind & sweet sister you will for give it. I must stop now much love & many kisses from your devoted br. Bob."

Bob was bewitched by proximity to Amélie, and the uncomplimentary suspicions that the Chanler girls were beginning to entertain regarding their glamorous sister-in-law seemed unworthy to him. Rallying to the defense of Amélie and her oscillating moods, he protested to "Dear Peg," who was sweating out another session of mud baths at Schwalbach:

"Poor Amélie has got neuralger, at a most unfortunate time. Archie had given us a bully dinner at a cafe, & in the midst of it Amélie had an attack of neuralger. I brougt her home & left Archie & Mr. B. to finish the dinner. If you knew how much Amélie wanted to be with you, you would feel ashamed of having thought anything against her. I will tell you a good proverb to follow, there are always two sides to a question, if you follow that you will never do anybody an injustiss, & will get on a great deal better in the world. . . ."

Bessie was lectured in the same vein when she expressed pique that Archie and Amélie had gone off to England for the season, instead of coming to Germany to see the sisters, as they had promised:

"If you have been complaining & grumbling at their apparent

neglisence of you, you will when you see them & talk [to them] you will be sorry at having done so. I am & am trying to make up for it now as best I can within my conciounce, heavens how it does kick & prick. Why it is worse than if a younge jack ass or bea was in it. But you are a more forgiving nature than me, for when you thought yourself slighted it might have occurred to you that they had some reason for their delay.

"Not so with me, for when I found they were going to Breed [Brede] & after that to Ascot, England, I was as mad as a march hair. But it has turned out right now. . . ."

Too much and too close association with Amélie was going to Bob's curly-topped head. Virile and without guile, he floundered toward an avowal the nature of which he did not suspect, and in bewilderment he translated his inner confusion into religious questioning. Undergoing a temporary loss of faith (or so it seemed to him), during which his thoughts and spelling alike whirled riotously, he struggled to sublimate the conflict by applying himself to a book titled *Why I Am a Christian, or Reasons for Believing in Christianity*. ("What a wonderful little work it is—just think of its being translated into Jappanies.") After much soul-searching he concluded that the meaning of life was inscrutable; "for if God took the trouble to form matter he must have done it for some purpose & I think our religion explains the reason as well as the Almighty ever intended it to be explained, for if it was explained there would be no such thing as faith."

Nevertheless, to avert a possible scandal, Bob was packed off to live with the French family near Blois where it was hoped he would at least acquire proficiency in spoken French. But the expedient failed to settle either Bob's seething emotions or his orthography. Reporting on a one-day return to Paris for the purpose of picking up passports, he told his sisters:

"Mr. B. & I sepperated after we had been to the legation—he to the Banck, & I to do some shopping—After I had done what I wanted I took lunch at a cafe on the 'rond poin de la Champdelissé' & did not have time to do justiss to the cooking which was very good.

"In the afternoon I went up the Iffell toure. I think the most appropriate name would be 'le tour de patience.' 'My heavens,' do you know that I took three mortal hours to mount. While I was going up I met Monsieur Carles the one who is doing Amélie's bust, he gave it up, as he had not time to waste in such a manner. . . . Indeed I did have a pretty poor time of it in Paris —I am glad I stayed though . . . & now I knowing the ropes can have some fun, without deppending on anyone to show me around. P. is undoubtedly the city to enjoy one's self in, as you will find out. . . ."

The country folk living around the village where he was boarding impressed Bob as "very stuppid & ignorant" but "very happy & good," and he liked them. The name of the spa where Margaret was putting in her third cure season he could never master. "How are you getting on at Schawarback?" he wrote, and again, "How wild Schwalback must be . . . I do pity you there if I was only an angle I would always hover arround it, & let the sheen from my golden wings cast hope & comfort on to many. . . ."

The nub of Bob's letters usually dealt with either esthetic reactions to sights, or his tumultuous emotions. Accounts of events were secondary. This contrasted with his brothers' and sisters' letters: they dealt with things factual, tangible, and visible; Robert groped introspectively. By 1891 he was sketching, and finding satisfaction in it. "I went into the garden of the Pettit Trianon & sketched & I liked mine immensely," he reported in June, 1891. "I got the broad effect well."

His letters thereafter became peppered with impromptu sketches. Writing from Milan during an educational tour of Italy, he recollected a "doctor who used to rinkle up his face when he came in to see me meaning to look happy and pleased, but made me think that his wife was accustomed to greet him 'd'autrement.' He was an Englishman and half Italian though he did not say so, but know [sic] Englishman ever dove into a room like he did." And there was a sketch of the little doctor, hat in hand, diving into a room.

Another sketch showed the interesting costume worn by the peasant women around Bad Liebenstein, in Germany. Still another went with a letter to New York showing the colonial-type costume in which Bob hoped to appear at a fancy dress ball in St. Moritz. (He appeared instead as Uncle Sam, striped trousers on his long, supple legs, bestarred blue coat, and "my hat was magnificent.") The creative urge was in him, and this, fanned by the equivocal sensations aroused by Amélie and his distaste for the banal existence of the expatriates he met, kept him resentful and rebellious.

"You wont catch me having anything to do with people who have taken up their abode at Paris, no not by a long short," he announced. "Will excuse Aunt Elizer, she is to old & to far gone to know whether people are lying or telling the truth. Heavens spear me from any more old dotage aunts of her species. . . ."

The emotional disturbance at length became so intense that Bob suffered what was then termed "nervous prostration," and complete rest—far from Amélie—was prescribed. The summer of 1891 he spent on a farm in Wales, in a remote spot devoid of excitements. His hosts were congenial, but the furnishings of their house moved him to esthetic groaning. ("O dear me the pictures & the conflomerations of furniture of every age, Egyptian mumies down to New Town chairs.") His eye caught the scene, clear-cut and vivid, as he verbally sketched his host's mother, Lady Prynne-Jones:

"Such a dear clear-headed far seeing old lady . . . I play Halma every evening with [her], & if you could see her smiling & chuckling over it with great fat spectacles on you would feel a lump rise in your throat & bless her as I do every time I move a pawn & look at her. . . ."

Enforced idleness and physical lassitude led him for the first time to apply himself to reading, and he discovered that he had a liking for books. He read haphazardly—Motley's *Dutch Republic,* Greek and Roman history, *Elsie Venner, The Story of an African Farm,* Amélie's *A Brother to Dragons,* and cousin Marion Crawford's *Khaled*—all in a jumble. Books in old French he balked at: "Montaignes Essays are to much for me—he spels 'fait Faict' & things like that all the way through."

From another drowsy retreat in Devonshire he told his sister: "I can't do much, and painting tires me—so reading is the only amusement I have, & I read all day long."

It was in this semisolitude that he began to get his bearings. His spelling became somewhat less erratic (although all his life

Robert Chanler would display a fine eighteenth-century disdain for consistency in spelling), and in an effusive letter written on July 16, 1891, he informed Margaret, who that summer was sampling the social whirl at Newport:

"I have been doing some little sketches & have fail[ed] several times, but I am not discouraged. I go to London tomorrow to see the doctor, & if he says I may I shall go to Brittany."

Two months later permission was granted, and Bob regained the Continent with steadied nerves. That winter he spent at St. Moritz, flirting, tobogganing, and (as brother Willie put it with the impatience of a man of action) making "glaring-eyed resolves to *do something* in this world—resolves so strenuous that they can be consummated only if the present is devoted to delicious repose." Bob was beginning to see his way, and it was not the way of his brothers. He told Margaret:

"I am sure I shall loath New Port & U.S.A. . . . I shall live over here until I become an artist & then go over with sanguin philanthropic ideas about elevating art."

But his affections and instincts were still deeply rooted in the family, and he was confident of their continued solidarity. He confided to Margaret:

"If we all work out our lives in large great works how sound will be our connecting links! We will not have any fear of out growing each others tastes & ideas. I think so far we bid fair to be a fine family, & one that our parents would have been proud of. Old Wintie will in turn do something when his family grows to such great proportions that he must support them."

This last observation had pertinence, since Daisy Chanler was expecting another child in three months.

Soon after this Bob took the plunge, and from a studio in Rome, on the Piazza di Spagna, he announced that he was formally embarked upon a career as an artist, always providing that his talent should prove substantial enough. His situation had nothing of the starveling Bohemian about it:

"My bed is kingly, exactly like a royal bed one sees in old

Robert Chanler in fancy dress at St. Moritz, 1889. "My hat was magnificent," he reported.

palaces. We have two servants, a German woman of good repute, & our boy Remo, who speaks Italian only. Jack says our apartments are the best he has seen in Rome. He comes around every morning & talks & smokes a friendly pipe."

"Jack" was John Elliott, the painter husband of Julia Ward Howe's youngest daughter, Maud. He had agreed to start Bob's instruction, the latter said, and "when he goes & even now will get Villagos the great Spanish painter & Coleman the great animal & landscape painter to come & help me. Also I am learning modelling & have been offered [a] place in the studio of Benluri, the great sculptor who did Grand Pa Ward's bust, & all this for nothing. O I am happy . . ."

José Villegas had painted Sam Ward's portrait in Rome during the last year of Sam's life. Mariano Benlliure y Gil had done a sparkling bust of Sam at the same time, admirably catching the old man's vitality and infectious twinkle. So Sam Ward was still opening doors and providing opportunities for the grandchildren

whose company he had been denied. They were constantly being
made to feel this remote beneficence: again and again people
would come up to the brothers or sisters and speak of their still-
warm affection for Sam Ward; and since Sam had traveled Europe
for decades, his name was an open sesame in unexpected places.

Elliott tried conscientiously not to be lenient in judging young
Chanler's ability. Maud Elliott, who was staying with her mother
in Boston, received almost daily letters reporting on Bob's progress.

"Of course, he is very anxious to know if I think he has talent,"
Elliott confided, "which is a difficult thing for me to answer as I
don't want to mislead him. I think he certainly has a great deal
of facility which may mean something and may not. As a rule it
is rather against a man than otherwise, but his ideas are so good
that if he can only be made to study seriously, I think he will
amount to something . . . I take him to all the studios and tell
him to admire what is good in every man's work, and not pin his
entire faith to any one man."

Regarding Bob's character, Elliott was puzzled. To the older
man he seemed excessively, even dangerously, pliant and open to
suggestions. Maud was told:

"This evening I went to see Bob who is a dear boy, and I think
I did him some good. He is more susceptible to good impressions
than to bad ones as far as I can see . . . Still I fear if he were to
fall into bad hands he would probably go to bits for he is easily
convinced. I spent two hours answering the most extraordinary
questions I ever had put to me in life about morality. I hope I
answered them well. I hope too he will follow the advice I gave
him."

Soon after this Elliott could report with more contentment that
Bob was "working bravely and well, and there is no doubt that
he has lots of talent. He is so much improved I don't think you
would know him. Steady occupation with sympathetic, hard-work-
ing people around him has quieted down his nerves to a wonderful extent."

There was just the one reservation about Bob's variability that
stuck in Elliott's mind. Bob, he still felt, was far too apt to be "in-

fluenced by the last person who has made some plausible remark to him. He is like a compass and people act on him like magnets, but when he is left alone he points in the right direction."

Delightfully settled in Rome, Bob had no longing for America and Rokeby. Rather, he professed to look back on his years there with positive distaste.

"Rokeby has no very dear remembrance in my mind," he assured "Peggoty." "So I don't think I shall live there much. And if I am an artist I shall live here & in Spain. . . . An author & an artist in fact any man of the arts can live where they like. They belong to a school & not to a country. . . ."

He knew his direction now, and in February, 1893, he wrote that Stanford White had been urging him to study in Paris; he added his own conclusion, based on sound instinct, that he was "not calm enough yet to stand the life, & the work in a studio with forty other enthusiastic students. The competition & keenness would be too much for me. Perhaps in two years I shall go & work at drawing there. . . . The artists here are not proud but talk & treat a student as an equal. So you see now my reasons for staying."

But Margaret did not see the validity of the reasons he produced. She could not grasp why he should be so absorbed in art, although Bob tried to explain:

"To me an artist is the most peaceful man alive, peaceful & sometimes joyfully happy & nearly every day sad. . . . And their ways of thinking are not given to the world except by pictures so the world calls them fools & empty. But they are deep-souled high minded & brave. . . ."

He was impatient for the day when he would come of age and be able to dispense with explanations to his elders. Upon Margaret's attaining her majority in 1891, he had written to her with determination:

"In a year and three months I shall be *21*. You will see me [at Rokeby] & not before."

And so it came about. On February 22, 1893—just two weeks after he had vented his musings on the dedication of artists to their high calling—Robert Winthrop Chanler became twenty-one. There was a celebration, Bob treating to champagne, and Elliott reproached himself later for having churlishly refused to drink a toast; champagne played hob with his stomach. "Still I think I ought to have toasted him," the painter ruminated.

Five weeks after that day of liberation, a cablegram was delivered at Lewis Chanler's law office in Exchange Place, New York City, reading:

ENGAGED TO JULIE HURRAH
TELL FAMILY RETURN SHORTLY
BOB

A Wedding in London

The news threw the clan into a Chanler tizzy. Not that the marriage of a younger son was an event of consummate importance in the family's social scheme, and Bob was always doing things in an unconventional way. But nobody had been *consulted,* and a marriage called for preliminary study.

"You can imagine the rushing to & fro, the conclaves, discussions, tête à têtes—maelstrom—which took place," Margaret wrote to Willie Chanler.

Wintie hurried into town from Tuxedo Park (where he had taken a house) for a confab at Delmonico's. Alida and Elizabeth, who were visiting relatives in Charleston, were recalled "on 24 hours notice," while Lewis suffered "a series of nervous shocks, culminating in silent hysterics. Brog on the other hand has reason to believe that Bob has an artistic future—et ça suffit pour lui."

Clearly the majority of the family was not satisfied; but in view of previous alarms over Bob, the preponderance of opinion was that the more speedily he was married, the better. This idea he had of devoting his life to painting was nonsense, of course; art was a suitable avocation for a man, but to speak of adopting it as a profession was ridiculous; an artist in the family, splashing about with paints and associating with Lord knows whom, would scarcely be a credit to the name.

Margaret had other reservations about the wisdom of the step Bob was about to take. There was the question of his health: had he fully recovered from that "nervous prostration" of two years before? She knew that artists led highly irregular lives, even dissipated, and Bob had shown himself absolutely reckless of consequences. Margaret kept her uneasiness to herself, however, until she should reach London, where she could judge the situation more clearly.

The girl whom Robert had chosen for a wife was no stranger to the Chanlers—she was Julia Remington Chamberlain, the younger sister of Alice Chanler, Lewis's wife. As a child, Julia, too, had lived in Red Hook, but she had been educated in Germany and England. She had been her father's favorite, but had been held in subservience by her domineering mother, and in New York the Chanlers speculated on how she had turned out under the circumstances. They little guessed that Julia was as flustered by the prospect of her imminent marriage as were her future in-laws. For the fact was that Bob had won her on the rebound from an unhappy love affair.

At twenty, Julia had fallen in love with an eligible young man, and he with her; but he had no fortune. This disqualified him in the eyes of her mother, and the romance had been broken up ruthlessly. Bob Chanler being at hand and eligible on the score of wealth as well as family position, the mother had engineered the match without either of the principals quite knowing how it came about. Julia had not been armed for defense, and while she was floundering in her unhappiness, she had listened to the sympathizing of Bob and had convinced herself that she loved him.

John Elliott in Rome had seen the match brought about with foreboding; it confirmed that reservation he had entertained regarding Bob's suggestibility. On March 20 Elliott had written to his wife:

"A very hectic day. Bob came back from Florence as I expected engaged to be married, and the ceremony is coming off on the 14th of April! I hope it won't be a case of marrying in haste and repenting at leisure."

And ten days later he advised Maud in strictest confidence:

"I think I can give you material for a chapter or so of your next novel on match-making mothers, coy daughters and opinionated

ABOVE Julia Chamberlain Chanler, shortly after her marriage to
Robert Chanler.

LEFT Robert Chanler shortly before his marriage in 1893.

not-to-be-caught-by-chaff youths, most interesting and pathetic. I am an old bird but I never saw a matrimonial race so jockeyed yet I suppose it happens every day."

In New York, the Chanler sisters scurried to get ready for sailing. As she did intuitively in moments of stress and excitement, Margaret turned to Mary Meroney, the factotum of Rokeby, for practical support in the crisis. In a hurried note she described Bob's cablegram as "the greatest shock I ever had, I think," and added:

"I hope you will come down with Jeannie if you want to and say good-bye to Bessie and Alida and take care of me until Wednesday when I expect to go too. But we will only be gone 2 months so it is not for long. Bessie and Alida have gone to bed worn out for they just arrived from Charleston. They send their weary love."

Alida and Elizabeth did leave New York on the first available ship; Margaret followed four days later, having stayed to shut up their New York house. But a storm drove her ship two hundred miles off course, and she reached London one day late for the wedding. Refusing to grieve over the contretemps (it was too late now to worry about Bob's health), she accepted the situation and three days later wrote a breezy account of the wedding to Aunt Julia Ward Howe in Boston, giving the details she knew her aunt would be eager to hear:

"Bessie found Bob so excited that she would not listen to his waiting for me as he and Julie wanted to do. So the wedding took place at 11 o'clock Wednesday morning in St. George's, Hanover Square." The rector of St. George's, the Reverend David Anderson, officiated, and "Alida was the only bridesmaid in white crêpe de chine & a big white hat. Bessie wore pink with green & gold over it & a marvellous bonnet of tinsel & eyes so that she looked like a dragon as she tells me with delight. The bride's family consisted of her mother, stepfather and Brothers. The Stanford Whites left their child in Paris & came over for the wedding & Bob had a dozen or so of English friends, so in spite of himself he was decently married.

"So much for the world," she went on to this great-aunt whom she increasingly emulated. "As for the flesh and the devil—Bessie says they are frantically, seethingly in love with each other, that Julie is humbly undertaking to try to soothe him. She thinks him the greatest genius alive, wants him to work 4 years in Rome, 'knows she isn't clever' and hopes she can take care of him. She is 'radiantly happy' under this—I don't know what to call it so will say unusual arrangement—& of course he, her great big baby man, thinks every thing is 'perfectly ideal.' . . .

"Before Bessie arrived a series of excitements arrived too, plans, decisions, hearts, minds, souls, had to be disposed of . . . clothes, food, sal-volatile. I found them quite exhausted, suffering from sympathy and hubbub, and at once they told me I must go to Paris. They have gone for 10 days. I haven't . . ."

Margaret's protective concern for her brother reconciled her to the marriage, although she still did not like it. And Robert's excitability worried her; it seemed to her un-Chanlerlike.

Those at home had only the brief, decorous accounts of the wedding cabled to New York newspapers to judge by. The *Times* pronounced the ceremony "a very pretty affair," and noted that among the guests was William Waldorf Astor, who had been young Bob's guardian. (Coincidentally, the same issue of the *Times* contained a lengthy account of William Waldorf Astor's purchase of historic Cliveden.)

Willie Chanler, who had gone back to East Africa, received a fuller account from Margaret, and to him she insisted that Bob was "madly in love," and the bridal couple were "as happy as people of that age and temperament most always are under like circumstances. . . . Bob is 'quite mad,' but loveable, in spite of his ridiculous personal vanity & other eccentricities. Julie seems a good wholesome armful with no nerves & otherwise healthy. . . . I could write pages that ought to be amusing about the whole thing, from Bob's cable . . . on March 26 to the morning I saw them off at Kings Cross on April 20. . . ."

Never was Margaret Chanler more mistaken than in her impression of Bob's bride. Julia Chamberlain Chanler was conventional, dressed beautifully, was self-effacing, shy in company, and was equipped to play the role of hostess deftly. But as a mate for Robert Chanler she was a total misfit. Underneath her surface coolness and reserve she was a woman of excessive timidity, easily frightened, shrinking from whatever was rowdy, bold, dogmatic, irresponsible, impulsive, rash, and above all loud. Alas! These were the very qualities that seemed to her to be personified in the Chanlers.

The newlyweds arrived in New York directly from their wedding and were whisked by Winthrop to Tuxedo Park. There they made acquaintance with the latest addition to Daisy's family— a girl, christened Hester Marion after her South Carolina great-great-great-aunt, the niece of the Revolutionary War hero. Wintie reported the pair "well & noisy," but admitted he was relieved when they talked about going to Bar Harbor for the summer. "Bully place for them," was his opinion. "Cool, conventional, & a long way off."

The pair stopped at Rokeby to be scrutinized by "Mulligatawny" (as Amos Tuck French had mistakenly caught Mary Meroney's name when first introduced), then moved on to Maine. But Julia could not feel at ease in America; the mere energy of the people exhausted her. Bob, too, was longing for Rome, so in the autumn they sailed back to Europe.

Bashaws and Belmonts

Before coming home, just prior to Robert's wedding, Wintie Chanler had emerged from a harum-scarum adventure in Morocco that for the time being made him appreciate the serenity of Tuxedo Park.

Willie Chanler, deep in projects of international scope that were sure to "make a packet" and bring fame to their promoter, had learned of the existence, or supposed existence, of an unexploited oil field in Morocco. Instantly he became fired with the idea of locating this untapped source of petroleum, and if it proved to be as rich as rumor indicated, obtaining a concession from the sultan of Morocco to work it.

Unfortunately, Willie already was deep in preparations for an exploration expedition into British East Africa, and he could not afford to leave London. Wintie was approached, and he jumped at the chance to go to Morocco and bring back samples of the oil. The mission would have to be carried out with utmost secrecy to avoid arousing international suspicions.

For the trip Winthrop teamed with Stephen Bonsal, a roving correspondent for the *New York Herald,* as reckless a daredevil as Willie Chanler himself. The two attached themselves unofficially to a British diplomatic party that was being sent to negotiate a trade treaty with the sultan, giving out the purpose of their journey as to hunt lions. In the guise of sportsmen they reached Fez without encountering any serious hindrance; but there they rashly became involved in a brawl with a mob of

Moslem fanatics, and in the running fight that ensued barely escaped being killed. The crowd had been incited by the bashaw, or governor, of the city, and the two young Americans vowed to pay him back. Assuming a lofty tone, they demanded redress from the sultan, who hated the bashaw anyway, and the governor was commanded to apologize to the Americans, humble himself publicly before them, and pay a heavy fine.

The ceremony of abasement was staged impressively. As a mark of respect, Wintie and Bonsal had been provided with chairs—two rickety gilt affairs, probably left by some French or Austrian embassy years before. At the crucial point the bashaw tried to wriggle out of confessing his complicity in the mob attack; whereupon Chanler arose in wrathful dignity and delivered an ultimatum, threatening that the guns of the American fleet would wipe out Morocco's cities unless amends were forthcoming.

The effect of this blood-chilling harangue was marred for Bonsal by the fact that, unknown to them, Wintie's chair was equipped with a music box that started to play as soon as he stood up; so that he was forced to hurl his thunderbolts to a tinkling obbligato of German beer-hall tunes. The bashaw, however, was awed (whether by Wintie's ferocity or by the music, Bonsal never was sure), and groveling in apology he paid the fine. With a lordly gesture the Americans flung this to the crowd of beggars clamoring at the gate.

Taking counsel of prudence, the adventurers decided that Fez thereafter would be too hot for safety, and they struck out with all speed for the coast. For three days they rode through blazing-hot, danger-filled country (sustaining themselves with their few remaining bottles of Veuve Cliquot drunk at desert temperatures) and reached Tangiers, where they learned that they had been reported slain, and their families already had ordered coffins to transport their remains to America.

But they did bring back samples of oil from Willie's field. These were smuggled past several customs barriers, and were submitted to two chemists for separate analyses. One chemist was German, the other English. The German unhesitatingly identified the oil as taken from low-grade deposits in the Harz Mountains. The Englishman just as positively identified the sample as coming from a worthless outcropping in Derbyshire.

So that ended the will-o'-the-wisp episode, which had kept Daisy

Chanler on tenterhooks of anxiety. To compensate, Wintie meekly allowed himself to be led to Bayreuth for seven days of Wagnerian opera. "It took a lot of beer but I got through it," was his summing up of the penitential ordeal.

By this time Willie Chanler was on his way to Zanzibar, and Winthrop was less than edified by a London newspaper account of the intended safari ornamented with Wintie's own Harvard class photograph, purporting to be "a recent likeness of the daring young explorer."

"I have already been married to Amélie Rives and now I have made extensive explorations in the Dark Continent," was his bitter-sweet comment. And off he set for America, vowing: "This is the last time I take my kids out of the country for five years at least. They have broke me flat."

A stay at Newport soon set him yawning again—tired out, he said, with the "giddy, goozy whirl of sassiety." He described the scene for his sisters with the dispassion of an autopsy surgeon:

"The poor dear millionaires are trying their damnest to have a good time. But the wind won't blow for the yachts & it rains whenever there is a particularly good polo game. Internecine strife divides society; many people don't speak, bow, or breathe the same air with others. The small fry are all as poor, or poorer, than usual. There is no good, cheerful, reeking scandal to comfort the women. The old men are all prophesying 'trouble in the Street.' And yet the same pompous procession of imported carriages, coachmen, harness, and clothes meanders up and down the Avenue every afternoon as of yore. It all looks as gay as a garden. The excursionists come in swarms to stare at the nobs, [who] turn up their noses & snort at the excursionists. And each longs to be having as good a time as the other."

No misanthrope could have painted a gloomier picture. But Wintie Chanler was no misanthrope; lightly stamping the dust of Bellevue Avenue from his English riding boots, with the advent of autumn he retreated to the house he had acquired in Tuxedo, where tranquillity and repose were in style. Amos French was rooted in that reservation of the rich, and Wintie had discovered it through him.

"Most beautiful and healthy," he had assured Daisy, "only forty miles from New York & with every kind of comfort. Lake to sail on & fish in—forty-two miles of roads through the woods. Tennis, swimming, etc. . . ."

Daisy did not care for the isolation: forty miles from civilized conversation, she was inclined to think, cut off from urban pleasures, theaters, music, socializing. But having paid $30,000 for the house, Winthrop proposed to enjoy it. He also expected to enjoy the poker games in the clubhouse, and the liberty to dash away for a while whenever the impulse seized him.

The accounts appearing in the newspapers about brother Willie's progress in Africa gave Wintie a particular satisfaction because they centered public attention on somebody in the family besides Amélie Rives. When a society reporter listed Alida Chanler as "receiving" at *the* Mrs. Astor's ball, Wintie wrote gleefully to Margaret that she had been identified as "the sister of the African explorer, and not as the sister-in-law of the novelist. . . . Aunt Tiny Griffin [former guardian], whom I saw yesterday, she has nervous prostration, was particularly pleased about this. She said that she was tired of seeing us all slated as the sisters and brothers-in-law of Amélie Rives."

Wintie's spirits were never low for long, nor was he capable of being bored at length. Finding himself in the city one evening with nothing to do, he scribbled a note to his friend August Belmont, who was living in the old Chanler mansion at 192 Madison Avenue:

"Dear Augie: Several young gentlemen whom I happened upon at the Opera told me that you were giving a small and early Children's party tonight. This roused my jaded spirit sufficiently to embolden me to ask your permission to come round and see the little ones dance. Waiting yours & Mrs. Belmont's kind invitation, to be returned by bearer instanter and no time wasted,
                              "I am,
                         "In hunger and thirst,
                         "WINTHROP CHANLER.

"P.S. I don't want to dance.
"P.P.S. I'm alone on the Town.
"P.P.P.S. May I come?
                         "W.C."

He came, was the life of the party, and after the guests, small and large, had departed, joined "Amoi" French and the three Belmont brothers—August, Perry, and Oliver—in the basement front room for a nightcap of champagne, during the downing of which he perched on the billiard table and howled the song:

> "I never like to wander
> From my own fireside . . ."

Eastward Ho!

Willie Chanler had made friends in England with a coterie of hard-bitten cavalry officers of the hunting set, and pending his return to Africa had been amusing himself by riding in break-neck steeplechases against the best gentlemen jockeys the turf and sporting clubs could muster—and by winning consistently. Beneath Willie's debonair exterior were extraordinary reserves of energy and tenacity of which few persons were aware; utterly self-reliant, he was ready for a fight or a frolic at any instant.

In some respects William Chanler was a model, and in sport he was a match, for his intense admirer, Theodore Roosevelt. Teddy, who was aggressively spreading the gospel of the "strenuous life," liked both Winthrop and Willie Chanler, for the three of them had been members of the Porcellian Club during their own years at Harvard, but he regarded the brothers in different lights. Wintie he loved for his wit and urbanity, indoors or out, while Willie he looked upon at times with a touch of awe. Willie could and would perform with nonchalance the sort of manly feats that Teddy worked himself up to by verbal breast-beating and figurative baying at the moon. Willie had no trace of the exhibitionist in him; whatever game he played, he played spontaneously and with utter concentration, concerned only to win. Tough, primitive, and single-minded, his capacity for action was enormous; dawdling or irresolution he despised. But his inherent pugnacity was disguised by effortless manners and aristocratic ease.

Willie's jaunty consistency in winning point-to-point contests did not sit well with some of his rivals in the dangerous sport. The fact that he was a rich upstart from America also told against him, and in certain quarters it was felt that he ought to be taken down a peg. Willie ignored hints and continued to ride hell-for-leather and to win. He would go to any lengths to improve his chances, even, at country meets where no sweat-box was available, sweating off weight by sitting for hours in a heap of steaming manure.

Finally a match race was proposed—Willie against the best of his English competitors. The stakes were substantial—two thousand pounds a side, winner take all. At White's and other West End clubs wagering on the outcome was heavy—so heavy that some of the bettors determined to make sure of winning by eliminating Willie. The sequel was a story long told in London sporting circles, although, like many stories revolving around William Astor Chanler, no documentary proof was ever allowed to exist.

A few days before the match (which is said to have been scheduled over the man-killing Grand National course at Aintree) two of the plotters were riding with Willie in a hunt. At a jump, these two closed in on Chanler from each side, lifted him clear of the saddle, and dropped him behind his horse. The tactic of "lifting" was well known, although frowned upon because such falls could be fatal. Willie escaped with a minor hip fracture; but the possibility of his coming up to scratch in the match race seemed taken care of.

His competitors misjudged Willie. On the appointed day he rode up to the starting line, strapped in the saddle with his hip in a cast, and went on to win.

This did not end the episode. Willie Chanler once described himself as "too mediaeval a person" to tolerate an insult or a defiance, and he set about evening the score. Singling out the man whom he believed to have been the instigator, he found his chance during a cross-country run, and just as his rival's horse rose to a fence, Chanler crashed his own mount into it. Both horses and riders went down in a tangle of lashing hooves. The action was seen by other riders, but such was the code of sportsmanship, nothing was ever said to Chanler about the matter; the unspoken consensus was that Willie had a legitimate grudge and was entitled to take his revenge, if he could do so without involving other parties. Willie sustained fresh injuries in this fracas, but luckily they were minor. His opponent never rode again.

To account for an enforced recuperation in London, Willie regaled his sisters with a tale about a sprained knee. From a hotel in Berkeley Square he groaned to Elizabeth:

"Was there ever such luck? A beastly frost for months & as soon as the thaw comes to be laid up. Well fate is against me. I am in town under the doctor's care while all the world is gay & hunting. I got a little fall & wrenched my knee. Of course I went on hunting & equally of course my knee swelled till it finally sent me to town. I go to the best surgeon here & he says it is nothing but I can't hunt for a week. So be it . . . I got a letter from Wintie the other day. He seems gay & festive and reports nothing of interest. Lewis & Alice are at Riverdale with three men servants a considerable number of maid servants and three horses. They think they are happy. . . . If I am fit enough I'll go to the Royal British Opera House Saturday night to hear Sir Arthur Sullivan's 'Ivanhoe.' The world says it is capital."

To Margaret went similarly cheerful misinformation regarding his injury, dressed up with an observation that would recur throughout William Astor Chanler's correspondence:

"The people here are very kind. I fancy, however, that they imagine me to be possessed of boundless wealth owing to the affluent sound of my middle name. . . . I am dreadfully hard up."

(Winthrop Astor Chanler had observed the same reaction. Willie would later contend that his brother took advantage of his simplicity by pointing out that they had the same initials, "W.A.C.," and they could "avoid confusion" if he [Wintie] simply dropped the middle name while Willie retained it. "I was gullible enough to agree," Willie groaned when Wintie thereafter gloated that his hotel bills had been reduced by one-half.)

In a subsequent letter to Margaret Chanler, written from new lodgings in Half Moon Street, Mayfair, Willie explained why he rode so recklessly—it was to keep himself cheerful:

"Chaff aside, I have been enjoying myself tremendously and am looking forward to a capital winter. Hunting does for me what nothing else can—it makes me good-tempered & keeps my liver from dictating to my character. A smile is often found lurking in the corners of my mouth now. No longer do I wear, as at New Port, the expression of a baffled tragedian. . . . Amélie's book is to be seen at the railway book stalls—people seem to think it is some sort of continuation of 'The Quick or the Dead?' . . . Kiss all the pretty girls for me. Get the others to write. Your loving brother, Willie."

But William Chanler's attention was fixed upon serious matters also—the preparation of an expedition which he planned to make into unexplored British East Africa, toward Mount Kenya. This time he would not be going "for fun," but at the head of a well-equipped exploration party, bent upon obtaining scientific information about a region that his friend Stephen Bonsal called "the last *terra incognita* of the habitable globe."

During the turn-of-the-century years, the beau ideal of a generation of American youth was Richard Harding Davis—the glamorous foreign correspondent and man-about-town. Manly, chivalrous, bold, and brave, Davis crashed through barriers impassable for ordinary mortals; he was petted by society and cheered along Broadway, and he was so good-looking that he set the standard of masculine beauty for the age. Yet in all these respects, Richard Harding Davis was merely the copy of an original, gotten up for popular consumption—and the original was William Astor Chanler. Davis was simply an over-statement of his friend. Davis spun his tales for a million readers; Willie recounted his true-life escapades to friends, and only in private. Willie was a headier yarn-spinner than Davis, a spellbinder, as Davis personally was not. The difference between the two friends was fundamental: by birth and heritage, William Chanler was a member of a certain social group, he was "in"; Richard Harding Davis was "out," and he would spend the better part of his adult life trying to crash through the one gossamer barrier that excluded him.

Davis and Chanler had met on Broadway before they encountered each other again in London in the summer of 1891, when Willie revealed his plans for Africa. Davis was enormously impressed, both by the scope of Chanler's preparations, and by the ease with which Willie was marshalling the enterprise. Davis particularly noted Chanler's surprising expertise. His conversation did not "teem with treks and Soudanese porters, and anecdotes of the slave trade and the quick effectiveness of jungle fever," Davis reported in *Harper's Magazine*. "So little given is Chanler to any one topic, that it was amusing, after he had interested those about him with anecdotes of Harvard or the boulevards, to ask him for a story of the land of the Masai, and to watch the faces of his hearers as the worldly, idle, and conscientiously dressed youth of the minute before told how men look who are dying of thirst, or how an elephant is liable to act when you fire at it."

The elaborate organization required for an expedition of the scope planned by Chanler astonished Davis. Government permission must be obtained to enter the territory, and arms and equipment of bewildering variety must be assembled. A working knowledge of photography, medicine, nutrition, agriculture, surveying, geography, military codes, cartography—all this was needed. Chanler's own refinements delighted Davis. Some of the aborigines who would be encountered probably would never have seen white men, and to impress these natives George Galvin was being coached by a professional magician in sleight-of-hand tricks. Chanler was taking a dozen pairs of flesh-colored rubber gloves, intending, while negotiating with tribal chiefs, to peel these off as if skinning himself, and giving the impression that he enjoyed the sensation.

So unobtrusively was this web of preparations being woven, Davis almost apologized for writing about it; and he lamented that "young men who do important things for the sake of the things themselves, and not for the afterclap of applause, are so few." The entire cost of the expedition, of course, was being borne by Chanler personally.

The sort of astuteness that underlay Willie Chanler's man-of-fashion air showed in the way he reached far afield to secure the right associate on the safari, which was expected to take two years and traverse a three-thousand-mile route through regions that were mere blanks on existing maps. His choice fell upon a lieutenant in the Austrian navy, Ludwig von Höhnel.

Von Höhnel was an experienced African explorer. In 1888 he had accompanied Count Teleki, the Hungarian explorer, on an expedition that struck northward from East Africa almost to Abyssinia, and discovered Lakes Rudolph and Stephanie. That expedition had been gone two years, and Teleki had lost one-third of his men by thirst and disease; so the dangers that would attend Chanler's undertaking were very real. Von Höhnel had been the cartographer of the Teleki expedition, and his brilliantly accurate maps had drawn Chanler's attention.

Early in 1891 Chanler wrote to the lieutenant, asking whether he would care to join a scientific expedition into East Africa. His laconic note gave no details, and since von Höhnel had never even heard the name Chanler the invitation mystified him. Nevertheless, for some obscure reason, it attracted him, although he had turned down several previous offers to return to Africa. While trying to make up his mind, he sounded out his naval superiors on whether he could obtain another extended leave of absence. Admiral Baron von Sterneck, the commander of the Austrian navy, said that he would have to meet this Mr. Chanler before a decision could be made, and von Höhnel communicated this fact in a reply letter. Back came a telegram from Sicily saying that Chanler would arrive in Vienna in a few days and would put up at the Metropole Hotel.

On the morning of the appointed day von Höhnel presented himself at the hotel, and was directed to Chanler's suite. The door was opened by a young man who seemed to be a sort of valet-secretary—George Galvin. Chanler was taking a bath, the lieutenant was told, and he retired to the dining room to wait. Shortly a slight, handsome, dapper man in his twenties appeared and introduced himself—William Astor Chanler.

At the first glance, von Höhnel was favorably impressed. Although eleven years older than Willie's twenty-four, he had never seen a man like this. Remarkably fine brown eyes, full of fire and challenge—pugnacious chin and resolute, firm-set lips—a hint of arrogance in the expression of the features that was not displeasing—the combination was striking. Chanler was dressed in quiet good taste, his suit beautifully tailored, and he carried himself with an air of superiority. Above all, to von Höhnel there

UPPER LEFT William Astor Chanler before his departure for second safari into East Africa.

UPPER RIGHT Lieutenant Ludwig von Höhnel, Chanler's companion on African explorations.

BELOW In camp in Africa. Chanler, left, in turban; Von Höhnel, center, and at right, George Galvin.

was an indefinable something about Chanler's whole bearing that stood out as unmistakably American.

Chanler's frank, unconstrained manner completed the conquest of the lieutenant, and as Willie rapidly outlined his plans, von Höhnel realized that he was a master of his subject. Together they drove off to interview Baron von Sterneck at the admiralty.

As they entered the great man's office, the admiral rose and welcomed his visitors pleasantly. In his youth von Sterneck had been a daredevil seadog, and von Höhnel, standing stiffly at attention, sensed that the two men of action took to each other at once. Courteously and fluently, speaking in English, which the admiral understood thoroughly, Chanler began to explain his proposals regarding Africa, speaking with a total lack of self-consciousness that embarrassed von Höhnel, inured to a world where subservience to rank was inculcated from birth. To the lowly lieutenant, the commander of the Imperial and Royal Austrian Navy was a demigod; yet here was this young American conversing with this exalted personage as if with an interested friend—and somehow the effect seemed just right. After a few moments, Chanler casually rested an elbow on a high desk at his side; this reminded the admiral that he had not invited his callers to be seated, and rectifying the omission, he led the way to a sofa. All three sat there while Chanler expounded his plans for an hour, holding the admiral's interest throughout.

One point puzzled him, von Sterneck confessed: how had Chanler hit upon von Höhnel, an officer in the Austrian navy, as his choice of associate?

When he was returning from his Kilimanjaro hunting junket, Willie explained, he reached the coast from the interior at Mombasa. There he was obliged to wait for a ship to Zanzibar. An Austrian corvette, the *Aurora,* entered the harbor, and Willie became friendly with her captain, Count Montecuccoli.* Also bound for Zanzibar, the count invited Chanler to come along as his guest; and during that voyage the neatness, discipline, and cleanliness aboard the *Aurora* had greatly impressed him, Willie said. Then at Zanzibar he had found everybody talking about the bril-

---

* Eventually von Sterneck's successor as commanding admiral of the Austrian fleet.

liantly successful Teleki expedition and praising Lieutenant von Höhnel.

The admiral listened to all this with great satisfaction. Then rising, he shook hands cordially and granted the lieutenant indefinite leave to accompany the Chanler expedition. The next day, after arranging to meet within the year for final consultation, Willie left Vienna—but not before dropping in for dinner at Vienna's famous Sacher restaurant, and making friends with Madame Sacher for life.

Months went by and von Höhnel heard nothing further from this American who so nonchalantly unsettled the sacred routine of Austrian officialdom. He suspected that Chanler had been side-tracked by some love affair, but then heard by chance that Willie was in England, amusing himself by fox hunting. Deciding to investigate, the lieutenant went to London and confirmed that Willie was hunting in the shires all right, but also that he had not neglected the preparations for the expedition. The quantities of supplies he had assembled for shipment had in fact reached such proportions that the nervous outfitter had inquired at the American embassy regarding Chanler's financial responsibility: was he good for the money? And what if he should have the misfortune not to return from so dangerous a journey? He was assured:

"If Mr. Chanler does not return alive from Africa, you will have your account settled promptly by the estate. If Mr. Chanler does come back, you may have to wait."

On June 11, 1892—his twenty-fifth birthday—Chanler left London for Marseilles, where he took ship for Port Said en route to Zanzibar. George Galvin was left to follow with the expedition's trading goods and other supplies; Chanler was to rejoin him at Lamoo (Lamu, in modern spelling), in British East Africa (now Kenya). Lieutenant von Höhnel left Vienna at the same time with the scientific and military equipment he had collected there. The two explorers rendezvoused at Port Said, where Chanler reported in high spirits to his family that his companion had brought, "among other things for convincing the natives that I am a 'dear sweet boy,' 4 savage Illyrian dogs, 200 rifles, and 35,000 cartridges." His health, he said, was excellent:

"I was examined by a doctor before leaving London & he pronounced me *sound* in every respect. I was gratified but rather surprised by his verdict. . . . If I have luck two years will see me more or less famous as an explorer & then I can settle down and tackle life at home. . . . Having this notoriety as a springboard I ought to get somewhere should I take the trouble to jump. If I fail in Africa I shall not be utterly cast down. . . . If I die, I die in a decent cause & leave my people nothing to be ashamed of."

Already he had told Richard Harding Davis that he hoped to enter public life and follow his father as a member of Congress.

From Aden, Chanler impatiently pushed on ahead, leaving von Höhnel to purchase camels and hire Somali drivers for them. Von Höhnel also engaged twelve Sudanese soldiers at Massowah to serve as escort, equipping them with Mannlicher repeating rifles in which they took great pride.

Meanwhile Chanler was busy at Zanzibar, rounding up the porters required for the safari. The supply of available men had been almost cornered by a missionary caravan heading into the backcountry, and Chanler had to offer high wages, and use the potent letters of recommendation he had brought, to recruit bearers. He finally got together one hundred and thirty men, but they were a motley lot. When von Höhnel saw them he was dismayed. Many were slaves rented out by their masters who took one-half of their pay; others were striplings incapable of carrying the standard load of eighty to one hundred pounds twelve hours a day. None of them had any experience in trackless country, or any notion of the harsh conditions they were certain to encounter, or of the fatigues and hardships incidental to African travel.

Since the success and safety of the caravan would depend on the loyalty and efficiency of its porters, von Höhnel protested against the folly of entrusting their journey, and perhaps their lives, to so unreliable a lot. But Chanler insisted that these were the only men available, and he felt confident that he could whip them into shape. Cautious and far-seeing in his planning, Chanler in action was often impulsive, impatient, and headstrong. Impatience was a fault common to all the Chanlers; they seldom could wait.

Von Höhnel especially mistrusted the headmen engaged by Chanler. The first headman, named Hamidi, had been with Chanler around Kilimanjaro, but he had never been in untracked country; von Höhnel disliked his sly, smooth manner. The second headman, Mohamadi, seemed no more capable or trustworthy. But Chanler stuck to his choices, and reluctantly his companion yielded; after all, Chanler was in command.

Embarking his bearers on a leaky Arab dhow, Chanler conveyed them to the mainland and to a base camp at Mkonumbi, about twenty miles inland from the island and town of Lamoo. George Galvin was waiting at Mkonumbi. Galvin amazed von Höhnel. Rather short, strongly built, cool-headed, calm in emergencies, George met every demand with practical handiness, and he had a definite knack with the men, being able to get cooperation without bullying or harshness.

The explorers had laid out their route with care. From Mkonumbi they were to ascend the Tana River as it wound north and west in the direction of Mount Kenya; then push north as far as the southern tip of Lake Rudolph. After exploring the country between that lake and Lake Stephanie, the caravan was to turn eastward and march through hundreds of miles of unknown territory to the Juba (Giuba) River, descend that stream to the coast, and come out near Kismayu in Somaliland, some hundred miles north of Lamoo. This was the country that Stephen Bonsal had called "a land without a name—but the Swaheli traders shudder as they call it 'the land of thirst and emptiness.'"

Willie explained this route in a letter to Elizabeth written at the Mkonumbi camp:

"Look up Lamoo on a good African map & you will see it on the East Coast about 200 miles north of Zanzibar. You will see a river called the Tana flowing from the interior & emptying near Lamoo. We follow the north bank of this river till we reach Mount Kenya. . . . We shall thoroughly explore it & then start north . . . penetrate nearly as far north as Abyssinia, then turn to the east & thence to the sea & home. . . . I will write you as often as possible during the journey; but don't feel frightened if you don't hear from me for 18 months as I am not certain that communication will be open to the coast from the interior. Now

I may as well tell you that if any expedition can travel with safety it is mine. It is perfectly armed & equipped in every way, and although I may seem reckless in little things I am very cautious when I have much at stake. Lieut. von Höhnel is a wonderful fellow & will do much to make my journey pleasant as well as successful. . . . If we are only moderately successful this journey should be attended with such valuable scientific results that it will make us famous. We have plates for more than one thousand photographs, scientific instruments of all kinds and last but not least von Höhnel knows how to use them all. You may be glad to hear that I have never been in better health; have a short brown beard and as I wear a white turban now instead of a hat I look more or less like a young Arab—perhaps dangerous when aroused. Tell George's people that he is very well & happy & is of the greatest service to me. Now I must stop for the sun is out of sight and it is getting dark. Love to Margaret & Alida to Lewis and Archie in fact to every one not forgetting Mr. Morris [the family lawyer]. I shall keep your last letter always with me. Your absolutely devoted & loving brother Willie."

"The Land of Thirst and Emptiness"

On September 18, 1892, Chanler marched out of Mkonumbi at the head of one hundred and sixty men, divided between the Zanzibari porters, seven Somali camel drivers, and twelve Sudanese guards. The pack train included fifteen camels and load-carrying donkeys; besides these there were oxen, sheep, and goats. The explorers themselves rode two tough Somali horses, but von Höhnel's "fierce Illyrian dogs" had turned out to be two retrievers and a scrappy fox terrier. The expedition was not cutting itself off from every civilized amenity: in Chanler's personal kit were half a dozen pints of champagne, a well-thumbed Plutarch, and Browning's poems.

A jaunty letter of farewell had gone to Margaret from Mkonumbi, mentioning, among more serious matters, Willie's disappointment that he had been unable to pick up any African songs worthy of adding to the Rokeby repertory. He had found one with a "pretty, broken rhythm," he said, but the words consisted of nothing but a "repetition of the exciting statement that a lady named Fatima is suffering from a prolonged attack of rheumatism."

His opinion of the inhabitants of the region he expressed forcefully in the same letter:

"The intellect of these children of the tropics is pitiably weak, and their morals of the lowest possible order. This is a dreadful place for slaves. The most popular occupation is selling one another to the Somalis, a neighboring warlike tribe who keep slaves. There are many instances where men have sold their sons, & brothers sell one another if the opportunity offers. These Swahili have been a great race. One may see ruins of their towns many hundreds of years ago abandoned & now half-buried ruins. Now the Swahili are perfectly depraved & have no ambition above eating and pleasure. It is time they made room for others more enterprising."

It would be months before the family would receive another letter.

From the start the progress of the caravan was slow. Von Höhnel's misgivings proved well founded, as desertions among the untested, incompetent bearers set in quickly. Here and there a man would throw away his load and slip into the bush. The first man to disappear took with him a load of ammunition, and though runners were sent to overtake him, neither man nor load was recovered. The difficulty the deserters would encounter in getting back to the coast seemed to make no impression on them; nor were they deterred by the prospect of incurring flogging and prison upon reaching Zanzibar, that being the penalty for desertion. Daily the Zanzibari melted away. Chanler tried reasoning with them, and invoked strict disciplinary measures, to no avail. In desperation he finally called the porters together at the end of a day's march, and told them that any who wished to return to the coast could go provided they set out at once; but starting with the next day, any man who tried to desert would do so at the risk of his life.

The next day a porter who had tried to desert once before tried it again. He was caught by one of the Sudanese guards, and Chanler ordered him to be marched in front of his captor. Watching his chance, at a favorable moment the prisoner darted into the bushes, and the Sudanese fired. Unfortunately his aim was only too accurate and the fugitive was killed.

Despite these discouragements, the expedition forged ahead, and after two weeks reached Hameye, a station on the Tana River that had been abandoned by the British East Africa Company. There a two-day rest was taken, and Chanler sent back to the coast five worthless bearers under a headman, who was instructed to bring back replacements. Since the round trip would take at least five weeks, Chanler and von Höhnel decided to make a side journey and if possible carry out one of the principal objectives of the expedition—to determine the location of Lake Lorian, a large body of water into which it was understood the Guaso Nyiro (Ewaso Ngiro) River emptied. No white man had seen the lake, which was believed to be the last undiscovered lake of major size in Africa, but natives placed it somewhere northeast of Hameye. On the Teleki expedition von Höhnel had scouted the headwaters of the Guaso Nyiro, but its lower course was still unknown.

The explorers also hoped to find a nomadic tribe called Rendile, who were said to inhabit a wide area nearby and to be well provided with herds of sheep and donkeys. From the Rendile it was hoped that food and additional beasts of burden could be obtained, to replace those that were succumbing to the bite of the tsetse fly.

On December 5 the two companions set out from Hameye. With them were eighty men and ten donkeys; the main supplies and the camels were left in Galvin's care at the station. Heading north, the explorers crossed a flat desert, dotted with flowers and butterflies brought out by recent rains. They then came to a rocky, hilly country where the going was rough, and at length reached a range of mountains covered with forests. This range they named the Jombeni. (Today it is known as the Nyambeni Hills.) They saw much game—zebra, oryx, rhinoceros, and now and then elephants—but no human inhabitants.

On the fourth day out, from a low rise they sighted a range of blue hills stretching far into the distance to the north, and surmised that these might be the southern outcropping of the General Matthews range. As Chanler stood examining these peaks, his gun bearer cried excitedly:

"Look, master! Down there is a large mountain! I think it is Kenya!"

Chanler turned his glasses in the indicated direction and beheld, standing nobly clear of the clouds, the snow-clad slopes of Kilimanjaro's mighty rival. At this proof that he was really in new country, Willie felt, he said, "as joyous as Moses when he viewed the promised land."

The route, however, lay in the direction of the blue hills north of Kenya, and day after day the explorers' elation rose higher. They shot game to feed the men, hippopotamus meat being specially relished by the porters, who gorged themselves on it until they became ill. Von Höhnel, in charge of the medical supplies, treated the resultant dysentery with heroic remedies—plenty of castor oil, or three or four "Livingstone rousers," topped off by ipecac and opium. The treatment seemed to work; at least the number answering sick call sharply decreased.

Chanler developed fever, but he would permit no pause. Coming to a river which they identified as the Mackenzie, they followed it to within fifteen miles of the distant hills, and could see on their slopes the smoke of countless fires. Could those be the fires of the Rendile?

Cutting their way through otherwise impenetrable bush, the party emerged on a grassy plain where the going was painful because of the irregular-shaped blocks of lava that lay under the tall grass, tripping one at almost every step. Frequently the caravan was charged by rhinos.

On December 17 the expedition had its first encounter with unfriendly natives. While investigating a forested hillside, they came upon a cultivated clearing where men and women were cutting brush. These ran off, and soon several hundred warriors came running, shouting and brandishing spears and poisoned arrows. They seemed to understand neither Masai nor Swahili, and Chanler, acting swiftly to head off an attack, seized several warriors who ventured close, and indicated by signs that they would answer as hostages for the caravan's safe passage.

The uproar increased, and in its midst, Chanler, overcome by fever, collapsed in delirium. Lying on the ground he kept yelling, "Attack! Attack! Cut them down!" terrifying von Höhnel. Then a tall man stalked out of the excited throng, speaking Swahili, and through him von Höhnel nervously negotiated a retreat. He released the hostages and gave each one a small present; then taking advantage of the crowd's surprise, he hastily bundled the delirious Chanler into an improvised litter and led the troupe out of that tight spot. The interpreter came along, volunteering to act as the expedition's guide.

Named Motio, he said he had been born near the coast, but had lived among various tribes in the mountains and spoke their dialects. The people who had blocked the safari's passage were called Embe, he said, and he seemed to know all about Lake Lorian and the Rendile. The lake could be reached, he said, by three days' march northward to the Guaso Nyiro River, and the Rendile were close by.

Von Höhnel hastened to set out. Chanler, much of the time unconscious, was carried in a hammock. Motio warned that the route lay across a waterless desert; and when Chanler recovered his feet, on the fourth day, they were in a sun-dried, almost treeless wasteland. The heat by day was intense, and the cold at night was bitter. As they approached the river, the ground became white with sulphate of magnesium, and its glare under the sun scorched the eyes. They had drunk the last of their water, and the porters were combatting thirst by chewing raw meat when at last they sighted the river on Christmas Eve. Jubilant because the course to Lake Lorian was now plain, and the lake must be not far off, the intrepid leaders relaxed over a Christmas feast—German army soup, fish from the river, oryx liver and oryx steaks, beans, biscuit, and coffee—with a pint of champagne.

The day after Christmas the journey was resumed, and that afternoon they came upon a major waterfall, where the river, tumbling in two streams over a lava precipice fifty or sixty feet high, churned away through a chasm filled with spray. This waterfall they named Chanler Falls, and pushed on. The terrain was rough; their feet were bruised by the lava rocks strewing the river bank, and the glare of the sun was blinding. Von Höhnel wrenched a knee and could not assist in hunting for food. Fish taken from the river provided a slight variation of diet until inspection of a catch during daylight revealed that they were alive with worms. Sleep was almost impossible because of the swarms of mosquitoes and flies. The horses sickened, and von Höhnel's died. Motio kept assuring them that Lake Lorian was not far off, that they would be able to see it soon from a high plateau just ahead.

On December 30 the caravan did reach this plateau (the Merti Plateau), rising five hundred feet above the plain on the opposite bank of the river. Chanler and von Höhnel crossed over, and after a struggle up the nearly vertical side, attained the top. From there

Chanler Falls. Photographed in 1923 when visited by a later American expedition.

they saw the river winding away for miles through a boundless desert, but no lake.

The next day they marched four miles along the base of the plateau and camped. Climbing to the top again, the explorers this time beheld, shimmering in the northeast, a large body of water —Lake Lorian! With the sangfroid of that stiff-upper-lip generation, the two men turned to each other and clasped hands in congratulation without a word. Von Höhnel estimated the lake must be at least sixty miles long, and Chanler tried to calculate the number of days it would take to reach it.

From then on the march became harrowing. Following the river, they passed through wooded areas teeming with rhinoceros that charged again and again. Chanler had several narrow brushes, and his tent boy was severely gored; Chanler put him on his horse and walked. The porters muttered about the madness of entering so perilous a country; both explorers suffered from fever intermittently; a bearer dying of dysentery had to be carried in a sling; others were very ill. One of the Sudanese guards hobbled along supported by a stick, babbling in delirium. The ground grew soggy, and at night it exhaled dank vapors that cut into the body like cold knives. For days there was no firewood, the river winding through tall grass, and the meat had to be eaten barely warmed over fitful grass blazes. Chanler urged the men on, promising them rest and plenty to eat as soon as they reached the lake, which could not be much farther off.

On January 12 a tall sycamore was sighted across the river, which had narrowed to less than ten feet in width and was only a foot deep; it seemed to be drying up, or sinking into the muddy soil. Climbing the tree to reconnoiter, Chanler and von Höhnel gazed ahead anxiously for a glimpse of the lake. All they could see, as far as the view extended, was a vast swamp covered with papyrus and water grass. The bitter truth was borne in on them: there was no Lake Lorian. The shimmer they had seen from the plateau had been a mirage; the Guaso Nyiro drained into a vast mud hole. The explorers climbed down and went to face their near-mutinous caravan.*

The return journey was a nightmare of thirst, hunger, and constant danger. The supply of dried corn and beans was wormy and about exhausted; the men were sickening on their unaccustomed diet of meat. The nearest food supply lay in the Jombeni Mountains, where grain and vegetables were cultivated by the inhabitants. To reach Jombeni before their food was entirely gone would require forced marches, and under the spur of this necessity the caravan slogged over the back trail. They followed the river bank, cutting their way through high grass that screened the crocodiles basking at the stream's edge. The trickle of food, except for meat, grew smaller and smaller. It was march, march, all day until night, and then long hours of darkness, shivering

---

* During World War II, South African troops in East Africa were intrigued by the name "Lorian Swamp" on their maps, in a region of almost virgin wilderness some two hundred miles northeast of Nairobi. A party of officers investigating the place found it to be a vast desert, just as described by Chanler, where a few water holes yielding a scanty supply of liquid mud, rather than water, were shared by nomadic Somali tribesmen and herds of elephants. Few white men had ever penetrated there, and the desolation and loneliness of the place made it as sinister and forlorn as Chanler and von Höhnel had found it.

cold, mysterious terrors, tormenting insects, and sleeplessness. Men died. But on the ninth day the Christmas camp site was regained.

Resting there only a day, the weary caravan struck out for the Jombeni hills, which Motio was sure could be reached by four days of hard marching. But they were slowed by the necessity of carrying the sick, and it was not until January 29 that the emaciated train reached a village of the Wamsara tribe on the Jombeni western slope. That night they camped, buoyed by the prospect of enjoying fresh milk, vegetables, and goat's meat as soon as trading would start in the morning.

But the Wamsara proved uncooperative, and during the night they set up a war chant. One of Chanler's porters died that night and had to be buried by stealth, in order not to reveal their desperate condition. The next morning several hundred fighting men milled angrily around the camp, and the only food produced was three yams. Chanler was faced with a crisis: his men were starving, and the shortest route back to the base camp at Hameye lay directly across the Jombeni range through the Wamsara territory. In the enfeebled condition of the caravan, it was folly to think of making a long detour through the desert.

Realizing that he must risk a fight, Chanler aroused the groaning men at two o'clock in the morning and distributed ammunition; three hundred rounds were held back as a last reserve.

At five o'clock, in bright moonlight, the caravan got under way. Chanler led with five Sudanese and Motio. To guard against treachery, Motio was bound with a rope tied around his waist, a husky porter holding the end of the rope in one hand and in the other carrying an American flag. Von Höhnel, with the remaining Sudanese guard and the camel drivers, brought up the rear.

Almost at once the sentinels posted by the Wamsara shouted the alarm from hill to hill. Since they had been discovered, Chanler ordered the tom-tom to sound, and to the beat of the drum he advanced until, shortly after daybreak, they were rushed by some two hundred screaming warriors.

Driven back by point-blank volleys, the tribesmen charged again and again. Three porters were killed and twelve were wounded, some with poisoned arrows. By eleven o'clock the attack had been repelled and the spearmen drew back. Profiting by the lull, Chanler rounded up all the food supplies he could commandeer in the adjacent villages, and soon had enough goats, cattle, and grain to support the caravan for eight days.

Driving the captured livestock before them, the explorers resumed the march, harried by warriors hovering on the flanks.

("These natives are fine fellows, spearmen, bowmen—poisoned arrows—and slingers. Stones as big as your head," Chanler would recount to his brother Wintie.)

The attackers kept up an incessant shouting and firing of arrows and stones, as Chanler pushed on, hoping to gain the crest of the ridge where Motio said the territory of the Wamsara ended and that of the Embe, who dwelt on the eastern side of the range, began. The Embe might be friendly. Several times the column was ambushed, and fought its way clear. Von Höhnel later described the running fight:

"Our route was uphill, across very intersected ground. We were in constant danger. Chanler led the vanguard, to clear the way. Our path led across a deep valley, into which we had to descend and ascend on the other side, advancing toward an enemy lying there in ambush. Chanler went ahead with a handful of men, while I with the remainder stayed behind to cover his advance. He had nearly reached the opposite height and was on the point of walking straight into the arms of a band of hidden natives, whom he evidently could not see. I began to fire shot after shot in that direction, [and] Chanler turned around to see what was the matter. At that moment he by chance saw a Wamsara armed with a spear approaching me from behind under cover of bushes, and without thinking of himself began to shout 'Look out! Look out!' I did not at first know what he meant, heard only at the same instant one of our Somali who rushed past me, saying, 'I'll kill him!' Then a shot rang in my rear and a moment later Mohammed Aman stood with a grinning smile before me, brandishing a fine Masai spear."

About six o'clock the peak was reached, and it was after dark when the caravan camped on open ground. Twenty goats were slaughtered, the cows were milked, and all through the night the exhausted men feasted while Chanler and von Höhnel treated the wounded. Willie noted that the wounds suffered by the Zanzibari were all in the back.

At daybreak, fearing a renewal of the attack, Chanler distributed the last rounds of ammunition and resumed the journey. But the Wamsara appeared to have had enough, and after two hours of unmolested marching, the crest of the summit was passed and a suspiciously smiling reception committee of Embe came forward to greet the caravan. It was evident that the chiefs were more eager to hurry the interlopers along than to entertain them. But a rest was imperative for the wounded, and a halt was made inside a stockade.

Although both explorers, in an attempt to placate the Embe, submitted to a ceremony of blood brotherhood (incidentally nearly fainting from the stench of the grease-smeared throng crowding close to watch the ritual), they wasted their time, learning afterward that the bond of friendship applied only in the one valley where they were camped. Soon bands of armed men were glimpsed scurrying to a rallying point somewhere on the path ahead, indicating an ambush. Then an attempt was made to poison the explorers with a pot of doctored honey, and Motio warned of worse to come. Breaking camp, the caravan set out again, and although there was a brush with some of the Embe's fighting men, the explorers suffered no further casualties.

On February 10, 1893, the base camp at Hameye came into sight, with the Stars and Stripes floating over it. Chanler's pulse quickened. "What news?" he shouted as George Galvin came running to meet him.

"Pretty good," came the answer, "All the oxen are dead—only three cattle are left—only five camels—and the donkeys are dying fast."

With flag flying and tom-tom beating, Chanler entered the camp from which he had set out sixty-five days before. In the interval he had traversed six hundred miles of unknown territory, discovered a range of mountains, exploded the myth of Lake Lorian, and had bestowed the family's name upon a major waterfall, which would appear on all future maps of Africa. All this at twenty-five.

The Fickle Ways of Fate

Both the Chanler family and the press, in Europe and America, had been receiving occasional and not always reliable rumors about Willie's progress, and direct reports arrived soon after his return to Hameye; William Astor Chanler was becoming a name widely recognized. What neither the public nor his family were apprised of, however, was that when he reached Hameye, Willie was desperately ill with fever and a disordered liver. He blamed the repulsive diet on which he had been subsisting. For a fortnight he was hardly able to leave his cot; nevertheless, he insisted that preparations go forward for resumption of travel as soon as he regained strength. He still had to find the Rendile, and to make his way through the unknown north back to the coast.

The expedition had been hit badly by deaths and desertions. Ten men had died on the trip to the Lorian Swamp, and ten more deserted at Hameye after hearing the tales of the survivors. The loss of most of the donkeys and all of the camels (the last five dying soon after Chanler's return) crippled the expedition's transport; nevertheless, Chanler was determined to push on. Before doing so he forwarded to the Royal Geographic Society in London a precise report on the Lorian exploration, with a map that von Höhnel had drawn. On March 6, 1893, he wrote to sisters Margaret and Alida an account of the Lorian trek, minimizing its dangers and glossing over his illness, saying:

"I am not very well & am very busy. I have had fever and lion trouble—those disagreeable incidentals to African life—but am getting rapidly better. . . . In a day or two with the whole caravan I go to Mt. Kenya, & then to the unknown north. I hope to be gone 18 mo's as there is a great deal of exploring to be done & should my expedition be the first to do it I should be famous forever. . . . I forgot to say that on the Guaso Nyiro River I discovered a most beautiful waterfall which I have called 'Chanler Falls.' So the family will be handed down to history after all. . . . This letter must go the rounds of the family as I cannot write any more."

And on the 9th he set out, hobbling at the head of the caravan, supported by a stick, his surviving horse being too weak to carry him.

Then, for the outside world, began a period of silence, and only months later would the story of Chanler's wrestle with adversity, privations, treachery, and disaster become known.

From the start he was dogged by hard luck. His horse died; for a time he camped among another unknown tribe, the Daitcho, who lived on the lower eastern slopes of the Jombeni Mountains, meanwhile keeping the moody Embe in check by simple feats of magic and firing off skyrockets at night, which threw them into panic. For weeks he was tied down by rains, his messengers drowned or eaten by crocodiles. A fire wiped out the camp, and he rebuilt it, meanwhile sending the headman Hamidi back to the coast to recruit a new force of reliable, experienced bearers for the big push into the northern country.

He found the Rendile, whom he described as never having even heard of a European, and a tribe named the Samburu who were subject to the Rendile. In parleys he learned the Rendile's customs, but he was rebuffed in his attempts to buy camels and donkeys from them. He collected for shipment back to the Smithsonian Institution in Washington, the Museum of Natural History in New York, and the Imperial Museum in Vienna hundreds of specimens of the wildlife of the regions he was passing through, the game, the lepidoptera and coleoptera. A new species of antelope he identified was later named Chanler's reedbuck, *Cervicapra chanlerii*. He took hundreds of photographs with a camera equipped with a rare telescopic lens.

Then August 24 brought a major calamity. Von Höhnel was

gored by a charging rhinoceros, and the caravan had to retrace its route to the Daitcho camp, carrying the wounded man in a hammock. The nearest medical aid was two hundred and fifty miles away, but George Galvin volunteered to get von Höhnel to it, and set out. Expecting the early return of Hamidi with fresh bearers, Chanler waited impatiently until October; then Hamidi did show up, but he brought eighty callow, unseasoned men instead of the strong, experienced porters Chanler needed. Rains kept him marooned at Daitcho week after week until December, when Galvin at last managed to make good his return, with a tale of brushes with elephants, apes, and lions, of hairbreadth escapes, of fighting fever and frustrations. Chanler was determined to press on, despite the loss of von Höhnel, and gave orders for the start; whereupon Hamidi and the entire force of bearers deserted, leaving only one Somali and the Sudanese soldiers faithful.

Stranded hundreds of miles in the interior, without means of transport, surrounded by restive tribes who had been kept pacified only by constant parleying and ruses, on January 7, 1894, Chanler bowed to the inevitable and abandoned the expedition.

A portion of the trading goods was distributed as presents to the Embe and Daitcho, and the rest destroyed with the surplus ammunition and rifles, out of consideration for future travelers that way. Then, with Galvin and the Sudanese, Chanler struck out for the coast. Marching eleven hours a day, through forests, swamps, and jungles, crossing rain-swollen rivers, they reached Mombasa half famished on February 10—one year to the day after Chanler's triumphant return to Hameye from the trip to the Lorian Swamp. He had been in the interior twenty months and was overjoyed to see the sea again, little guessing the storm that awaited him in Zanzibar.

For the moment, he was most eager to get news of von Höhnel. It developed that after receiving medical treatment, the lieutenant had been shipped home, and the prognosis for his recovery was favorable. A lasting affection had been formed between the two men, so dissimilar in temperament, and Willie had been able to open his heart to this friend as he could to no one else. In the first days of shock after the accident, while the wounded man was being carried to a medical station, Chanler had impulsively dispatched letters to overtake the lieutenant, recollecting the many times von Höhnel had borne patiently with his outbursts of temper and rashness and irascibility.

"I cannot tell you the full extent of my feelings at your departure," he wrote, "because I do not yet realize all that you were to me. . . . From the moment when you lay breathless & bleeding under the tree in Subugo forest I realized that you could no longer hope to continue your journey; but what your absence would mean to me I had not the courage to conjecture. . . . It was not until you were out of sight that the cold fact of your situation & my loss became plain to me. Day by day it grows stronger, and like the features of a landscape in a melting mist, the different points your absence touches become plainer & more visible.

"We may not see one another in this world so that I can speak my mind freely to you. Your companionship during the past months has been one of the pleasantest incidents in my life. Your influence has been all for the good and I must tell you that I feel to be a better man since I have known you. I fear many & many times I have caused you pain & now I ask your pardon. I have a bad—really bad—temper & on looking back I wonder at the kindliness with which you often met my roughness. If we should be permitted to meet again I hope there will occur some opportunity for me to prove my affection for you."

As for his future plans, Chanler wrote to his absent companion that rumors had reached him of a financial crisis in the United States (the panic of the 1890s) "& my ignorance of my own affairs is so astounding that I do not know whether or not I may be affected in some way . . . But you know me well enough to be sure that in the end I will probably throw all ideas of debt to the winds & push on northwards. Oh! How I wish you were here. Were you by my side I should not think a moment, but steer, 1st to Borama & then to the northern coast. . . . Now, my dear Höhnel, I will say good night—I pray God you will reach Europe restored to health & it is my one hope that we may again travel together in Africa. Till then Goodbye & God bless you."

But the news from Zanzibar that greeted him at Mombasa aroused all the combativeness in Willie Chanler's combative nature. It appeared that Hamidi and the absconding porters had flocked back to Zanzibar with accounts of frightful cruelties suffered at the hands of Chanler, hoping by these tales to justify their desertion. They claimed that men had been shot for sport, flogged to death, starved, and subjected to revolting barbarities. Public opinion in Zanzibar had been inflamed, and Chanler found awaiting him a letter from Sir Lloyd Matthews, the sultan's prime minister, curtly advising him to instruct his agents to pay off the porters (they were claiming $8,000 in wages) and disappear from Africa as speedily and secretly as possible; Sir Lloyd said that he could not answer for Chanler's life, should he show up in Zanzibar.

Willie's reaction was instant. He cabled the prime minister:

RENT ME A VILLA. INTEND TO STAY IN ZANZIBAR TWO MONTHS.

And five days later he sailed to face his accusers.

With him went the Sudanese and one Somali camel driver who had remained loyal. On reaching Zanzibar, these men went before the American consul and unanimously refuted the porters' charges. Chanler offered to pay the customary blood money to the family of the man who had been shot while trying to desert, and also offered to allow Matthews to bring suit on the porters' behalf in the United States consular court.

Sir Lloyd would have none of this, insisting that the suit must be heard in the British court. He refused to listen to testimony by the Sudanese, informing the American consul that it was not necessary inasmuch as he had "formed his opinion and quite understood the case." In reporting all this to the State Department at Washington, the consul said that Matthews had denied Chanler "even common justice," and termed the treatment of Willie "outrageous in the extreme."

Political currents were at work of which Chanler gradually became cognizant. The British East Africa Company, which claimed a trading monopoly throughout the area that Chanler had explored, had become suspicious, and had stirred up the colonial office in London to question the motives of the young American who was carrying the American flag through territory over which Great Britain exercised a protectorate. What, it was asked in London, did this action mean?

With such high interests involved, the cards were stacked against Chanler; and so, having remained for the promised two

Portrait bust of William Astor Chanler by Augustus St. Gaudens, done on Chanler's return from Africa, 1895. (*Courtesy of William Astor Chanler, Jr.*)

months in the villa he had so cavalierly commanded the sultan's prime minister to rent for him, on April 3 Chanler sailed without concealment for Aden. With him went the Somali and the Sudanese, to be paid off at Aden.

At that port Willie's steamer for Trieste was getting under way, and rather than miss it he roused his Hindu banker out of bed at midnight to pay off the faithful escort. They then accompanied him to the dock, begging him to return soon. As the tender pulled away, Willie noticed a bag of rupees that had been left over after the reckoning; snatching it up, he tossed it to the weeping Somali with a wave of farewell.

At Trieste, von Höhnel was on hand, quite recovered from his gruesome wound. From there Willie hastened on home, landing in New York on June 12, 1894—one day after his twenty-seventh birthday. Going to the Brook Club (of which he was a founder), he planted himself in a chair and for three days and three nights (the Brook being one club that never closed, but like the brook "flowed on and on forever") recounted his adventures in the masterful Chanler voice, quitting his seat only to visit the lavatory.

On the third night, it is said, the stunned and jaundice-eyed club members decided that this was too much, and expelled Willie Chanler on the spot. Whereupon his four brothers resigned in protest.

Chanler's expedition, the largest sent into East Africa up to that time, while it had not achieved all its goals, brought back a mass of scientific data and opened up a hitherto unexplored region that today forms an important part of Kenya. Honors were showered upon the intrepid adventurer. He was elected to membership in geographical societies in England and Austria. Harvard University took another look at its ex-sophomore, and conferred a master of arts degree. Augustus St. Gaudens did Chanler's bust. ("It is not bad, I believe," Willie confided. "He says it is simply an épanche—whatever that may be.")

But from this time on, William Astor Chanler would nurse a prejudice against British colonial policy, against the English and English "sportsmanship," that would grow steadily more pronounced with the passage of years.

An Old Knot Unraveled

and the End of the Beginning

During Willie Chanler's absence in Africa much had occurred in the family. The three girls, having hastened to England for Robert's wedding, had remained to take in the London season. It was a brilliant time. Thanks to the intercession of Henry White at the embassy, Alida was presented at court, and this time there was no omission of the curtsey. Margaret Chanler declined the offer of a presentation for patriotic reasons. White House etiquette, she pointed out, made no provision for curtseying to the President, and she would not pay greater deference to any foreign sovereign than she was expected to pay to the head of her own nation. Underneath their cosmopolitanism, the Chanlers were intensely aware of their American roots and proud of them.

Margaret did commission that expatriate American, John Singer Sargent, to do a portrait of Elizabeth, and the painter was much taken with her beauty: "the face of the Madonna and the eyes of the Child," he said. Women with large, regular features were most admired then; they were spoken of as "extremely handsome."

(Bob Chanler scoffed that Sargent "must have an eye of the old monks," and teased Margaret with being "next in line for Madonna honors.")

The Chanler sisters watched the military spectacle of the trooping of the colors before the sovereign from the library of 10 Downing Street that year; while they were glued to the windows,

LEFT   John Singer Sargent's portrait of Elizabeth Chanler, London, 1893.
(*Courtesy of Chanler Armstrong Chapman*)

RIGHT   Alida Chanler in ball gown, London, about 1893.

the prime minister, Gladstone, strode restlessly up and down behind them pursuing his own thoughts.

Alida had a thrilling taste of the glittering society of London, and she enshrined herself in the family tradition by her unorthodox contact (literal) with the future Nicholas II of Russia, then the tsarevitch. Nicholas, in London for a royal wedding, was given a ball by the Prince and Princess of Wales, which Alida Chanler, thanks to the thoughtfulness of the Henry Whites at the embassy, attended.

Lloyd C. Griscom, youthful Philadelphian and friend of the Chanlers serving as private secretary to the ambassador, Thomas Bayard (the first United States diplomat to hold the rank of ambassador and an affectionately close friend of Sam Ward), in his memoirs described the resplendent company—princesses and dukes, gorgeously uniformed men and duchesses sparkling with jewels. The royal party opened the ball with a quadrille, followed by a waltz. During the latter, one of the numerous court chamberlains, equipped with gold and silver staves seven feet long, rapped in front of Griscom and said, "His Royal Highness wishes you to dance." Griscom espied Alida Chanler across the room, the only girl present whom he knew, and hastily claimed her for a partner. Then, said Griscom, edging gingerly into the circle of dancers, they were making their turn of the floor when the tsarevitch bumped into them and trod heavily on Alida's foot. With an "ouch!" she continued to limp along (she was a notoriously bad dancer anyway), and a few moments later was petrified to see the stocky, unsmiling Nicholas bearing down on them again. Griscom braced his shoulder for the crash, and the tsarevitch was sent sprawling. Leading quickly to the far side of the room, Griscom held his breath; and his heart stopped beating when a gold stick tapped his arm and said, "His Royal Highness wishes you to stop dancing." But to his relief he saw others being requested to withdraw, and it became clear that the prince merely wished to thin out the crowd on the floor. No charge of lèse majesté was brought, and Alida took away a souvenir of her brush with royalty in the form of badly bruised toes.

This was Griscom's after-the-event account. Alida's was different. According to family legend, she was escorted to the ball by Griscom, a very junior secretary at the embassy at that time. When the music struck up, they were approached by a chamberlain who "invited" them to open the ball. Despite their consternation, they could only comply, for the request was in fact a royal command. By this means, Alida was placed opposite Nicholas, the guest of honor, and it provided the only expedient by which, under court protocol, she could dance with him. Had Nicholas spotted her in the crowd and arranged it? The question would be debated endlessly around Chanler dinner tables.

In any event, under the "jealous glares of ugly duchesses" (Alida's words) she went through the quadrille with the future tsar, and the family legend persisted that Nicholas was deeply affected by her beauty—so deeply, it was said, that a year later he chose for his bride the celebrated beauty, Princess Alix of Hesse-Darmstadt, who closely resembled Alida and would go down in history as Alexandra. Looking back, the Chanler clan would shudderingly speculate on what might have happened had Nicholas wed Alida instead of Alix. Given the former's subsequent hare-brained impulses and her erratic mysticism, Rasputin might have gained control ten years sooner and the revolution have been advanced by that much!

Willie Chanler, in Africa, was kept faithfully informed of Chanler doings during these months by long reports from Margaret. Confessing to a queer feeling when she sat down to write realizing that he might never receive or read the letters, nevertheless she rattled along:

"Alida has been presented & much admired though she is hardly having a 'season' as we know so few people. . . . I took a nice little house opposite Albert Gate. We give little dinners twice a week to which Bessie brings M.P.'s & 'souls' while Alida's are frequented by young lawyers. . . . A year might have changed us but it hasn't. Alida is still 'growing up' of course but on the same lines. Elizabeth leaps from friend to friend the world over; she is rather like a humming bird . . . beautiful with the sunlight she reflects. Wintie has a 'black' daughter to be called Hester Marion after the general's sister from whom he & Daisy are descended. His being in business is splendid & he & Archie see each other every day & get on deliciously. The latter has 100 irons at fever heat & his wife under Weir Mitchell. He travels from one interest to the other & looks well content with this state of things. He has made great good friends with the Stanford Whites, St. Gaudens & other men of their successful artistic calibre & you will see how good this is for him. He is much more what he was years ago than what he was two years ago. It has been splendid for Lewis. By going into the criminal courts he comes in contact with such a world of realities & crises & has his interest in people widened wonderfully. He is very good at it & we are proud of the position he has made for himself already. . . . Such Uncles & Aunts as we have are where they were a year ago. Uncle Frank [Delano] can't cross the ocean so he and Aunt L[aura] move from Monte Carlo to baths & back again. I see as much of Aunt Julia [Ward Howe] as I possibly can, she is one of the dearest & most gifted creatures that ever lived. . . . Marion Crawford has written a play for Daly's which is coming out soon. . . . Your letter to Alida & me I have read aloud till I know it by heart. The Royal Geographical Society in its annual report the other day mentioned you so delightfully that I have asked Harry [White]

to convey your sisters' thanks as he knows the President infor-
mally. The papers at home have left off explaining us as Amélie
Rives' sisters-in-law. On her presentation they chronicled Alida
as your sister. It is very amusing that W.W. Astor has bought
Cliveden on the Thames from the Duke of Westminster, also a
large town house on Carlton Terrace & the Pall Mall Gazette. . . .
Home Rule makes the House the House of Discord. I went one
night & heard Chamberlain & Gladstone. . . . We go home in
July . . ."

The chatter ran on; and somewhere in Africa Willie would
gulp it down and bless Peggy for her scrawl.

Willie was not told about Elizabeth's fey experience, which
had filled the sisters with dread. It had occurred about the time
of Robert's wedding. Elizabeth had gone to stay at Wells, and the
eerie episode had shaken her as evidence of "powers unseen."
She had recorded the vision on the spot, using scraps of paper
taken from the waste basket. The hurried account read:

> *Wells, June 5th, 1893. I have just waked from the most
> awful dream of my life. I cannot tell what hour it is. The
> cuckoo is singing & from a faint light through the curtains
> it must be dawn*
>
> *I was at a party in London. I was coming down the stairs
> as many others were coming up. I held Alida by the arm.
> She said, 'Look at that beautiful man.' He was a tall Eng-
> lish soldier, but I don't remember what he looked like for
> I turned from him to see Willie stand[ing] on the steps
> below me coming up. He was dressed in one of his summer
> suits of black camels hair. He was very pale, his face in a
> sweat. When I first looked his face was turned. He was
> speaking to a man beside him with a rather grim self-con-
> scious little look on his face that he often had when em-
> barrassed in public. He raised his eyes to mine and took
> my hand. I screamed 'Willie!' He looked at me with a
> grim smile and I think said 'Yes.' Then everybody on the
> stairs clapped their hands, and as he held my hand so that
> I couldn't clap I struck my right arm & my breast loudly
> with my left hand, with a feeling of triumphant joy. He*

*shook his head a little from side to side with the same sad
grim smile—a gesture that was common with him. I saw
that something was wrong. I said 'Willie, is George dead?'
He said in a rather hurried & 'cross' tone still with the
grim smile on his face, as if I had been stupid & misunder-
stood him, 'He never was so well in his life. You see I died
first.' I seized both his hands & said 'Willie are you dying?'
He nodded his head or said 'yes.' I must have screamed or
made a noise for he tried to quiet me by pressing both my
hands very hard &* LOOKING *at me. Oh those eyes, those eyes
—God grant I may never forget them for* Christ's *sake
Amen.*

*I have counted the quarters from St. Cuthbert's tower. 1st
it struck one, then the half hour, & the ¾, & now 4 o'clock
so I must have waked just after 3.*

The night on which this apparition came to Elizabeth Chanler
in England, William Chanler had spent with von Höhnel, camped
in the crater of an extinct volcano, wondering whether he would
ever see home again. So dubious had he been regarding his
chances of coming back, on leaving the base camp at Daitcho, he
had given George Galvin a letter, instructing him to wait at the
camp until January 1, 1894; and if he had received no word by
then, to conclude that both explorers were dead, break camp, and
head back to the coast.

The heritage of Rokeby, the faith in dreams and portents, was
strong in Elizabeth, and was not unknown to other members of
the family.

But Willie had returned in good health and spirits. After paying
his visit to New York and home, he had returned to Vienna to
supervise the publication of von Höhnel's maps, the lieutenant
having been recalled to naval duty. He combined this task with
all the pleasures the Austrian capital could provide. The hunting
and titled sets lionized him, and his comforts were taken care of
scrupulously by Frau Sacher.

Willie had not seen Robert since the latter's marriage, but he
was skeptical about the success of that match. The Chamberlains
were not conspicuous for warmth of feeling; and Willie suspected
that Bob's blazing impetuosity could be rendered productive only

by some influence more sustaining than a passive partnership. Writing to Margaret in October of '94, he stated his misgivings frankly:

"I am, of course, interested in all that concerns Robert & therefore look forward to meeting Julia. But I must confess that I cannot arouse any enthusiasm in a young man's choice. His notions are almost always wrong to begin with, and almost inevitably, particularly in independent people like ourselves, lead to regrets after a few years. The romantic marriages which turn out well are only in the eyes of the ignorant possessed of romance. There must be something else besides affection. In these days I should say particularly money . . ."

Matured by experience and very much a man of the world, Willie found no difficulty in accepting the values of the world. He went on:

"I am going to put in my spare time learning a little French. I feel *almost* shame when I recognize my inability to talk anything but African & English. . . . I have been junketing too much—opera & theatres & actually I danced once or twice! Think of that!"

Von Höhnel would hardly have recognized his friend in this guise; Willie's ultramasculine manners had more than once startled the conventional Austrian. Coming into Chanler's hotel room one day, he found Willie stamping inside a trunk with his shoes on, trampling down clothing. Von Höhnel asked what on earth he was doing. "Packing," Willie replied nonchalantly, and went on with the operation.

The youthful, handsome explorer was in demand. At Monte Carlo, where he had just scored a gambling coup, winning $20,000 at a sitting (sensibly he never attempted to duplicate the feat), he ran into Henry M. Stanley, the explorer of the Congo, on the steps of the casino, and was told that "the king of the Belgians wants to see you." It was in regard to the leadership of an expedition the king was preparing, to open up a region in the Congo Free State lying north and east of the Kasai River. Stanley had been offered the job, but his health was poor and he had just been elected to parliament; and he had recommended Chanler. Willie went to Brussels and was received immediately by the king, who described the purposes of the expedition—to open up the territory to agriculture and industry—and offered mouth-watering terms. Willie's suspicions were aroused because the terms were just too magnanimous to be meant seriously by a man as notoriously miserly and shifty in his dealings as Leopold. It seemed clear to Chanler, as the king talked on, that the offer was a trap; that should he lead the expedition successfully, he would never collect his winnings because he would not come back alive. He was fairly certain that the stated aims of the expedition were window-dressing, and that in reality it would be a foray in quest of gold and ivory. Turning down Leopold's offer, he beat a retreat to Paris.

Another man led the expedition, which turned out to be just what Chanler suspected—a pillaging sweep through the backcountry—and Willie was not surprised when dispatches reported that on the return march the leader had met a violent death by the "accidental discharge of a rifle."

While in Paris, Chanler received a cablegram from von Höhnel saying the latter's ship was to call at New York shortly, and hoping they might get together again. Dropping everything, Willie caught a fast liner and was on hand when the corvette dropped anchor in the Hudson. Whirling his friend ashore, Willie launched into a description of the program of activities he had laid out for the next several days, until von Höhnel protested that it was out of the question, that he could never afford it, inasmuch as the only money he had to spend on his holiday was a small sum saved out of his pay.

"Give it to a pretty girl!" cried Willie gaily. "And don't mention money again as long as you are in New York!"

The three weeks that followed were the maddest of von Höhnel's life. Chanler was proud of his city and his country, and he wanted his friend to see everything and meet everybody. Nightly they were entertained in the homes of millionaires (or so it seemed to the Austrian), until the lieutenant gave up inquiring whose hospitality he was enjoying at the moment. He was introduced to famous sportsmen, travelers, political figures, businessmen, and artists; he was astounded at the number of prominent people whom Willie knew. Theodore Roosevelt invited him to Oyster Bay. The Boone & Crockett Club gave him a dinner that led to a great deal of drinking, with Willie chanting Masai war cries and regaling the company with tales of apes and elephants and crocodiles, of fights and fever, of slave caravans and the dives of Port Said, and of the satisfaction derived from reading "Pippa Passes" in a jungle camp while hyenas howled and lions roared close by.

Chanler took his friend up the Hudson to Rokeby, where the three Chanler sisters were staying, and von Höhnel was tremendously impressed by them. He deduced that Willie's exuberance they found trying at times, particularly after the two friends had spent a session in the tower, drinking and trolling African chants. Both Elizabeth and Margaret had become converts to the cause of temperance; they dreaded to see their brother becloud his future by a bent toward dissipation. One evening Elizabeth took von Höhnel aside and begged him to undertake another expedition into Africa and take Willie with him. The lieutenant tactfully alluded to the dangers inseparable from such a journey, especially to a man like her high-spirited, impulsive brother. But Elizabeth drew herself erect, and in von Höhnel's words "seemed actually to grow, as with glowing eyes she replied, 'I would rather see him die gloriously in Africa than lead a dissipated life in New York!' She was quite Roman!"

Back to New York the friends hastened, where the Austrian watched St. Gaudens at work on Willie's portrait bust. Then in a yacht that Chanler chartered they sailed to Newport, where von Höhnel was entertained by Daisy and Winthrop Chanler at Cliff Lawn; and all in all, as he put it, "with the best will in the world, I could not give an adequate description of the many and varied experiences I lived through in those weeks." His departure for the Azores rang down the curtain on an extravaganza of hospitality that he would never get over.

Willie's return from Africa had coincided with the passing of a major milestone by the Chanlers, when, ten days after the explorer landed with triumphant loquacity in New York, Alida Chanler came of age and the family estate could be settled. This

Reunion, about 1886. Winthrop (standing) and William Chanler, with their sisters, Elizabeth, Alida (standing), and Margaret Chanler.

involved a division of property held in New York City, at Newport, and elsewhere, and specifically the disposition of Rokeby. What should be done with the old home? It had left its mark on them all and its associations were dear. All the brothers except William were married, with households of their own, and Willie gave no indication of settling anywhere. To sell the property seemed out of the question. A solution was arrived at which satisfied everybody, namely, to transfer the estate to the three sisters for their permanent home.

The transfer was effected by swapping city property which the girls owned for the brothers' shares in Rokeby. Armstrong took nothing in return, inasmuch as he had spent the $100,000 that his father had left to him for Rokeby's upkeep.

The buoyant air of 1893 had been propitious for Amélie also; late that year she was discharged from Weir Mitchell's care, her nerves restored. And in 1894 she went abroad again with Archie. In London her social and literary triumphs were repeated. An incident occurred at this time that would later be recalled with an uncanny shiver by some members of the clan. At a crowded reception in London, Armstrong waved toward a tall, athletic-looking, strikingly handsome young man on the opposite side of the room and said:

"There is the man Amélie should marry." He had no idea who the man was.

At that moment Oscar Wilde came up to Amélie, who was sur-rounded by the customary cloud of admirers, and said:

"You are the most beautiful woman in this room, and I must present you to the most beautiful man in this room. You two must be seen together."

And he led her to the man Archie had indicated.

The man was Prince Pierre Troubetzkoy, a half-Russian, half-American expatriate painter, in England to do a portrait of Gladstone.

Shortly after this, Armstrong returned to the United States alone, and again he and Wintie saw much of each other in con-nection with their joint business ventures. Wintie and Daisy had suffered their first bereavement in the death of their son, John; but another son being born to them shortly thereafter, their grief was partly assuaged.

A major project occupying the two Chanler partners was the establishment of a water power plant and cotton mill in North Carolina. The idea was Archie's, and both he and Winthrop in-vested heavily in it. A town was created, called Roanoke Rapids, and Archie spent much time at the site personally supervising the construction. Stanford White designed the buildings, with un-happy results; for while attractive externally, the interior was unsuited to any utilitarian purpose; cotton mills were out of Stanford White's line. The many changes in the plans that were necessitated sent the costs up and up and contributed to much ill temper.

In altercations with his brothers, Winthrop Chanler's voice could soar to shouting pitch, as it did in the rows around the Rokeby table. Wintie was impatient of contradiction, and in deal-ing with his brothers he could adopt a tone of assumed authority that did not in any way reflect lessened regard for them. With money tight during the depression of the nineties (Wintie had no conception of how to live within his income), he reminded Willie of the help he had rendered at the time of the African

safari—"15,000 golden smackers I tossed into your maw . . .
Those at least you must leave me in your often discussed & frequently altered will. If you marry rich I expect the money in
6 months after receipt of the bride's settlement. If you die poor,
at least provide for *them*. May you live a thousand years & leave
a fat family, only don't forget that you did me there. . . ."

But good humor came quickly after Wintie's fits of temper;
in fact, his friend Owen Wister insisted that with his short,
pointed, light-brown beard and twinkling hazel eyes, Winthrop
Chanler was the very model of Frans Hals's "Laughing Cavalier."
Even his sarcasm was without malice. He could write to Henry
Cabot Lodge:

"My Amélie Rives brother landed last Wednesday according to
the papers and is I suppose in Virginia. . . . My African sportsman brother (I give them their well earned titles) landed on
Saturday and is to meet me in New York tomorrow at 2:30. (This
will require a good deal of drink.)"

At the time of this brotherly dig, Winthrop was unaware of
the actual situation between Archie and Amélie. In January of
1895 she had returned from Europe alone. The newspapers, which
long since had decided that anything Amélie did was "copy,"
noted that she was not met by her husband, who was supposedly
at The Merry Mills, the name of the estate he had recently acquired in Virginia not far from Castle Hill. Reporters on hand
when Amélie came down the gangplank of the White Star liner
Teutonic were refused an interview, but no reporter was prohibited from describing her appearance as "almost as girlish-
looking as when she was Amélie Rives and sprang into fame."
And there were references to "a sylph-like form . . . soft violet
eyes under sweeping coal-black lashes . . . a veritable Cupid's
bow of the mouth . . ."

For all this seductiveness, Amélie's Virginia neighbors observed
that her knack with horses had not been impaired by residence
abroad.

But it was months before the real news of 1895 regarding the
"Amélie Rives Chanlers" leaked to the press and public. Then,
in October, word got out that during the previous spring Amélie
had quietly obtained a divorce in South Dakota. There had been

Amélie Rives Chanler, about 1893.

no contest and the decree had been granted on grounds of incompatibility. No alimony had been asked, but Chanler had voluntarily settled upon her a lifetime income of three hundred dollars a month.

This was sensational news, for in 1895 a divorce was scandalous. That was the year when Alva Vanderbilt divorced William Kissam Vanderbilt in order to marry Oliver H. P. Belmont, and became the first woman of prominent social position to defy the wrath of public opinion. And even after that, acceptance of divorce came about very slowly; for years to come a divorcée would remain socially suspect if not absolutely cast out.

Insiders were hardly surprised by the sequel to the Chanler divorce, although the public was taken aback. On February 18, 1896, Amélie was married to handsome Prince Pierre Troubetzkoy, in the same parlor at Castle Hill where she had been unevenly matched with John Armstrong Chanler nearly eight years before. Only members of the Rives family attended the wedding, the press reported, and the couple left shortly for a long stay in Europe.

This wrote finis to the episode that had caused so much heart-burning in the Chanler circle. As Princess Troubetzkoy Amélie ceased to exist socially for the Chanler sisters, although Alida did enjoy the titillation of being indirectly allied with a creature as shocking as a divorcée. To Margaret a divorce was heinous, although she was willing to stretch a point in Armstrong's favor because she had come definitely to resent Amélie. What Margaret would not condone was what she called "plural marriage," the remarriage of divorced persons while the first partner was still living. To Margaret such remarriages were a blow against the sanctity of the family, and of course Amélie Rives by her offense placed herself beyond the pale of Margaret's forebearance. For the Chanler family generally, with their facility for opening and closing chapters of experience without reference to preceding or succeeding events, the incident was closed. But for the public, to the end of his life, Armstrong Chanler would remain and be identified as "the former husband of Amélie Rives."

October of 1896 brought two events of major importance in the Chanler annals. On October 8, Lewis Stuyvesant Chanler startlingly announced his retirement from the practice of criminal law in New York County; and on October 27, Alida Chanler became the bride of Christopher Temple Emmet of New York, a young lawyer and sportsman.

Lewis announced his withdrawal from practice in the course of summing up the defense of a penniless client accused of killing his wife. When he entered upon criminal practice, Lewis told the jurors, he had expected that he would be accorded the courtesy given to any mercenary lawyer, but he had found out his mistake. The systematic slights and prejudices to which he had been subjected by certain judges of the criminal courts of the city had become intolerable, he said, and he would never practice again in the courts of New York County.

There were private reasons for Lewis Chanler's action, also. His wife's health again was unsatisfactory, and a milder climate had been recommended for her. Hence Lewis planned an extended sojourn abroad, preferably in England. A second child had been born to him and Alice, a daughter who was named Alida for her aunt, and the whole family would go abroad as soon as he could wind up the cases to which he was already committed. His retirement, and the stated reasons, were widely discussed in legal circles and much sympathy was expressed for him. The *New York Tribune,* citing his painstaking work, commented that he would be missed in the Tombs.

But the center of attention that month of October was Rokeby, where the pageantlike wedding of Alida was held, under the artistic supervision of Stanford White. Temple Emmet came of a distinguished Irish family, of which Robert Emmet, the martyr to the cause of Irish freedom, had been a member. Temple Emmet's immediate ancestor, Thomas Addis Emmet, Robert's brother, had been implicated in the 1798 uprising and had been arrested, but was released upon consenting to go into exile. Coming to New York, he had prospered as an attorney and political ally of De Witt Clinton, and had founded a line of successors eminent in the professions. To the Chanlers' relief, Temple Emmet adhered to the Protestant faith of his ancestors.

Alida had often been teased by her brothers about her fear of becoming an old maid, and they averred that she had accepted the first man who had proposed; her heart, however, had been won, and hers was a love match.

The engagement had been announced in September. Word of it reached Margaret in Europe, where she was visiting that summer, and she hastened home to make preparations, but found that Stanford White had taken charge. There was to be a mighty gathering of the clan, of course, and only Daisy Chanler would be unable to attend. She had been called to Rome by the failing health of her mother, Louisa Terry, but Wintie kept her informed of the developments, step by step.

A special train was to bring the guests from the city, he wrote, and "the entire family, with the melancholy exception of you, will be assembled at Rokeby for the wedding. Just think of it! There is talk of Aunt Julia Howe, Aunt Tiny Griffin, and Aunt Betty White coming up for the night . . . Robert talks of coming over. . . . Archie says he will be here 'drenched in calm'—ominous outlook!"

The festivities came up to every expectation. The special train brought two hundred guests from New York, and the ceremony was held in Christ Church in Red Hook, with the rector and Bishop Henry Potter officiating. Winthrop Chanler gave his sister away, and brothers Willie, Lewis, and Robert were ushers; the bridesmaids were all cousins of the bride except one; and the guests passed under an arch of autumn leaves and evergreens, erected by the country folk, as they left the church for the reception and breakfast at Rokeby.

There Stanford White had lavished his effects. Across the front of the house were draped tapestries, and strolling around the grounds, mingling with the guests, were Neapolitan minstrels strumming mandolins. A canvas pavilion with a wooden floor had been set up on the lawn for dancing, and the Hungarian orchestra that was the current rage of New York provided music there. The festivities went on all afternoon until the special train whistled for the return trip to the city.

Only one sour note intruded: at the last minute Armstrong Chanler had telegraphed from Virginia that he was ill with pleurisy and could not attend. He sent his blessing and a present.

To the Chanlers, this behavior was incomprehensible and inexcusable. "The man is daft!" Winthrop exclaimed. As the head of the family, Archie's place was at his sister's side on her wedding day, even if in a wheelchair, Wintie felt, and his brothers agreed. Bob echoed Wintie's exclamation, saying Archie must be "looney"; that was the only possible explanation. Alida cried for hours upon receipt of the telegram, sure her brother was dying, and Winthrop filled in for the absent head; but the affront was not forgotten or forgiven.

Armstrong himself offered nothing in extenuation of his remissness, and a short while later turned up unconcerned in New York at the Horse Show in Madison Square Garden, an annual event to which he was devoted. While in the city he attended meetings of the directors of his various companies, but soon hastened back to The Merry Mills.

Then rumors began to filter north about strange doings at that estate. Armstrong was said to be shutting himself up for days, refusing to see visitors and conducting mysterious psychological experiments. His New York clubs rarely saw him, and after March of 1897 they saw him not at all. In reply to inquiries, the family intimated that he was in Europe.

The sensation was great, therefore, when, in October, 1897, one year after Alida's marriage, New York newspapers disclosed that John Armstrong Chanler was in Bloomingdale insane asylum at White Plains, north of New York City.

Interestingly, the commitment papers under which he was held had been signed by two of his brothers, Winthrop Astor and Lewis Stuyvesant Chanler, and by a cousin, Arthur Carey, of Boston.

Archie already had been in the asylum seven months.

PART THREE

Arms and the Man

Of the Consequences That May Flow
from Going into a Trance

The Chanlers were formed by their heritage and by the conventions and social patterns of their time, but they were never dominated by them. At all times they exhibited an extreme degree of personal independence and self-sufficiency. Heritage contributed heavily to the latter; they were born self-sufficient, and their extraordinary upbringing and education among social inferiors had completed the work. Many of their distinctive traits set them apart as a group, easily recognizable—their voices (those attention-compelling "Chanler voices"), their high-bred manners, their vocabulary and diction impregnated with obsolete overtones. As a family, among themselves, they exhibited highly complex and individual reactions, differing widely in their creeds and their conduct. Daisy Chanler had been struck that although the Chanlers quarreled violently, they never quarreled over the things that divided most families—money or property rights. The Chanlers quarreled over moral or theological questions, or over issues concerning precedence and social propriety.

It would seem out of character, therefore, for Winthrop and Armstrong to have had a falling out over a matter of business; but such were the unexpected turns that the Chanler temperament could take. Fundamentally, of course, the disagreement was the culmination of long-continued rivalry on both sides.

Archie and Wintie were the principal stockholders in the Roanoke Rapids Power Company in North Carolina, which they had started largely through Armstrong's initiative. In December, 1896, Archie called a meeting of the company's directors in the New York hotel where he stayed, the Kensington, at Fifth Avenue and 15th Street. A dispute over policy arose, and the brothers took opposite sides. Winthrop was still resenting Archie's failure to appear at Alida's wedding, and the Rokeby-style argument grew so heated that it almost led to blows.

The next day Armstrong received a letter from Winthrop, written in a rage, stating that he would neither speak to his brother nor communicate with him from then on except in writing or through a third party.

Just as heatedly, Armstrong sent back word accepting his brother's ultimatum, and adding that he proposed to send an auditor to look over the books of his father's estate, of which Wintie and Lewis Chanler were executors. Archie pointed out that no accounting had been rendered for five years, and in view of what he was beginning to consider Winthrop's faulty business judgment, he wished to satisfy himself that there had been no mismanagement of the estate.

This step Winthrop construed as a further personal affront, but he returned word that his brother could do as he pleased.

Meanwhile, there had arisen another point of difference between the brothers concerning their joint investment in a second company at Roanoke Rapids, the United Industrial Company, which had been formed to operate the mills. In this company Armstrong held stock having a book value of $175,000 and Winthrop held $50,000 worth. Elizabeth Chanler was a minor stockholder, and so was Stanford White. In addition, Winthrop Chanler was the salaried president of this company, and both he and Armstrong were directors.

Reflecting that it would be difficult to do business with a man who refused to speak to him, Archie relayed a suggestion that his brother resign as president and director of United Industrial. Wintie complied in a flash, and in January, 1897, Armstrong reshuffled the board and elected himself president of the company.

A distressed witness of the brothers' estrangement was Stanford White. He also had a stake in United Industrial. Archie had been talking about taking a vacation from business in order to carry out certain psychological experiments that interested him; and to give him leisure for this, White proposed that Armstrong empower him and their trusted mutual friend, St. Gaudens, to act for him in the business for a while. St. Gaudens, however, declined the responsibility. Archie approved the idea and gave White his power of attorney, reflecting that business was slack, and he could revoke the power of attorney at any time.

This took place in January, 1897, and Archie withdrew to The Merry Mills to continue the investigations in which he was interested.

Armstrong Chanler had always been conspicuous for intellectual vigor. After taking his M.A. and law degrees at Columbia, he had studied at the Collège de France and the École des Sciences Politiques in Paris, and he had never ceased to be mentally curious. In college he had majored in philosophy and psychology, subjects then closely related, but he had not kept abreast of the proliferating literature of psychology or with its emergence as a separate science.

John Armstrong Chanler possessed charm. He was fairly tall (although not when standing beside either of the family giants, Lewis and Robert), with sharply chiseled features and hypnotic eyes. He was slim and athletic; his mental perceptions were keen; but his mind was not disciplined or orderly. His frustrating marriage to Amélie Rives had aggravated in him a tendency to solitariness and erratic behavior; a discerning medical friend would describe him as "a man of sound common sense, but marked originality and pronounced force. While not prone to take offense where none is meant, he is sensitive and keenly alive to insult or injustice." Like all Chanlers, he was impatient.

During the closing weeks of 1896 and the opening weeks of 1897, Archie was exploring a newfound faculty in himself that lay outside the range of his experience up to that time. (The faculty would later be identified by such an authority as William James as mediumistic.) The first intimation had come in a curious manner. One evening at The Merry Mills he had been idly knocking the balls around the billiard table when he noted that they had stopped in the pattern of the constellation known as the Great Dipper, or Great Bear. He set up the balls again, struck them, and they came to rest in the same pattern. He tried a third time and got the same result. He was sure there was no flaw in the table, and his curiosity was excited. Taking a pencil from his pocket, he started to make a note of the occurrence on the back of an envelope, and was astonished when his hand refused to answer his thought; instead, moving involuntarily, it wrote, "Get a planchette."

A planchette is a form of ouija board. Chanler was certain that he had not consciously written the command, or advice, or whatever it might be; his hand had moved without his volition and without his having the least notion of what it was going to write.

Determined to look into this strange manifestation, he procured a planchette, and after a few tries found that coherent messages began to evolve under his manipulation, although he was mystified as to what produced them. He definitely rejected the theory that "spirits" or other-worldly forces were at work; he felt that the phenomenon had a rational explanation, and he became eager to track it down. Up to this time he had never even heard the word "subconscious," which was coming into use among psychologists; and since he was unable to say whence this mysterious faculty came, he called it his "X-faculty," X being the algebraic symbol for an unknown quantity.

Some of the messages spelled out by the planchette directed him to carry out definite actions. To test their validity, Archie acted on one that purported to be a tip on the stock market. The tip proved reliable, and he made $1,300 profit. But this test was crude and Armstrong did not repeat it, although he kept practicing with "automatic writing," as it was called (though "graphic automatism" was his preferred term), and finally was able to dispense with the planchette and write directly on a pad of legal foolscap with a lightly held pencil.

But he found that his X-faculty was not always trustworthy, and at times it misled him. Once it told him that he could carry live coals in his bare hand; he tried it and was painfully burned.

The most startling demonstration, however, came when his X-faculty told Chanler that if he would stand at a window facing west at a certain hour holding a mirror in one hand and his pearl stickpin in the other, and gaze intently into the mirror, his eyes would change color from light brown to gray. He made the experiment, and according to him the transformation was completed "in about fifteen minutes." *

Changing the color of one's eyes by premeditation was a feat of such rarity that Chanler became infatuated with his mysterious X-faculty, and he was in a credulous mood when it indicated oracularly to him that he was destined to carry out some lofty mission in life, the nature of which was not defined.

Word of the live-coal experiment, followed by talk of a change in the color of his eyes, alarmed Archie's friends and relatives. Stanford White, who as holder of Archie's power of attorney was in a position of special delicacy, decided to look into his friend's condition personally, and dropped a note to Chanler saying he would visit The Merry Mills shortly.

To this Archie replied by telegram, advising White not to come because he was "too ill" to receive visitors. This increased White's uneasiness. Disregarding the message, he made the trip south and knocked unannounced at the door of Archie's secluded home. With him he had brought a physician, Dr. Eugene Fuller.

Archie was taken aback at sight of the uninvited callers, and showed annoyance when both men rudely pushed into the house. White introduced his companion by name without revealing that he was a medical man, and gradually thawing Archie's coolness chatted about business affairs, protesting against his friend's hermitlike existence. He pictured the benefit Chanler would derive from running up to New York for a few days and "plunging into the metropolitan whirl"; and in the end, under White's charm and persuasiveness, Chanler agreed. All three men took the train back together.

---

* Oculists who examined Chanler's eyes after 1896 agreed unanimously that his eyes were then dark gray in color. A highly qualified doctor who had known Chanler in the years *before* 1896 testified that they had then been light brown. And Amélie Rives Troubetzkoy would swear in an affidavit that from 1888 to 1895, the years when she had been Chanler's wife, his eyes were light brown, just as she had described them in *The Quick or the Dead?*, published in 1888. The hero of that romance was modeled exactly upon Chanler, she stated, feature for feature, including eyes "the color of autumn pools in sunlight." Any Virginian, she said, would know the color indicated, the color produced by the sunlight playing on dead leaves at the bottom of a forest pool, giving the water a sparkling, light-brown hue.

During the ride Chanler talked freely about his experiments, about the amazing feats of his X-faculty and about automatic writing. White's friend seemed particularly interested in this subject and put many questions, which Archie answered frankly.

In New York, Armstrong checked into the Kensington Hotel, and there he received a clear communication from his X-faculty (this time by means of "vocal automatism," or involuntary speech), saying that it wished him to go into a "Napoleonic trance," during which he would "reenact the deathbed scene of Napoleon," his features taking on an exact resemblance to the emperor. How the trance would be induced the X-faculty promised to disclose when the propitious moment arrived.

Shortly after this, St. Gaudens dropped in, and during their conversation Archie was given to understand by his X-faculty that the moment had come. He asked St. Gaudens whether he cared to observe the experiment, and the sculptor said he would. Since he had never been in a trance, Archie was rather relieved to have a friendly observer present.

Acting on the instructions of his X-faculty, he stretched out on the bed, and taking a shaving mirror in both hands held it at arm's length above his head and stared fixedly at the reflection. He felt that he might be making himself ridiculous, but persisted, and after a few moments began to experience an eerie sensation: his mouth gaped, and he gasped for breath convulsively. This went on, he estimated, for perhaps ten minutes; then his hands slowly placed the mirror on the bed, his eyes closed, and the trance began. He retained entire consciousness, and was aware that St. Gaudens, greatly affected, was pleading with him to break off the experiment. With perfect composure, Archie did, and St. Gaudens left, much upset and earnestly requesting that Chanler never repeat the performance in his presence.

The next day Stanford White and his companion on the Virginia trip, Dr. Fuller, called at the Kensington, and during the conversation worked around to the subject of the trance concerning which St. Gaudens had told them. They expressed a wish to witness the experiment themselves, and Archie consented to oblige. Everything passed off as before: Chanler lay entranced, with eyes closed, and while in that state he heard White's awed whisper:

"It *is* exactly like Napoleon's death mask! I have a photograph of it at home."

A couple of days after this, unpleasant consequences started to unfold. Dr. Fuller called again, saying he had brought a friend, an oculist, who was intensely interested in the change of the color of Chanler's eyes and wished to examine them. Archie happened to be in no mood to receive callers, but Fuller pleaded so insistently, he relented. The three men had a long discussion about what today would be termed parapsychology, although the word had not been invented yet, in the course of which Archie expressed some unflattering opinions about the medical profession in general. The oculist examined Chanler's eyes in different lights and was full of questions.

The next evening, as Archie lay in bed reading, the door was pushed open without a knock by the self-styled oculist of the day before. He was accompanied by two rough-looking attendants. Brusquely he introduced himself as Dr. Moses Allen Starr, professor of nervous diseases at the College of Physicians and Surgeons in New York, president of the New York Neurological Society, and also president of the American Neurological Association. To this array of credentials he added another—medical examiner-in-lunacy.

Informing Chanler that he had a court order for his commitment on grounds of insanity, Starr ordered him to get up and come along quietly, warning that resistance would be futile, that force would be employed if necessary.

What happened next Archie would recount with sardonic humor. He told Dr. Starr "very quietly," he said, that he declined to obey the doctor's command, and "finally succeeded in convincing him, without the slightest show of force, that he had not brought enough men with him to carry me off that night."

Later he would amplify the account. His subliminal self, he said, had warned him of some imminent danger, and he had placed under his pillow the loaded revolver that he always carried when traveling, and had carried since his days on the plains with General Crook. When Starr caught hold of Chanler's left wrist, Archie slid his right hand under the pillow, and pointing the gun "straight at the middle button of Dr. Starr's waistcoat— he was in evening dress," announced calmly:

"Doctor, I've got the drop on you and you know it."

"I guess he did all right," Chanler added, "for he went pale and let go my hand."

"Will you come quietly?" Starr demanded.

"No," replied Chanler, "but I will sit up and discuss the matter with you if you promise not to try any rough tactics."

But Starr said he would discuss at another time, and backed out of the room.

The next day two detectives from police headquarters appeared with a warrant for Chanler's arrest as a dangerous lunatic exhibiting homicidal tendencies. The proprietor of the hotel, a personal friend of Chanler's, examined the warrant, found it in order, and advised Chanler to submit.

"I've half a mind to let these scoundrels have all the rope they want and see if they won't hang themselves," Archie exclaimed; but he got up and dressed, with the help of his valet.

In the lobby the detectives displayed their warrant and said they had been told by Theodore Roosevelt, the police commissioner, to show Chanler every consideration. A closed carriage was waiting. Archie got into it and with his captors was driven to Grand Central station, chatting amicably along the way.

"So little did these men think I was insane," Archie would point out afterward, "when we got to Grand Central station and one of them got out to get the tickets [for the train ride to White Plains], the other one, thinking he had been gone too long, got out and went after him, leaving me alone and unguarded in the cab. I got out and went across the street and bought some cigars and was back in the cab again before they returned."

Confident that he could soon rectify the mistake of the arrest, Chanler felt no alarm; he accepted the occurrence fatalistically.

The twenty-mile ride to White Plains was brief, and late on the evening of March 13, 1897, John Armstrong Chanler passed through the gate of the asylum for the insane maintained by The New York Hospital, commonly called Bloomingdale. He was thirty-four years old—certified to the world as hopelessly insane.

Of Love and Lunacy

When John Armstrong Chanler was hustled into Bloomingdale asylum, his family was widely scattered. Lewis Chanler was in England; Willie Chanler was at sea; Robert Chanler was in France; and Elizabeth and Margaret Chanler were in India. Winthrop Chanler alone was nearby, at his home in Tuxedo Park. (Alida, although she was honeymooning at New Rochelle, was seldom consulted about family affairs, being considered too scatter-brained to grasp grave questions.)

Lewis had been in New York recently, having come over in response to a summons from Wintie, inspired by Archie's announced intention to examine the books of their father's estate. When Lewis arrived, Wintie laid before him the whole story of Armstrong's recent behavior, his growing "queerness," his erratic decisions, and those "crazy" experiments he was conducting in Virginia. Stanford White added his own apprehensions, and the logical conclusion seemed to be that Archie had become deranged —a victim of prolonged mental and nervous exacerbation, dating from the time of his marriage to Amélie—and for his own safety should be placed under restraint and medical care.

To anyone with Astor blood, insanity was a touchy subject, in view of the seldom mentioned imbecile son of the first John Jacob, and at a later time Henry, with his bull-of-Bashan sermonizing and other eccentricities. Concerned for the family name, Lewis advised that word of Archie's condition be withheld from the press. Wintie was just as concerned about this. After all, it was possible that with rest and total seclusion Archie might recover, and on this basis Lewis consented to join Winthrop in seeking their brother's commitment to an institution where he could receive adequate care. Wintie enlisted the cooperation of a cousin, Arthur Carey, who more than once had told Archie to his face that he was "cracked." Lewis took care of the legalities, and on March 10 Justice Henry A. Gildersleeve of the New York Supreme Court signed commitment papers, acting on the application of the three next-of-kin, supported by the finding of Dr. Moses Allen Starr, examiner-in-lunacy, that John Armstrong Chanler was insane.

Word of Archie's confinement reached the other members of the family as a *fait accompli,* and they accepted the judgment of Wintie and Lewis as undoubtedly sound. To the family's friends word was passed that Armstrong had gone abroad for an extended stay.

Archie's downfall had occurred at a time of another emotional upheaval among the Chanlers, but one that at the moment touched Elizabeth and Margaret alone. During the last couple of years, the Chanler sisters had formed a warm friendship with a Boston couple living in New York, the John Jay Chapmans. Mrs. Chapman, the former Minna Timmons, was half-Italian, a woman of passionate temperament. Minna and Elizabeth had been drawn to each other from their first meeting, the ardor of Minna's character counterbalancing the reserved glow of Elizabeth's, disciplined by long years of invalidism.

John Jay Chapman came from a line of strong-minded New England reformers. Intellectually gifted—too gifted for common usage—he was subject to psychic storms of a bizarre nature and overwhelming intensity. While at Harvard (where he was a contemporary of Winthrop Chanler in the Porcellian Club) and courting Minna, he imagined that another student had spoken of her slightingly, and waylaying the young man he had beaten him mercilessly. Then learning that he had been mistaken, he had done penance by thrusting his left hand into a fire and holding it there until it was so charred it had to be amputated. A man capable of such violence on behalf of principle was not commonplace, yet the dark depths of Chapman's troubled nature would never have been guessed from his witty urbanity and his irrepressible enjoyment of laughter. With all his humor, Chapman was like his forebears in passionate dedication to the causes he espoused. As a spokesman for the municipal reform movement in New York City, he had been a principal organizer of the Good Government Clubs that aimed at combatting corruption and civic misrule—"goo-goos," these amateur crusaders were scornfully called because of their devotion to "visionary ideals" like honesty in office and a decent regard for the rights of citizens.

Throughout 1895 and 1896 the Chanler sisters saw much of the Chapmans in New York, both in society and more intimately in the Chapmans' home at 325 West 82nd Street. By profession Chapman was a lawyer in Wall Street, although he disliked the law and practiced only for a livelihood; literature, philosophy, and reform were his interests. The sympathy between both Chapmans and the Chanler sisters ripened steadily throughout 1895. Chapman related to his wife the sort of telepathy that had developed among them. At a dinner party, he wrote to Minna:

"Elizabeth C. was in the dumps—way down in Hades and could scarcely make conversation, and though I went determined to be cheerful and succeeded—for if one has not got absolute self-control in such matters one is a boor—it was all I could do. I then went to the Century [Club] shindy, where I had a good time. Then I wrote to Elizabeth Chanler a note:

" 'My dear Miss Chanler
" 'I have a desire to write to you and it is no more than speaking —it's not about anything in particular. . . . There is a certain cut fate has for us—against which there is no defense—namely the misfortune and unhappiness of other people. I had a sort of feeling that you had had some form of this dealt to you recently. . . .'

"Now the electric flash in this [Chapman went on to his wife] was that she in casual conversation had mentioned going to see Amélie Rives and her brother, who were passing through town, and though I don't know either of them—the whole bogey flapped its wings all over the drawing room—I mean a cat-and-dog life in the Rives family. Now do you see the dangerous sort of creature I am? I don't do these things, I don't think or care about them, but the air is full of voices, demons—and angels speak and struggle in people's hearts, and trumpets blow that drown the dinner table small talk, and I need all my wits and all my prophets all the time. . . ."

The drift of these two persons—John Jay Chapman and Elizabeth Winthrop Chanler—was not perceived by either; but when Margaret Chanler returned from abroad for Alida's wedding in the autumn of 1896, she took in the appalling situation at a glance: Elizabeth was desperately in love with the husband of her best friend! Chapman liked to read aloud, and he read well. One evening, while he was reading to their circle, Margaret saw a look on her sister's face that revealed the dilemma into which Elizabeth, so self-possessed, so self-controlled, had fallen. Margaret was horrified, for the situation not only contained all the ingredients of heartbreak, but threatened to precipitate a crashing scandal: not only were the Chapmans congenially married, but they had two small sons, Victor and John Jay, Jr., and were expecting a third child imminently.

Margaret reacted energetically. Assuming command immediately after Alida's wedding, she snatched Elizabeth away on a long voyage to India and Japan, propinquity being one factor in the equation that she could eliminate. After a pause in England to pick up letters of introduction, the sisters' route lay through the Mediterranean, the Suez Canal, and on eastward. Letters streamed back to Mary Meroney at home. As their ship, the *Valetta*, neared Ceylon, the old nurse was assured that "we are both well when we are not sea sick & it will be delightful to land on a tropical island & see the forests of cocoanut trees. They say the monkeys jump right into the carriage & sit on your shoulder, & there are flying foxes. . . . All the sailors on the boat are Indians from Bombay dressed in cotton things & turbans. Miss Chanler is going to get some of their dresses to wear for painting aprons. I think I will bring you a big red turban, it might scare away the tramps. They are as big as the biggest pumpkin I ever saw & if you dont hold your head up very proudly they fall off."

In Ceylon the travelers were entertained officially, everywhere impressing their hosts by their dignity of bearing and the remarkable clarity of their diction. After luncheon at the residency, they

visited a Buddhist monastery where Elizabeth discoursed philo-
sophically with the monks through an interpreter. Crossing to the
mainland they stopped at Madras, and then proceeded to Oota-
camund, where the wife of the resident proved to be a New York
acquaintance. ("Coticummond," Margaret called this "Queen of
the Hill Stations," with untroubled disregard for the pedantry of
spelling.) There they encountered a general who had marched
with Roberts to the relief of Kandahar in 1880, and he laid out
an itinerary for them that took them clear to the Khyber Pass,
bowed along from residency to residency in carriages with footmen
and outriders. Elizabeth applied herself to compiling a voluminous travel diary which she intended for Minna Chapman. Then
at Calcutta they received shocking news: ten days after the birth
of her third child, Minna Chapman had died. The child, a boy,
had been named Conrad, and in a letter to Elizabeth conveying
the information John Jay Chapman wrote:

"I do not want you to come home. . . . The family and all
Minna's and my friends have done what mortals could do, and
are taking care of me. . . ."

Elizabeth felt otherwise. Waving aside Margaret's objections,
she resumed the ascendancy she normally exercised, and with all
speed crossed to Bombay and there caught a fast steamer to
Brindisi. From that point the sisters traveled overland to France
(pausing fleetingly at Monaco to pay their respects to their now
aged and widowed Aunt Laura Delano), and sailed for New York
on April 7.

On their landing, the full story of the crushing blow to Chapman, and of Armstrong's no less crushing misfortune, was imparted by Wintie. Elizabeth promptly visited Archie in Bloomingdale, and found no reason to differ from Winthrop's judgment.
Her brother appeared rational to her on all subjects except one,
but that one seemed preposterous to her. Archie had convinced
himself that his detention was due to a deliberate conspiracy on
the part of his brothers, aimed at gaining control and eventual
possession of his inheritance. By their father's will, should he die
without issue, his share of the estate would pass to his brothers
and sisters in equal portions. What better way to insure that he
would not contract a second marriage and have children than
by having him declared insane? What woman would marry a

certified lunatic? In the meantime, should the courts rule him incompetent to manage his affairs, his brothers and sisters would have the practical control of his property. Add to these motives the resentment caused by Archie's proposal to obtain an up-to-date auditing of the administration of his father's estate, and bad feeling harking back to his marriage with Amélie, and then Alida's wedding, and the picture seemed complete to Armstrong Chanler.

To Elizabeth the idea was fantastic. Chanlers never haggled over money, she pointed out, and she was certain her brothers' motives were honest. Archie indicated the bars at the window: was that sort of thing expressive of brotherly concern and pure motives, he asked. Elizabeth smiled. The bars were there "to keep you from running away," she said lightly; and the airy carelessness with which the words were spoken awakened a suspicion in Archie's mind that "Queen Bess" was in the plot, too. Until now he had refused to believe this. Visibly excited, he requested Elizabeth not to visit him again, for he had no need of her sympathy, although his brothers would need it, he added, "by the time I get through with them." Seeing the effect her visit produced, Elizabeth did not call again.

The conditions under which Chanler was held were strict but not unnecessarily onerous. Bloomingdale asylum was a private institution, a branch of The New York Hospital, the governors of which comprised the most respected and eminent citizens of the metropolis. The patients paid for their care, and Archie was assessed one hundred dollars a week for board, lodging, and medical care, plus the hire of two keepers, one of whom was always with him. He was forbidden to have any money, but could order luxuries to be sent in, at his expense. He could communicate with no one outside the asylum, whether by letter, telephone, or telegraph, except through the asylum authorities, who had full power to censor or suppress any communication at their discretion. He was allowed to have books and newspapers, and could take exercise inside the grounds, but always in the custody of a keeper.

Chanler found much to object to. He spurned the asylum food, terming it "badly cooked, adulterated, or decayed," and subsisted mainly on rations purchased from nearby grocery stores. Although a member of the medical staff visited him every day, the visits seemed to be for the purpose of getting him to agree that he was demented, something he steadfastly refused to admit. This refusal was put down as confirmation of his insanity, indicating inability to cope with reality.

He had awakened to the gravity of his plight only when it was too late. His first reaction had been one of profound humiliation, and for shame he had resigned from all his clubs—the Union, Manhattan, Knickerbocker, Democratic, Metropolitan, Century, University, Racquet, Calumet, Lambs, Players, St. Anthony, the Sons of the American Revolution, and the Alumni Association of Columbia College. (He failed to resign from the French Club, for what reason he never said; perhaps it was overlooked.)

Next he cast about for means to effect his release. He must, first of all, procure competent legal counsel. He was sure that the asylum authorities would never allow any appeal to pass them addressed to a lawyer, who might "make trouble." And even if he should succeed in smuggling out a message, who would take seriously the statements made by a certified madman? "Give a dog a bad name and hang him"—the adage ran through his mind. No, he would have to present his case with irrefragable logic and absolute conviction if he were to overcome the natural skepticism with which an appeal would be received, and also the natural reluctance any attorney would have to interfere in a family matter of such delicacy—especially when the family concerned was as prominent and as powerful as the Astor connection.

After several attempts, Archie gave up in despair of being able to draft the sort of appeal required. He had no skill in writing; in fact, he had often jokingly said that the only thing he could write was a check.

In this dilemma, his X-faculty came to the rescue. He had kept up the practice of automatic writing, and one day the pencil in his hand spelled out the words:

"I will write you a letter that will get you out of this hell-hole."

Thereafter, little by little, a letter took form. Running to several thousand words, it was a remarkable production for a man of supposedly weak wits.

The letter was dated from "The Society of The New York Hospital" (the legal name of Bloomingdale asylum), at White

Plains, New York, July 3, 1897. Chanler had then been incarcerated nearly four months. It was addressed to Captain Micajah Woods, commonwealth's attorney of Albemarle County, Virginia, who also practiced privately at Charlottesville. Woods was known personally to Chanler, and as a Virginia lawyer he might be presumed to be outside the range of Astor influences. Deferring to the Southern weakness for honorific titles, the letter began:

"My dear Captain: You probably will be surprised to hear that I am not abroad, as is generally thought; but am confined without due process of law, in a New York private insane asylum, whither I was brought by force against my expressed will; having been arrested by two officers in plain clothes on an order from a judge of the Supreme Court of the State of New York.

"You will pardon the length of this letter when I say that I wish to employ you as assistant counsel in cooperation with [State] Senator John W. Daniel [of Virginia, a friend] as leading counsel, in a habeas corpus proceedings which I wish instituted without delay.

"I enclose a certified copy of my commitment papers, which I suggest that you defer reading until you have finished this letter, as they are a tissue of perjuries from beginning to end."

So that Woods might understand the handicaps under which the letter was being drafted, Chanler mentioned that "the sum total of my law library consists of the Constitution of the United States in the back of a dictionary, and selections from a list of legal maxims in the same book." Then he delved into the causes of his imprisonment as he saw them.

Chief among these he placed the long-continued estrangement from the rest of his family, dating back to 1888 and his marriage in Virginia. A climax in the progress of this ill-feeling had been reached at the time of Alida's wedding; Elizabeth Chanler had told him, he stated, that his incensed brothers at that time had called him "crazy" repeatedly. He had paid no heed to her use of the word at the moment, he said, because it had long been customary, "whenever, in the course of an argument . . . I said anything which they found difficult to combat," for his brothers to retort, "You're crazy!"

The letter described the recent business quarrels with Winthrop

Chanler, and Armstrong's giving Stanford White the power of attorney in order to be free to carry on the experiments in "esoteric Buddhism" in which he had become involved. He recounted White's uninvited appearance at The Merry Mills; how White had induced him to come to New York under false pretenses; of his session with the pretended oculist; of his trance and the color change of his eyes. This last detail was relevant, he stressed, because the first count in the commitment papers stated that the examiner-in-lunacy had concluded "I am insane because I say that my eyes have changed color."

Archie outlined the conditions under which he lived in the asylum—"in solitary confinement in a two-roomed cell. A keeper sleeps in one of the rooms . . . and he is always with me. When I take exercise in the asylum grounds the keeper is always with me." His razors had been taken away, and he was forced to let the asylum barber shave him, although the man's clumsiness produced a painful rash. Because he found the institutional food indigestible, he had been reduced to a diet of "baked potatoes, lettuce, fruit, and crackers" brought in from a nearby store.

"In the meantime, I am living in a madhouse. Every 'patient' in the building in which I am imprisoned is hopelessly insane. At times some of them become violently, homicidally insane, when, after yells and struggles with keepers, and a siege in a straitjacket, they are forcibly removed from this building for having become 'violent,' as they call it here.

"Nothing prevents a patient from becoming homicidally insane at any time. In one of such fits of frenzy the lunatic might take it into his head to walk into my cell and attack me. The cell doors are unlocked, and although there is a keeper on watch on my floor, he is not always there. To give me warning of the approach of prowling inmates I put a table against my door at night."

One night a muscular inmate did invade Chanler's cell and was only routed by keepers.

"This will give you an idea of my surroundings," Chanler continued. "I think that you will agree with me that they are calculated to drive a man insane. When you add to these 'surroundings' the active and sustained efforts of the resident doctors to talk me into becoming insane by declaring to my face that I am insane, and attempting to argue me into admitting that I am; when you consider this, you will, I think, conclude that I have my nerves and will-power under effective control in being able to remain sane. So much for my life for the last four months."

Turning to the commitment papers, Chanler developed his contention that he had been illegally arrested and imprisoned. His address, as stated in the commitment papers, was given as the Hotel Kensington, New York City, although he was a bona fide resident of Virginia, and had never been registered at the Kensington except as a transient guest. The statement of the proprietor of the hotel confirmed this, as did entries in the New York City directory, which gave his home address as "Virginia." In 1895, he had gone to the office of the commissioner of taxes in New York City and had formally entered on the tax books his residence as Virginia, in order to fix the amount of his personal tax. Finally, even the complaint sworn to by his brothers and cousin referred to him as having been "for several months . . . at his home in Virginia."

Because of his clearly established residence in Virginia, and his being a citizen of that state, he charged, the New York courts had no jurisdiction in his case, and he was being detained illegally.

Other irregularities and inconsistencies in the commitment papers were pointed out, and the charge of perjury was pinned directly on his brothers and cousin. They had sworn, he said, to having personal knowledge of certain acts said to have occurred in his home in Virginia when they could not possibly have had such personal knowledge since not one of the three—Winthrop Chanler, Lewis Chanler, or Arthur Carey—had ever set foot inside his home. In fact, at the time the acts were alleged to have taken place, Lewis was in Europe, and Armstrong and Carey had not met since 1894. Nor had Archie seen Winthrop Chanler since the previous December, although the actions complained of were supposed to have been committed in February, to Winthrop's "personal knowledge."

Next the attesting doctors were taken apart legally, and their statements analyzed to show a clutter of contradictions. Dr. Starr was especially excoriated, accused of deceit, moral turpitude, and medical ignorance of subjects ranging from the subconscious mind to the effect produced by a porous plaster on a tender skin.

"It looks to me like perjury," Chanler told Woods. "How does it strike you?"

Point by point, Chanler demurred to or denied the medical examiner's allegations. He had not, he said, "limited myself to a peculiar diet"; had not frequently gone into a "trancelike state . . . exposed myself to cold, neglected or injured myself . . . threatened other people . . . been confined in an institution for the insane in 'New Paris, France,'" and so on down a long list. He admitted that he had carried a revolver, and always traveled with one, but he denied that he could be described as "going armed." He admitted that he said the color of his eyes had changed from brown to gray, and so it had. He admitted that he had been in a trancelike state, but not "frequently," and confirmed that when in a trance he sometimes spoke French, as he sometimes did when not in a trance. He denied that he suffered from "delusions," and offered in support a voluntary statement by his keeper: "I didn't describe no gradual development of no delusion for I didn't see none."

In conclusion, Chanler demurred to the charge that he had become unduly suspicious of his friends, commenting:

"My friends so called—family and friends—ran me in here. Had I been more suspicious of my friends I should not be in the hole which I occupy at present."

Chanler turned his fire also on Justice Gildersleeve's obtuseness in ruling that he was a maniac "with suicidal as well as homicidal tendencies"; he cited his peaceable surrender to the arresting officers, and his exemplary conduct since entering Bloomingdale, where he had threatened no one and had committed "not a single act which in the remotest degree resembled either violence or insanity." He conceded that he had, quite calmly, "frequently warned the authorities here that I would seek legal redress for the false imprisonment that I was undergoing, and that I would hold them legally responsible for their share in it."

As for why the doctors did not discharge him as sane, Chanler suggested that it was to their pecuniary advantage to retain a patient who could be gouged out of one hundred dollars a week "in exchange for a two-roomed cell, a keeper—and baked potatoes."

The summation of this brief was devastating:

"The ground work of the commitment papers is an amalgam of avarice, malice, and mendacity. I was accused by persons who were not in a position to know whereof they—not merely spoke, but duly swore. These said accusers were all and severally on bad terms with me for years . . . [and] it was to the unmistakeable interests of two of the said accusers, Messrs. Winthrop Astor Chanler and Lewis Stuyvesant Chanler [as executors of their father's estate], that I should be disfranchised, as an insane person, of my property as well as of my liberty. . . . It was to the equally unmistakeable spite and malice of the third said accuser, Mr. Arthur Astor Carey, that I should end, after years of every description of violent altercation with and opposition to me, in a madhouse."

Justice Gildersleeve's having signed the commitment order "without ever having laid eyes" on the condemned person was bitterly protested:

"Somebody takes it into his—or her—head, for certain reasons, that you are crazy. It seems fair that you should be allowed to confront your accuser—a common murderer has that privilege— and be heard in defense . . . before being summarily arrested like a malefactor, as I have been, and put behind bars without a trial for an indefinite period, perchance for life."

What Chanler wanted of Micajah Woods was to bring, in cooperation with Senator Daniel, a habeas corpus action in a federal, not a New York State, court. The exact procedure he left to the attorneys, but urged speed:

"I have been given to understand that when my unknown term of imprisonment here is ended, I am to be shipped off to Europe. I caution you not to write or telegraph me, nor mention to a living soul, save Senator Daniel, anything connected with me or my whereabouts. It has been given out by certain interested parties that I am in Europe (I find that is the stock term used when a man is sent here). Let it be so considered as long as possible. . . . Above all I warn you and Senator Daniel to be on your guard against all the doctors here. For they are all of them as smooth-spoken and deceptive in their manner as any set of confidence men. . . . As you may gather from my letter, I mean war. . . .

"Speed and secrecy are the watchwords. . . . Let a Federal judge examine into my sanity for a change. Examination at the hands of a distinguished and honest man is the last thing I should avoid. . . .

"As I am allowed no money—I haven't seen a dollar bill in months—and as I am not allowed to communicate with my New York office, I am unable to send you and Senator Daniel cheques for retainers and disbursements. So I must ask you to charge all traveling expenses and disbursements to my account until I am liberated."

At length the letter was written, but the problem remained: how to get it into the hands of Micajah Woods, in Charlottesville, hundreds of miles away. The asylum authorities would never allow it to pass.

Weeks and months went by while Archie watched for an opportunity.

Pirates Ahoy!

While his brother Armstrong grappled with subliminal enigmas, Lewis Stuyvesant Chanler had been pursuing the paths of peace and improving his time and talents at Cambridge University, in England. There he combined the study of international jurisprudence with participation in the debates of the Cambridge Union. As Willie Chanler had often remarked, in tones of toleration, admiration, endearment, or irritation, depending upon the mood and the occasion, Lewis dearly loved to make a speech. But then, Willie himself was never reluctant to shine as a spellbinder of a different sort, before a different audience.

The English climate was proving beneficial to Alice Chanler; in fact, the whole English way of life suited her; and the family's contentment at Cambridge was completed by the birth of a second son, who was given the name William Astor Chanler II. Lewis was no such facile letter writer as was his brother Winthrop, but he kept the family informed of his activities, or lack of such, including his interest in horses on and off the race track. He badgered Margaret constantly for news of Rokeby—the farm, the "house people," the affairs of Christ Church in Red Hook, of which he had become a trustee.

"Hoping for a letter from you tomorrow although I am conscious of not having deserved any further consideration at your hands," ran a typically desultory greeting from Gogmagog Hills,

Family of Lewis Stuyvesant Chanler in England, about 1900. From left, Lewis Stuyvesant Chanler, Jr.; William Astor Chanler II (later William Chamberlain Chanler, to avoid confusion); Mrs. Lewis Stuyvesant Chanler (née Alice Chamberlain); Alida Chanler. (*Courtesy of Mrs. William Christian Bohn*)

Cambridge. ". . . I am now going in for literature & am to edit one of the University papers; it may teach me to spell. . . . There is not much news. Term is over & so is my hard work. The Union has taken up much spare time—I am now Vice President. . . . Next week or rather on a week from Monday I expect to be the President and then vacation. Tennis, real tennis, is my chief amusement. . . . On Thursday I go to Oxford to make a speech, after which I shall keep silent unless a general election comes along and I get a chance to go on the stump a little for the Radicals. . . . Bob writes that what he misses most is my fat sleepy face at breakfast—fear I am losing my dignity & find it hard to be in a bad humor long—both signs of moral degeneration. Come over and brace me up."

A chance to speak for the Radicals did come with the general election of 1897. Sympathizing with the Irish Nationalists in their struggle to gain home rule, Lewis campaigned for them under the sponsorship of John Redmond. A bellicose speech in Dublin, which the London press described as "breathing no end of threats against England," caused his Anglicized cousin, William Waldorf Astor, to deny testily that Chanler spoke for the Astors. But Redmond offered Lewis a seat in parliament from an Irish constituency, an offer that was declined, to the immense relief of Margaret Chanler; she lived in dread that her brother would settle abroad permanently and become one of the rootless exiles whom she regarded with mingled pity and aversion. But Lewis reassured her; the Chanler roots were sunk too deeply in American soil for easy transplanting; and he wrote that he was "quite as eager as ever to return & do not see the slightest sign of a growing liking for life over here." He added a word of advice to Margaret about her habit of fretting over her sisters:

"You must not take life so hard; remember that you ought not to do the thinking for three & a little self-indulgence is a good thing as a rest."

Willie Chanler was often seen at Tammany Hall, on New York's East 14th Street, during these days, and he reported that Lewis's stand for old Ireland was warmly applauded there. Willie still had his eye upon a political career, and he took naturally to the shillelagh type of electioneering practiced by the Tammany braves. The boss of Tammany, Richard Croker, found a Chanler connection useful, and Willie enjoyed the roughhouse tactics by which Croker sometimes "persuaded" the votes to fall on the right side. Several Tammany district leaders became Chanler's firm friends, notably Tom Foley, leader of the Irish-Italian district east of City Hall.

Willie had kept up a correspondence with Theodore Roosevelt, and toward the end of 1896, when Roosevelt was about to become Assistant Secretary of the Navy under President McKinley, Teddy turned to Chanler for practical help in the fight to annex Hawaii.

"At the waterline partisanship ought to disappear," wrote Republican Roosevelt to Democrat Chanler with his customary vigor, "and I know you are as strong in your views of foreign policy as

Cabot [Lodge] and I are. It seems incredible that the Democratic party, the historic party of annexation, should be inclined to go against the annexation of Hawaii; but so it is. . . . There are several . . . Democratic senators who would be for it if their party did not commit them against it. I think this is the time when you could use your influence in a way that would be invaluable to America on one of the very points which you and I regard as most vital. Could you not see Croker and get him to use his influence with Senator Murphy to go for the annexation treaty? It should not be a party measure at all . . . and if we win we must win by Democratic aid. I wish you would attend to this at once."

Despite this junction of forces, the annexation treaty failed to pass at that time.

The most explosive foreign policy issue at the moment was provided by Cuba, where insurgents under the leaders Gomez, Garcia, Maceo, and others were fighting a guerrilla war against the Spanish regime. The "jingo press" * was broadcasting propaganda provided by a revolutionary committee, or junta, headed in New York by a refugee school teacher named Thomas Estrada Palma, and whipping up sentiment for intervention by the United States. William Randolph Hearst's *Journal* and Joseph Pulitzer's *World,* the two newspapers boasting the largest circulation in the nation, led in this inflammatory campaign, publishing lurid accounts of supposed Spanish atrocities. Estrada Palma handed out his propaganda in an office maintained by Horatio Rubens at 66 Broadway; Rubens, a lawyer, had subterranean connections with shadowy characters all over Latin America, and he and Willie Chanler became very friendly.

Another activity carried on by the Cuban junta was the smuggling of contraband matériel of war to their comrades fighting on the island. The risks involved in this traffic, not only in the way of possibly compromising American neutrality and drawing the nation involuntarily into war, but directly to the smugglers, were

---

* So called from the popular song:

> "We don't want to fight, but by jingo, if we do,
> We've got the ships, we've got the men,
> We've got the money too!"

real enough. Not only must the vigilance of Spanish gunboats be circumvented, but also the opposition of the navies of the world whose governments were at peace with Spain. One filibustering ship had been captured and an American in the crew had been sentenced to death by a Spanish court-martial, and grudgingly reprieved when an uproar of indignation arose in the United States.

William Chanler itched to take a hand in this dangerous game. He sympathized with the Cuban revolutionaries, and he also believed that the interest of his own country required the expulsion of Spain from Cuba. In this conviction he was not alone. In December, 1897, Roosevelt had written to him, endorsing the letter *"Private and Confidential"*:

"Dear Willie: Your letter pleased me very much, and it will delight Cabot [Lodge]. I will now say what I did not write before, because I feared you might misunderstand it. . . . My feeling about this matter is just this: I wish we had a perfectly consistent foreign policy, and that this policy was that ultimately every European power should be driven out of America, and every foot of American soil, including the nearest islands in both the Pacific and the Atlantic, should be in the hands of independent American states, and so far as possible in the possession of the United States or under its protection. With this end in view I should take every opportunity to oust each European power in turn from this continent, and to acquire for ourselves every military coign of vantage; and I should treat as cause for war any effort by a European power to get so much as a fresh foothold of any kind on American soil. . . . So that I believe you have done a wise and patriotic action, and I congratulate and thank you with all my heart. . . ."

This praise of Chanler's activity was significant because it came from a member of the government of a nation at peace with Spain, and the action alluded to was Chanler's smuggling of arms to the Cuban rebels. The letter of course was unofficial and repudiatable; Secretary of State John Hay had in fact plainly told Chanler, "If you get caught, we won't even know you."

Months before, Chanler had unfolded his plans to von Höhnel, regretting that his companion of Africa could not share the adventure, but the lieutenant was on sea duty. As a substitute, Willie had joined forces with a daredevil known as "Dynamite Johnny" O'Brien, well known at trouble spots around the Caribbean.

Chanler and Dynamite procured two coastal steamers which they loaded with arms purchased secretly by the Cuban junta. To get the cargoes out of American ports required ingenuity. It involved forged manifests and recruiting crews of rough characters, picked up largely on the Philadelphia waterfront. Chanler's craft was the *Bermuda,* and he appeared on the ship's papers as the supercargo, under the name "White." George Galvin was signed on as an able-bodied seaman, passing as a stranger to "Mr. White."

In February, 1897, Galvin had written a farewell letter to von Höhnel from Chanler's New York apartment, at 83 Clinton Place (now West 8th Street). The note was not gay:

"Just a few hurried lines to bid you farewell. I leave this morning for Philadelphia where I ship on a steamer as an A.B. Our destination is the insurgent camp, Cuba. I sympathize deeply with them in their fight for liberty and only hope to be of some slight help to them in the field. I will go into a cavalry troop. Mr. C. too will be on the same vessel but we will have to be as perfect strangers. It is a risky trip with little glory attached and very little chance of promotion, but there will be plenty of bad food, hard work, and a good chance of getting one's head blown off. However I don't care and only wish you too was with us. . . ."

Two months later, Willie, back from one successful trip, wrote to von Höhnel from a dingy hotel in Jersey City where he was lying low, rejecting his friend's remonstrances against taking such risks:

"I am afraid it will be impossible for you to understand my motives in undertaking this business. First I am, as you say, young & reckless. Second I sympathize with the Cubans in their gallant efforts in behalf of liberty, and third, I, being an American, feel it necessary to do what I can to separate entirely this continent from Europe. I have had not the slightest influence brought to bear on me in this matter; but on the contrary have met with discouragement & obstacles from all my friends to whom I have spoken on the subject. The delays, etc., have but strengthened my purpose & I hope that by the time this reaches you to be with either Gomez or Garcia doing what I can to drive Spain from the island. . . . It is no easy matter to get to Cuba I can tell you. We are chased from pillar to post by police, revenue cutters & warships. I have narrowly escaped capture twice but my old luck seems to stand by me. . . . Keep your heart up & dont picture me shot in the stomach, lamed, maimed, or hanged. . . . If I am killed it will be in a good cause. . . . Now good bye & good luck . . . Don't say anything of this letter. Wintie will write you when he hears that I am in the island."

Willie's family saw nothing of him while he played at cat-and-mouse with the Spanish gunboats. He had not particularized to von Höhnel the "narrow escapes" alluded to, and regarding some of them, details would be revealed only years afterward. One of these von Höhnel belatedly recounted as an example of Willie's nerve and quick wittedness in an emergency.

The *Bermuda* had been blocked from making a landing until its water supply gave out, and Willie was compelled to return to the Bahamas to replenish. The port authorities there became suspicious of the craft, and the governor sent an aide to verify the ship's papers. This officer, it turned out, had met Willie in London years before, and as soon as he came over the side he spotted the bogus supercargo.

"You are not Mr. White," he challenged. "You are William Astor Chanler."

"Right, I am Chanler," Willie replied coolly, "and you are so-and-so (naming him) and you were kicked out of your club in such-and-such a year for cheating at cards."

All which was true. The aide reddened and any question of the *Bermuda*'s true identity or mission was waived.

A second narrow escape was more hair-raising. Obviously no verification of this story from documentary sources can or ever could be produced; but true or not (and it is by no means certain that it is untrue), it reflects Willie's resourcefulness and his intrepidity.

Willie had several navy deserters in his crew, and in order to give them some diversion during the tedious lurking off the Cuban coast awaiting the signal to land, he had a light naval gun mounted on the *Bermuda*'s forward deck under a camouflaged housing. The deserters who were good marksmen were allowed to use this gun occasionally for target shooting.

On one trip, the *Bermuda,* after standing off for days, at length received a signal to land its cargo in a little harbor on the southern coast. As the ship boldly turned into the narrow entrance channel, directly ahead was seen a Spanish gunboat at anchor. The space was too cramped to allow the *Bermuda* to turn around; she was trapped.

Whether any command was given was never made clear; but in a trice off came the bow gun's housing and the gunners opened fire. With their first shot they struck the gunboat's magazine and blew the craft out of the water.

Frantically backing out of the cove, Chanler considered what to do. His situation now was perilous, for sinking a warship was an act of piracy, for which the *Bermuda* would be hunted down by every navy in the world. Filibustering was one thing, piracy was infinitely more dangerous; under international law, the fate of pirates was hanging.

Acting with characteristic nerve, Chanler headed for the Florida coast. Calling the crew together, he explained their predicament and warned that their necks would be in danger if they ever breathed a word about what had happened. To drive home the warning, he stopped at a lonely key and put ashore several of the toughest men, stripped to their shorts. All day he left them to the sun and mosquitoes, and when they were taken off in the evening they were in pitiable condition. That, Chanler told them, was only a taste of what would be their fate if they ever talked.

That night, off the Florida coast, the *Bermuda* was hove to and the crew was put ashore and told to scatter. Then Chanler scuttled the *Bermuda,* and with one seaman (presumably George Galvin) set out in an open boat for Cuba. He made the island safely, and managed to get into Havana without detection. There he took refuge in an elegant bordello kept by a *déclassé* titled English-woman, as the least likely place where the authorities would be apt to look for him, and stayed there until he believed the furor over the gunboat had sufficiently died down. Then he quietly made his way to New York.*

---

* Years afterward, a fictionalized account of this episode was published in a pulp magazine, where one of Willie's sons read it. Knowing that his father had run guns to Cuba, the boy asked whether the incident could be true. Willie was startled, but confirmed that the account was essentially accurate, and that the ship in question was his own. Trying to guess who might have broken silence, he finally narrowed the probabilities down to an army ex-sergeant, who was both literate and foolhardy enough, Willie thought, to have taken the chance.

> "I know not if the truth it be,
> I tell the tale as 'twas told to me."

"Give a Dog a Bad Name"

Throughout his recent business altercations with his brother Armstrong, Winthrop Chanler had lost none of his bounce. About the time when Stanford White was intruding upon Archie's psychological investigations at The Merry Mills, Wintie had been peppering his friends with chaff as though he had not an anxiety in life. Dropping into the Wall Street offices of his friend French early one morning, he left this memo scribbled on the laggard banker's desk:

> "Manhattan Trust Co.
> 10 Wall Street
> Thursday, 9:10 A.M. Feb 1897

"My dear Amos,

"I really want to remonstrate. Here it is after 9 o'clock and neither Mr. Waterbury, Mr. Kean nor Mr. French at his post. Shocking sloth, most dilatory dawdledom. Yours in sorrow more than anger.

> "W. Chanler."

In September, 1897, Daisy Chanler's mother, Louisa Terry, died, and Wintie and the children moved to Rome to stay with Daisy's father, who was eighty-four. And it was in Rome in October that Winthrop received word that the New York newspapers had found out that Armstrong was in Bloomingdale asylum, and were airing the information in a ridiculous manner.

The publicity had been brought about unwittingly by Archie himself. Since July he had been watching for some means to smuggle out his laboriously drafted letter to Micajah Woods, soliciting that attorney's help. No opportunity presented itself until October 13, when a newspaper reporter who had been in the asylum taking the cure for morphine addiction was discharged. He volunteered to carry out Chanler's letter. Being a reporter, he also carried word of Chanler's whereabouts to New York City news rooms.

The next day *The New York Times* revealed the mental breakdown of "the former husband of Amélie Rives." His commitment had been procured by his "nearest relatives and friends," the *Times* said, "upon the advice of physicians, and after careful deliberation," because of an "alleged tendency to hallucinations and the manifestation of symptoms of nervous collapse. . . . He was taken to Bloomingdale quietly, and in order that his privacy there might not be intruded upon, the impression was allowed to obtain that he had gone abroad." This story was published under the somewhat dubious headline: "Some Queer Hallucinations."

Both the *Tribune* and the *Times* interviewed Armstrong's law partner, Harry Van Ness Philip, and were given a version of the circumstances which must have made frustrating reading for Archie when he opened the papers the next morning in his barred cell.

"In the first place," Philip was quoted as saying, "let me say that I do not consider that Mr. Chanler is an insane person by any means. I saw him yesterday and he talked with me in a perfectly rational manner. Of course he realizes his condition and is sensible of the necessity of having absolute rest. His nervous system was undermined by hard work and too close application to important interests which he has in the South. . . . His mind became overtaxed, and some months ago his relatives and friends saw that he was getting into a bad way and needed the change and rest which only perfect seclusion could give. It was deemed wisest to place him in a large institution where he would not only have all the advantages of experienced and skillful treatment, but would also have the protection of an adequate discipline."

This final phrase may have seemed to Archie an overglib description of barred windows and twenty-four-hour surveillance.

Philip insisted that Chanler himself had wished to keep knowledge of his condition and whereabouts from the public, hence the reports that he had gone abroad.

"The last time I saw him the question of newspaper publicity came up in our conversation and he urged me to keep his matters out of the newspapers," said his partner. "I feel confident that Mr. Chanler will recover his mental vigor, but I am afraid that this newspaper talk will retard his recovery. He is comparatively a free agent where he is now; he sees whomever he wants to and he reads the newspapers. It is to be regretted that he cannot have perfect quiet and protection from worry. But now that the main fact is known, I think the best way is to tell the exact truth about the case."

This ostensibly candid account hardly squared with information that the *Times* gathered from other sources. To some of his friends, said the *Times,* Chanler had "evinced a disposition to object to his commitment to Bloomingdale asylum. Although manifesting no bitter feeling toward his relatives, whom he regards as being mistaken and ill-advised, he has expressed strong objection to his incarceration. To at least one friend he raised the point that his commitment to an institution in New York state is illegal, because he is a citizen of Virginia. At no time has Mr. Chanler shown any violent symptoms of insanity. One of his hallucinations, which are said to have aroused the suspicions of his friends as to his mental soundness, is a belief on his part that he had succeeded by will power in changing the shape of his face and the color of his eyes. Other alleged hallucinations are that Mr. Chanler believes himself to be a reincarnation of Napoleon, and that he could make a great fortune at Monte Carlo by a system of play devised by himself."

The *Tribune* succeeded in reaching one member of the Chanler family, Willie, at his apartment on Clinton Place, but he had little to offer.

"My brother has been in the asylum for a few months, but is improving, and we hope for his complete recovery," Willie told reporters. "He has a splendid constitution, and there is every reason to expect that with rest he will cease to suffer from the nervous exhaustion which has been his trouble."

In the absence of Winthrop and Lewis Chanler, both in Europe, Willie wrote hastily to sister Margaret cautioning her and

Elizabeth not to "volunteer information about the case. If people (relatives or friends) should ask for information, the formula pitched upon & given in your letter is just the right one and covers all necessary ground. I did what I could to stop publicity, but as you see failed. There is more in this than meets the eye, and I'm, you may be sure, on the qui vive. It is odd that it should all come out only after Stanford's & Wintie's departure. Don't worry. What is, is, & cant be changed. I'll try to see Alida on Sunday. . . ."

Alida was occupied with her first child, a daughter, born a month previously, and at the moment was regarded in the family as even more scatterbrained than usual.

Willie had not been consulted about Armstrong's commitment, and while he was inclined to rely on the judgment of Winthrop and Lewis, the inconsistencies being brought out by the newspapers were disquieting. A fact of which no word had yet reached the public was that there had been an estrangement between Archie and Willie, also, dating back nearly a year. It had been caused by an argument over a horse. Willie had acquired a racing stable and a breeding farm near Leesburg, in Virginia; registering his colors (light blue, gold stars, blue and gold cap) with the Jockey Club, he was racing his horses with some success on the New York tracks.

In December, 1896, he and Armstrong met by chance on the train going south; Archie was on his way to Virginia, and Willie was headed to look over his yearlings. The conversation turned to a race recently won by a horse of Willie's named Salvacea, and Archie commented that he had read in a New York newspaper statements about the running of that race that seriously reflected upon the honor of the owner. "No sensitive man," he said, would let such an insinuation pass without challenge; he would "either demand a public apology, or at once institute a libel suit." Since he had seen no apology and had heard nothing about any libel action, he asked Willie plainly whether the innuendo had been well founded. Willie winked and laughed, implying that there might be something in it. This struck Archie as no laughing matter, and a hot argument followed, almost leadiing to blows. Finally the brothers separated, withdrawing to opposite ends of the car, and the ride was continued in a mutual glower. Since then there had been no communication between them.

In the present emergency, Willie urged Winthrop to return, and this Wintie did in November, Robert coming with him. In a letter to Daisy written aboard their ship, Wintie's blithe spirit seemed in no way troubled. It started:

"Dampfer 'Fulda,' Saturday, November, 1897

"Dearest Woof:

"This steamer that I don't care a *damfer* sailed at 7 last night. It was cloudy and one could see nothing. Bob and I dined sumptuously at a private table with Papa Roelker who is returning to his grindstone in Providence leaving Mamma Roelker and the *Roelkerinis* in Florence with his brother. The chief steward is our slave. To my huge delight I found that he had given my cabin to someone else & so prepared to dance an imitation war dance, whereupon he instantly offered us two rooms right next to the saloon, large, airy, & clean. I gave him two golden sovereigns & he nearly fainted with surprise. . . ."

In New York, Winthrop had need of all his diplomatic finesse to soothe the extensive Astor connection, wroth at being dragged into the distasteful Bloomingdale business; the newspapers were constantly referring to Archie as "lawyer and clubman and great-grandson of John Jacob Astor." Ruffled feathers had to be smoothed, and the situation in regard to Archie himself had to be reviewed to make sure that there would be no fresh embarrassment. And as the event turned out, the press received private assurances that the medical experts held little hope of Armstrong's early recovery, and that concern for his welfare should preclude any further public canvassing of the case. The *Times* responded to these discreet suggestions so cooperatively as to volunteer that friends who had heard Armstrong's own statement of his condition and wishes did not feel "called upon to interfere with the policy pursued by those responsible for his commitment."

This proved to be the feeling of Micajah Woods after he had read Archie's appeal for legal representation. The situation was one of extreme delicacy, and interference might be wholly unjustified. In reply Woods sent a friendly but noncommittal acknowledgment of receipt of Armstrong's letter, and advised patience.

To the man in Bloomingdale, this was a bitter setback, and the adage again came to mind—"Give a dog a bad name and hang him." His brothers and sisters seemed determined to prove that he was demented, and the doctors now were diagnosing his malady as progressive paranoia. Yet he felt rational, and responded favorably to all the stimuli indicating sanity of which he had any knowledge. But how could he establish the truth and regain his freedom? Who would accept his word? Where could he apply for help? Finding no key to the enigma, he resigned himself to doing what Woods recommended—to practice patience and do everything required of him except one thing—never, never would he admit that he was insane. Archie settled down to wait.

And outside the walls of Bloomingdale, the other Chanlers went about their affairs. In England, as war with the Boers erupted, Lewis Chanler found increasing difficulty in suppressing his indignation at the bullying policy of the British; his sympathy was with the Boers. At home, Willie Chanler, following the example of his father, was at length embarking upon his political career, and in the autumn of 1897 won election to the New York legislature as the Tammany candidate in the Fifth Assembly District. During the session of that winter he entertained handsomely in the house he had rented in Albany, while dealing with questions of patronage and legislative bills instead of contraband munitions of war. Margaret Chanler, her interest in political activity spurred by the example and counsels of her Aunt Julia Ward Howe, served capably as her brother's hostess.

In January, 1898, Winthrop, his mission accomplished, sailed for Rome, wife, and home, with liveliness undampened; not foreseeing that within three months he would be hastening back under circumstances far different from those he left.

Domestic Breezes Blow Hot, Blow Cold

Though public affairs were about to engross the Chanlers, their private concerns continued to be worked out within the clan in the usual diverse ways.

Upon their return from India, Elizabeth and Margaret Chanler had found John Jay Chapman in a state of shock caused by his wife's death. Outwardly calm, he seemed cheerful, but inwardly he was disoriented—near collapse and unaware of his peril. He had three small boys on his hands, the eldest only six; he was yoked to a profession that he disliked; he was burdened with debts, was intellectually overintense, and he had been cut adrift from his emotional moorings.

During the summer of 1897 he took the children to Saunderstown, Rhode Island, across the bay from Newport, where the Chanlers were summering. There had been visiting back and forth, with the inevitable result that he and Elizabeth recognized that they were in love, and came to an understanding that they would marry soon.

To contemplate marriage, and especially a marriage involving the heavy responsibilities of a ready-made family and an unstable husband, required courage on Elizabeth Chanler's part. Her health was precarious; periodically she was troubled by recurrence of her lameness; while her prospective husband, a widower with three sons, was a man of extraordinary independence and stormy impulses. Chapman never had ridden on an even keel, but had spent his life asserting an identity that eluded him, striving to reform customs and institutions while his own nature was constantly bursting out of bounds. To ally herself with such a man, under such circumstances, meant for Elizabeth the abandonment of the teachings of Mary Marshall, an action demanding both fortitude and love. Fortunately Elizabeth Chanler was amply endowed with both. In the hope that her stability might bring repose to Jack, she was willing to risk not only physical danger, but the possibility of a demoralizing failure. And Chapman responded.

Their courtship was quaintly subdued, neither being demonstrative. They clung to their privacy and avoided being seen together, meeting surreptitiously in unlikely places, such as a Paulist chapel on Tenth Avenue in New York, where no acquaintance was apt to be encountered. These furtive meetings amused Chapman, for neither he nor Elizabeth was romantically young; he was thirty-six and she thirty-two. But he entered into the spirit of the adventure, assuring her gaily:

"You shall have all the fun of it. I will wear a cloak and give the countersign, evade the eyes of hotel clerks, pass you in public, and leap through your casement to the sound of twangling instruments."

Chapman viewed the Chanlers sympathetically, although he felt that their cohesiveness limited them at the very time it made them stand out exotically from their social background. To him, as an inward-looking personality, the exuberant extroversion of the Chanlers was a source of constant amazement.

When Elizabeth informed her brothers of her proposed marriage, they were seriously alarmed. Chapman himself they welcomed; his background, New York connections, and brilliant mind were congenial, although his reformer zeal was not. It was for Elizabeth they feared, for they had accepted unquestioningly Mary Marshall's dictum that Elizabeth must never consider marriage. But their reluctance gave way before the serene determination of "Queen Bess," and reconciling themselves to the fact, they hoped for the best.

Margaret Chanler meanwhile had been elaborating her own life style. She did not contemplate marriage, but wished to live independently. With this end in view she persuaded her sisters to relinquish to her their shares in the ownership of Rokeby. Then,

Margaret Livingston Chanler, 1893–1894, during extended residence abroad.

with possession of Rokeby assured, Margaret cast about for a town house in New York, and under the guidance of Stanford White purchased a small dwelling at 317 West 74th Street, just off Riverside Drive, on the upper West Side of Manhattan. It was agreed that the sisters should live with her in town, at least temporarily, and for their convenience Margaret ordered alterations, including an elevator for Elizabeth and a studio on the top floor where "Queen Bess" could continue her painting.

These changes had been completed when Margaret and Elizabeth returned from India, and the three sisters moved in; Alida with her husband, to stay until the house they were building in Portchester was ready. So at last the family seemed to have settled into some permanent pattern, which Bob alone appeared likely to upset.

Robert Chanler's marriage had been navigating torturous channels, skirting disaster, for some time. The family did not know the full story, but they surmised much. The truth was that on his wedding night Robert discovered that he had taken a totally frigid mate. The physical aspects of marriage filled Julia with a disgust that she could neither conceal nor overcome. To this was added her cringing from the sheer vitality of her husband and his family. She was twenty, unversed in the world, and basically incurious. She craved orderliness, decorum, primness, and security; the furious way the Chanlers hurled themselves upon their pleasures and objectives terrified her. She shrank from their assertiveness, from their apparently haphazard existence, and their mental and physical boisterousness.

The first evening she and Robert spent at Rokeby, on their honeymoon visit, an argument had arisen at dinner, and the brothers soon were shouting at each other with such fierceness that Julia fled to her room. Bob found her there, packing to leave, declaring that she would not pass the night in that house where a murder was likely to occur at any minute. Bob laughed. That had been no *argument,* he explained, it was merely a *discussion.* What happened during an *argument* he promised to show her at breakfast the next morning, which he did, pointing out the knife gouges plainly visible in the mahogany dining table.

Another sample of the Chanler turmoil that unnerved Julia had occurred shortly after her marriage, at a large reception given by the Winthrop Chanlers. Pounced upon at the door, Julia had been marched across the room crowded with loud-talking persons (those Chanler voices!), plumped down on a sofa, and given the hissed command:

"Sit there! Don't move! Spread out your skirts! Willie is dead drunk underneath!"

Such incidents were not conducive to the elimination of Julia's inhibitions, and time brought no easing. She tried to be a wife in fact, and she sensed her husband's talent and wished to further it; but from the overwhelming manifestations of that talent she recoiled.

Bob's Bohemian ways and friends shocked her. Even wealthy Henry Clews, who had taken up sculpture seriously, Julia kept at arm's distance, although he and Bob were the closest of friends. Unlike in temperament, the two men shared artistic enthusiasms and disagreed ribaldly about almost everything else. There was a record of their carrying on a discussion of art and life at the Deux

Magots for forty-eight hours consecutively. Clews, whose social foundations were comparatively recent (his fortune dating from his father, who had made it in Wall Street), contended that Bob cheapened himself by riotous living, and Bob retorted that Clews would never become a real artist until he shook off his worship of social standing. After each monumental disagreement, Bob would charge at his work again with a fury that his wife could not comprehend and that repelled her.

When no child appeared, the Chanlers hinted at some deficiency in Julia. Willie scornfully believed that his sister-in-law was more interested in being fashionably gowned than in having a child; he put her down as heartless. Bob's inner rage and frustration finally drove him to the point of asserting his conjugal rights regularly on Sundays, and on those days Julia would faint in anticipation of the ordeal.

Bob was still groping—but toward what? Margaret Chanler could see no future for him in art, and to his brothers—Archie excepted—he seemed unlikely to amount to much anyway, so he might as well paint if that gave him satisfaction.

Such was the family's situation in 1898, when suddenly public events eclipsed private considerations, for the Chanlers as for the nation.

No Place for a Married Man

As 1898 approached, a cry was being raised in the nation's sensational press for armed intervention by the United States in behalf of the Cuban insurgents. Public indignation was whipped to a froth by fictitious accounts of revolting bestialities supposed to be practiced by the Spaniards upon the defenseless Cubans. The demand was for war, and President McKinley was resisting it as well as he could.

Theodore Roosevelt, now Assistant Secretary of the Navy, fretted at Washington's inaction, and prayed for some event that might bring about the intervention which he believed to be inevitable. The Cuban rebels were reported to be in desperate straits, their forces threatened with collapse unless help came soon. On December 23, 1897, Roosevelt shared his bellicose apprehensions with Willie Chanler in a private letter from Washington:

". . . As you know, our squadron is going down to gulf waters this year. I do not believe that the administration will admit even to themselves that our hand may be forced in the Cuban matter; yet I firmly believe such to be the fact. I do not believe that Cuba can be pacified by autonomy and I earnestly hope that events will so shape themselves that we must interfere some time in the not distant future."

Events did so "shape themselves," although whether accidentally or by a premeditated act of provocation will never be known for

certain. On February 15, 1898, the battleship *Maine* was blown
up in Havana harbor, with loss of hundreds of American lives.
In the press, Spanish treachery was blamed, and that interpreta-
tion was trumpeted by the interventionists. The day after the
tragedy Roosevelt unburdened himself to a fellow Porcellian, Benjamin Harris Diblee:

". . . Being a Jingo, as I am writing from one Porc man to
another, I will say, to relieve my feelings, that I'd give anything
if President McKinley would order the fleet to Havana tomorrow.
This Cuban business ought to stop. The *Maine* was sunk by an
act of treachery on the part of the Spaniards, *I* believe, though we
shall never find out definitely, and officially it will go down as an
accident. . . ."

The prospect of imminent fighting came as a deliverance to
Willie Chanler, bogged down in the humdrum preoccupations of
the state legislature. Although he discharged his responsibilities
loyally as the representative of Manhattan's Fifth Assembly District, he had little heart for them. At the residence he had leased,
at 114 Lancaster Street, in Albany, he held open house to advance
measures favorable to his constituents; his hostess, sister Margaret,
pleased by being "very quiet in manner and good-looking," although she was outspoken in stating her views and capable of dis-
concerting brusquerie.

Two bills that Chanler worked wholeheartedly to pass had to
do with liberalizing the Sunday closing law for New York City's
saloons and amending the code for regulating prize fights. The
latter subject held personal interest for Willie because he owned,
jointly with several other sportsmen, a stable of fighters and often
worked out with them at Stillman's gymnasium, housed in a building that he owned in the city.

In February Willie paid a surprise visit to his brother Armstrong in Bloomingdale asylum; it was their first meeting since
their row over a horse race. Willie wished to look into Archie's
condition himself, although Archie suspected that his brother had
come as a spy for the family. But he greeted Willie cordially, and
they talked for a couple of hours about Willie's political career,
which Archie approved, and other matters. Finally, when Willie
prepared to leave, Archie gave him a message to deliver to Lewis

and Winthrop Chanler and to Arthur Carey. Speaking with utmost earnestness, Armstrong said that the papers committing him to Bloomingdale bore "indisputable proof" of perjury, and much as he shrank from having "the brand of felony" placed upon his next-of-kin, the law must take its course—a course which would, on the evidence, lead "to a convict's cell in state's prison." As a lawyer, Armstrong had only one piece of advice to offer his brothers and cousin, and this was that "the said three gentlemen together with their wives and children emigrate without delay to the Argentine Confederation," where he understood that extradition did not run.

Willie promised to transmit the message. And that was the only time Armstrong saw William Chanler at Bloomingdale.

Willie's attention thereafter was concentrated upon matters other than his brother's plight: war with Spain was imminent, and he was determined to have a part in it. He told the family of his intention, and brother Lewis wrote back to Margaret from Monte Carlo:

"Willie says I must be back by summer or it will be too late. I suppose he knows all about it, he knows."

On March 11 William Astor Chanler resigned from the Assembly. He was spurred to this action both by his own eagerness to fight (what von Höhnel called his "blood-letting propensities") and by pressure exerted by former associates in gun-running. One of his fellow filibusters, reduced to editing a newspaper in Buffalo, had written an appeal similar to others addressed to Chanler:

"Let's go to Cuba! Let's get Captain Ed. Murphy & Capt. [Dynamite Johnny] O'Brien and a few other choice spirits such as were congregated on the old *Bermuda,* and fight the beasts!"

Willie was not the man to resist such a call to manifest excitement, but he needed reliable information regarding the intentions of the government at Washington. His close friend Roosevelt should know what was brewing, and to him Chanler turned. But at that very time Roosevelt was looking to Chanler in hope of seeing service himself. On March 15 Roosevelt wrote glumly:

"Dear Willie:

"This is the first letter of yours that I have ever hated to receive, for I have been on the point of writing to you to know if

you were going to raise a regiment, and to know if I could go
along. I shall chafe my heart out if I am kept here instead of being
at the front. . . . If nothing else happens I hope I can get with
you in any capacity. . . . I have a man here, Leonard Wood, who
is also very anxious to go. He is an Army surgeon, but he wants
to go in the fighting line. He is a tremendous athlete. Can't you
come on here? I will take you to Alger [Secretary of War], and I
will get Wood, and you and I and he will go over the matter together. At present I am utterly in the air as to how to advise you,
because I haven't the slightest idea what I could do myself. . . ."

Willie answered that he intended to raise a regiment of volunteers, and on March 26 Roosevelt wrote back urgently:

"Things look as though they were coming to a head. Now, can
you start getting up that regiment when the time comes? Do you
want me as lieutenant colonel? Also, remember that to try to put
toughs in it—still worse to try to put political heelers in—will
result in an utterly unmanageable regiment, formidable to its
own officers, and impotent to do mischief to the foe."

Which was the advice of an amateur in the fighting line offered
to a professional.

With things humming at home, Winthrop Chanler could not
abide lying sluggishly in Rome, and despite his wife's misgivings,
in March he crossed to New York again. On March 31 he reported
to Daisy, in a note written from the Knickerbocker Club:

". . . The war talk is as furious as ever. It is impossible to say
what will happen. . . . It all looks very black."

Off to Washington he posted to consult Lodge, assuring Daisy
from the train that "I am not off to Cuba, my Honey, only going
to Washington." Later, from Lodge's home, he relayed a second
message stating that there was "no manner of doubt about [the
Maine] having been blown up by a mine . . . It is all very
beastly and the United States are almost a unit in demanding
reparation complete and instant for the 264 poor boys killed in
their sleep. . . ."

The President was preparing a message to Congress, but its tenor
was unknown. The clamor for war was incessant, but on April 7

Roosevelt wrote to a fox-hunting friend, Austin Wadsworth, of Geneseo, that "if you are puzzled you can imagine the bitter wrath and humiliation which I feel at the absolute lack of plans. . . . If I were you I should get hold of Willie Chanler, who now intends to raise a two or three battalion regiment, to be commanded by a regular officer. With he and myself as lieutenant colonels, I am sure he would be delighted to have you as a major; and I should like to put Wood in as a major. We will have a jim-dandy regiment if we are allowed to go. . . ."

Three days after this note, McKinley transmitted his message calling for intervention, and on April 20 Congress voted and the President signed a declaration of war. Back in New York, Winthrop Chanler wrote excitedly to Daisy:

". . . War—War—War—Extras are being shouted now under the Club windows. . . . I doubt if the Spanish will fight. They will back down and out at the last minute. Our army is being rapidly mobilized in Tennessee and the S.E. The call for volunteers and militia is ready to be made. It is really an exciting time, & we who think about it don't sleep well. I was surprised to find so many men who say that they can't sleep at night for thinking, thinking, thinking. . . . I can't leave now. The chances are that I would be called back. God knows when I can get away . . . it may be all over in a month. . . ."

The day after war was declared, the following advertisement appeared in the New York newspapers:

A CALL IS HEREBY ISSUED FOR
ALL ABLE-BODIED MEN
between the ages of eighteen and forty-five years who wish to enroll in an infantry regiment of United States volunteers in case of a war with Spain. Recruiting office, 140-142 Sixth ave. Hours 9-12 and 5-7:30. WM. ASTOR CHANLER.

The recruiting office occupied the ground floor of a vacant office building. The street windows were draped with American flags, and chairs were lined up for applicants waiting to be interviewed.

The response at first was slow, but before evening a rush had set in, and within a few days 1,550 men were signed up. Temple Emmet, as hot for action as any Chanler, helped in taking applications; he expected to be an officer in the regiment himself.

In the midst of this excitement, Margaret Chanler announced that she was going to the front as a Red Cross volunteer. She had been urging the men of her circle to enlist, and reflected that it behooved her to follow her own advice and join up. She had no skills, but registered with the Red Cross for service in any capacity, meanwhile enrolling in a course of training in basic hospital routines; since she spoke Spanish, she thought she might be useful to the nurses as interpreter, and she was prepared to fight their inevitable battles with bureaucratic red tape.

Margaret's decision cast Elizabeth's situation in a fresh light. Temple Emmet was heading for the war, and Alida had said that she would go at least as far as Florida with him, so "Queen Bess" would be left alone. Her immediate marriage to Chapman seemed advisable, "so that he can look after her when the others are away," as Wintie put it.

The wedding (a "war wedding," the newspapers called it) was held on April 24 in the parlor at 317 West 74th Street. Wintie described it to Daisy:

". . . Nobody but the family—Willie & Temple fresh from the recruiting office . . . Bess had a little bunch of orange blossoms and I ran out & got some lilies of the valley for buttonholes. It was done by my advice as I wrote you. Bess was simply going to pieces and Jack looked like an undertaker in the healthy season. Beatrice [Wintie's seven-year-old daughter] came in in the middle of the service & Alida's baby was present. Afterwards we all sat down to luncheon & drank healths. Margaret was literally at the end of the telephone wire waiting to sail for Key West with the Red Cross people. But the boat went without her for no women are allowed to go till the Army moves into Cuba. She may therefore wait three weeks or three months or six. . . .

"Jack Astor [John Jacob Astor IV] has offered the government a battery of artillery equipped & furnished & the use of two of his railroads for transportation purposes in exchange for a staff appointment on some general's staff who is going to Cuba. . . .

Austin [Wadsworth] is wild to get a job & fight before he dies
. . . and everybody you ever heard of. I am like the man who
couldn't get into the Ark. . . ."

Willie, meanwhile, was meeting with obstacles in regard to his
regiment. Politics complicated the picture. The Chanlers were
Democrats, and the Republicans were in control in Albany and
Washington. Willie was told that neither the army nor the state
militia could use his volunteers immediately. He appealed to
McKinley, who was sympathetic, but pointed out that there was
no provision in the army's plans for volunteers.

Roosevelt was powerless to assist; on the day after the Chapmans'
wedding he wrote to Willie Chanler:

". . . Everything here is as yet undecided. I am trying my best
to get a chance to go myself, and even that is still uncertain. . . ."

A postscript to this letter broke the news somewhat lamely that
Congress had authorized the raising of three regiments of volunteer cavalry (not infantry), and that Secretary of War Alger had
offered Roosevelt the command of one. Considering himself not
qualified, Roosevelt had declined, but had offered to serve under
Leonard Wood. He thereupon was named the regiment's lieutenant colonel, and his postscript of April 25 informed Willie:

"P.S. I have just been offered a lieutenant colonelcy in a regiment of mounted riflemen, and the Secretary tells me that only
some such regiment will be raised outside of the militia force at
present. In that case your regiment would have to come in at the
second call. If I was not limited to westerners, at least at first, in
my regiment, I should feel very much like getting you and Emmet
to get a company of good horsemen and good riflemen to come
with me."

As matters turned out, only this regiment—the First United
States Volunteer Cavalry, the famous Rough Riders—was raised,
and the command and subsequent glory remained in Republican
hands.

Realizing that he had been checkmated, Chanler reluctantly
disbanded his regiment and made plans to go to Cuba and join
General Gomez's forces. Choosing a handful of picked adventurers
on whose fighting qualities he could rely, he set out for Tampa,

Florida, the staging ground for taking off to the war zone. *The New York Times* suspected that Willie's band of irregulars was entrusted with some secret mission, the desperate nature of which was suggested by the *Times'* description of its members:

". . . A man named Galvin, who went with Mr. Chanler on his African trip; a German army officer who came to this country to offer his services to the government, and who, on finding that the government had no place for him, joined Mr. Chanler's regiment; and two other men whose identity has not been disclosed. They are said to be close friends of Mr. Chanler. The party are supplied with Cuban uniforms, and took very little luggage with them. It is understood that Mr. Chanler is to pay all the expenses."

Left behind, Winthrop fretted over his inactivity, but kept reminding himself that he was married and had numerous dependents. Of Roosevelt's good sense in throwing up an assistant secretaryship for a subordinate commission in the army, Wintie had a poor opinion. He told Daisy:

". . . Theodore has resigned . . . and goes to Cuba before long with a regiment of cow-boys from Arizona & New Mexico. I really think he is going mad. The President has asked him twice as a personal favor to stay in the Navy Dept., but Theodore is wild to fight & hack & hew. It is really sad. Of course this ends his political career for good. Even Cabot says this."

Then casually, with an air of abstraction, as if unaware of what he was saying, Wintie conveyed to his anxious wife the possibility that he might take some part in the show. Not in the actual fighting, of course, but in an observer role, out of danger.

"I don't know what I can do yet," he edged into the subject. "They are sending arms & ammunition & clothing & food to the insurgents next week so that Gomez & Garcia . . . can fully equip & arm their men & cooperate with the U.S. fleet in the blockade. . . . The Cuban general [Emilio] Nuñez who goes in charge of the expedition . . . has promised to take me, and the War Department will give me safe conduct & transportation by sea & land. It will be very interesting—no fighting, of course. . . ."

A week later he was in Tampa, and writing:

"We got here last night after a dreadful railway journey of 42 hours from New York. 'We' consisted of Willie, Temple Emmet & myself & 5 men whom Willie picked from his abandoned regiment . . . and who are to accompany him through the campaign. George Galvin was already here, having been sent on ahead to buy horses for Willie's party. What I wrote you at last I have decided to do. Nuñez is here & will take me on his staff when he starts in a few days. . . . Cabot has got me passes which practically put the army & navy of the U.S. at my disposal, so that I can leave Cuba when I get tired of it or sick or anything. . . ."

In far away Rome, where the prevalent belief was that the Americans would be mopped up by puissant Spain, Daisy Chanler quaked at the transparent protests that no peril existed in the theater of war. But she knew there was no penning her Winthrop's roving spirit, and she kept up a brave front, praying and sending Wintie miraculous medals which she entreated him to wear. Wintie kept cheerily, even cheekily, in touch.

"The plan," he wrote, "is to send about 5,000 U.S. troops as a base of supplies for the Cuban army under Gomez. . . . As soon as we land, we, that is Nuñez and his men, will go straight to Gomez, who is waiting for us, with arms, food, & clothing. . . .

"Another man has joined Willy's party, a Dr. Abbott of Philadelphia, whom he found camped at Taveta on Kilimanjaro, the first time he went to Africa. . . . Several men have tried to get in with Willy. He has applications every day from New York & even here. He refuses all, as he only wants to be 10 in number."

Dr. Abbott was a collector (later curator) for the Smithsonian Institution; he rode into Willie's camp unannounced one night after traveling halfway around the world to join the expedition, and was greeted with shouts of welcome. Other members of Willie's motley band, as portrayed by Winthrop, were:

". . . The Sergeant, a lovely 'tommy' who has ten years service in the crack cavalry regiment of our army, the Sixth, and who left Buffalo Bill's Wild West Show and all his worldly goods to follow Willie to Cuba & see some real service. . . . Grover Flint who was a trooper in the regular army for two or three years . . . another regular army boy, also resigned from Buffalo Bill's Show to join Willie . . . Geo. Galvin . . . then the Kentucky grandson of Daniel Boone, fearful braggart and the worst (so far) of the party. Then Dr. Maximilian Lund, the hero of a thousand German duels, with a face like a scarred gridiron and mustachioed like a Tom Cat, but a punctilious German gentleman, very formal, good-natured & childlike. We all like him & laugh at him . . . then Temple, always cool, phlegmatic & very careful of tiny details . . . young Hood, son of the famous Confederate general of that ilk, a nice gentlemanly fellow . . . next to him your Hubbie with a machete & revolver strapped to his little person, his hair cropped short, very dusty & dirty & feeling rather a fool but enjoying himself. . . ." *

On May 11 a new note was introduced into Wintie's reports when he wrote that "we are said to be off day after tomorrow *mañana por la mañana* as they say over here . . . Willie has been made a colonel in the Cuban army & has had an adjutant & interpreter & secretary given to him, one Captain Ramirez. Rumor has it that the Government (U.S.) has given Willie a Lieutenant's commission in the U.S. Volunteers, but he knows nothing authoritatively. . . ."

The rumor was correct. In Washington a list of officer appointments had been released, and included were a commission as assistant adjutant general with rank of captain issued to John Jacob Astor IV (in return for his gift of a battery of artillery and other favors), and a captain's commission issued to William Astor Chanler.

"Lawks! There's promotion for you!" Wintie exclaimed at the news, and then went on: "All is changed. Willie has accepted his Captain's commission & is on Gen. [Joseph E.] Wheeler's staff here in Tampa. At first he did not want to accept his commission, as he was already a Cuban colonel and besides was pledged to take

---

* Dr. Maximilian Lund had been interviewed by the *New York Morning Telegraph* on his way to Tampa and had stated his fighting record as follows: "I have fought more duels than any other man alive, forty-seven in all—forty-four with swords and three with pistols. I won twenty-seven and lost seventeen sword duels and lost one pistol duel. I still live." A Dane by birth, although a naturalized American citizen, Lund had seen service in the German army, at one time in the bodyguard of King Albert of Saxony. He had received a medical education and told of operating upon himself in his room one night in St. Petersburg. A pistol bullet scar near his mouth he thought disfiguring; so he cut it out and sewed the edges of the wound together so neatly it became hardly noticeable.

Willie Chanler's band of desperadoes headed for Cuba in 1898 to fight with the Cuban insurrectos. Leadership later was taken over by Wintie Chanler. Willie on horse at far right.

his ten men into Cuba. As all these men serve without pay, he of course has to treat them with some consideration. He did not know what to do. Temple & I insisted on his taking his commission. . . . It is very nice to have when one considers that the President gave it to him among the first & without ever being asked to do it. In order to salve his conscience about his men, I could do nothing but offer to take them in myself. This satisfied the Cubans and the men too. So here I am with 10 troopers at my back going in with Nuñez or Castillo as their personal escort. It is safe enough now. The Spaniards are all cooped up in Havana & the large towns. We shall have a bully time with flies & bugs & rain & the war will soon be over. . . . Theodore has got his band of rough riders all organized at San Antonio, Texas. If I get on the island first I shall be happy. Maybe I'll join my band to his. . . .

"I know your dear heart is going 'pitty-pat' at the mere idea of my going into danger," he soothed his wife. "Don't worry. I have no notion of running unnecessary risks & there is really very little to fear. . . . I see little difference between serving under one flag or the other, except that with the Cuban, I can see service which may lead to a job with my own government. With the Americans I can see nothing but a drill ground in some God-forsaken spot. . . .

"Willie [is] kept as busy as a bee in Gen. Wheeler's staff. He drinks nothing. He does his work well & cannot get away if he tried to. From a political point of view it will be of great advantage to him also. . . ."

But days passed—all May and into June, and nobody moved. In New York Margaret Chanler still awaited call by the Red Cross, her patience quite exhausted. Wintie commiserated:

"We are still here. Daisy writes wishing I was in the U.S. Army instead of the Cuban (they have made me a Lieut. Colonel) but I cannot see what difference it makes. I am serving the same cause & have managed to retain my personal liberty of action. In the U.S. Army I should have to koto to Tom, Dick & Harry & go where I was put & stay there. Now I can go to Cuba which is what I want to do & leave when I wish to leave. Moreover I can be of infinitely more use to the Cubans . . . & incidentally whack Spain much harder.

"Good-bye, old girl. You are the right sort. Alida is here looking after Temple. Willie is well & really useful. His fellow officers say he is the only civil appointment they ever saw worth a damn."

Alida broke up the family's united front when it dawned on her, somewhat belatedly, that there were risks inherent in a soldier's life. The family version of her reaction to this amazing realization, while possibly untrue in detail, represented Alida as driving into camp in a buggy one day and beckoning Temple out of line.

"You must come home, Temple," she stated in her silvery, far-carrying Chanler voice. "I find that this war is dangerous."

Whatever the manner of Temple's recall, the fact was reported to Rome by Winthrop:

". . . Alida & Temple & Jane Emmet (Temple's sister) leave for the North tomorrow night. It is like losing a leg to lose Temple, he is so useful & sensible & nice. All the men like him & are sorry to lose him. . . . Willie sailed away with Gen. Wheeler day before yesterday. He goes I think to Santiago. We go to Gomez in Santa Clara province (the middle of the island), where there are few, if any Spanish troops. . . . Don't worry your head about false reports in the European papers about Spanish victories. They have not won a single fight. . . . Theodore got off finally the day before yesterday. I saw him the day before he sailed. He was in fine fettle perspiring profusely but healthy. . . ."

At last, on June 14, Wintie could write gleefully:

". . . Great news! We are to have a boat—a big one—given us at once. We shall carry 325 Cubans under Nuñez including our good selves . . . also quantities of arms, ammunition, food, clothing, boots, etc., and 150 horses to the insurgents under old Gomez. . . . Have no fear. Nuñez has landed over twenty-five expeditions when both America & Spain were trying to stop him, so he is not afraid of meeting any gun boats. Besides, we shall carry guns and men who know how to use them, though naturally our object is to avoid all trouble."

But it was another nine days before Wintie could finally write that he was on his way, aboard the steamer *Florida,* accompanied by a supply ship, the *Fanita,* heading for Key West and an unannounced landing place in Cuba.

"Altogether it is lots of fun," he admitted unabashedly to his wife. "All well on board and happy . . . There is a splendid Cuban *gobbo* [hunchback] on board going to fight for his country, so we are sure to have luck. . . . Theodore got to Cuba before me after all. . . ."

In his band of freebooters all were well, he reported, except Grover Flint, who had a broken leg; but "Dr. Max Lund has put it in a plaster cast & as it is now a fortnight since he broke it & he has at least four or five days before he need ride, he will probably be able to go along with the best of us. . . ."

This letter was written on June 23, and then there was silence for three weeks. What occurred during that period was recounted later by a seventeen-year-old Cuban participant named E. J. Connill.

During the run down to Cuba and around the island to its southern side, the transports were joined by the American gunboat *Peoria* as naval escort. The first attempt to land was made at a point between the towns of Casilda and Trinidad, at the mouth of the San Juan River, in almost the exact center of the island. A boat was sent in and was fired upon. Scouting parties revealed a strong enemy force, and the next day, June 30, the flotilla steamed sixty miles eastward and anchored west of Tunas, opposite a Spanish blockhouse defended by about a hundred Spanish regulars, well entrenched. General Nuñez ordered the blockhouse shelled by the *Peoria*, and then sent in two boats with Cubans and Chanler's irregulars. General Nuñez's brother, Colonel Indalecio Nuñez, commanded the Cuban detachment. As the boats approached the beach, the Spaniards opened fire, and young Nuñez was killed by a bullet through the head, his boat was sunk, and several of his men were wounded. The rest, with Chanler's band, scrambled ashore, took cover wherever it offered, and returned a vigorous fire.

Chanler soon was shot through the right elbow, and Abbott was wounded more seriously by a bullet through the shoulder. The command having devolved upon Wintie, he kept up the attack until dusk, then ordered the wounded evacuated. Seventeen were crowded into the remaining boat, and Wintie, Abbott, one Cuban, and Lund stayed on the beach. And there (as Chanler put it) "we sat in the woods and fought the mosquitoes who were much worse than the Spaniards, until almost eleven o'clock, when we could see by the moonlight if a boat came."

Aboard the *Florida*, anxious watchers scanned the shore for some sign of life. At about eight o'clock a man was discerned swimming toward the ship with a knife clenched in his teeth. Hoisted aboard, he proved to be Lund, stark naked. He reported that Chanler and his companions had disappeared, and it seemed certain that they had perished. Lund told of fighting off sharks during his swim out to the ship, but the Cubans were scornful of the story, and despised him for having deserted his comrades. Lund insisted, however, that they had vanished, and there was no sign from shore.

General Nuñez waited several hours longer. Then, giving up hope, he ordered the anchors weighed. But Grover Flint, who had stayed aboard the *Florida* because of his broken leg, begged permission to scout the beach once more for the missing men. Nuñez consented, and Flint was lifted over the side with his leg in the cast, and with two other Americans rowed stealthily toward the beach. Soon they were lost to the view of those on the *Florida*.

At four o'clock they returned, bringing with them Chanler, Abbott, and the Cuban, with a diverting story of how they had been found. Flint said that as his boat slipped noiselessly along the shore, expecting in the moonlight to hear the crack of a Spanish rifle at any minute, he heard faint whistling—first "Yankee Doodle" and then "Pop Goes the Weasel." It was Chanler, whistling softly in hope that he might be heard, the tune recognized, and help come. Flint whistled back, and guided by the sound came up to the three men standing up to their necks in the water, where they had been driven by the ferocious mosquitoes. Only their faces were exposed, and these were so blotched and swollen that Wintie was recognizable only by his short golden beard.

As he was hauled into the boat, he was heard to mutter, "This is no place for a married man."

Abbott had lost much blood and was weak, but the bullet that had passed through Chanler's arm had hit no artery and he suffered little.

The next day Nuñez made a successful landing forty miles to the east, and General Gomez came down to the coast to meet them. Wintie was impressed by the old fighter—"a wonderful little old man, active as a boy, with an eye like a hawk and charming manners." Gomez promised to take care of Winthrop's band, and Abbott, despite his wound, insisted on going with the insurgents.

On July 10 the *Florida* steamed into Tampa Bay, its mission accomplished, and by July 15 Wintie was back in the Knickerbocker Club in New York, scrawling a lighthearted account of the adventure to Daisy. His arm was healing, he said, and as soon as it was normal again he proposed to rejoin his "brigands" in Cuba.

"I am living in Stanford White's empty house, having my arm

massaged every day & taking a course of weight-pulling to get the stiffness out of it," he scribbled. "Willie is with General Wheeler at Santiago and has been recommended for promotion for gallantry; so you see I did him a good turn when I took his men off his hands. Good-bye, my Honey—Lord knows when I'll get back to you and my Puppeties. It is all very uncertain. Theodore is now Colonel of his regiment, and Wood is a Brigadier General."

The official report submitted by Captain Carter Page Johnson, senior American officer with the Nuñez expedition, praised the bravery of Winthrop Chanler and his picturesque desperadoes, saying:

"I cannot speak too highly of the gallantry of Mr. Chanler's men, who fought overwhelming numbers until dark, when they withdrew under cover of darkness, with the loss of one killed (Gen. Nuñez' brother) and seven wounded out of a party of twenty-eight men."

To sister Margaret, Wintie confided lightheartedly:

"I got it through the elbow like an ass at Tunas & had to go back. So far I haven't found fighting as amusing as fox hunting. If it hadn't been for Willie's band of brigands, I'd have been with Theodore at Caney and Santiago. The Lord probably wanted to chasten me elsewhere."

Margaret Chanler, having at last got to Cuba with a group of Red Cross nurses, had narrowly missed meeting Wintie on his return to Key West, their ships passing each other just off the port, headed in opposite directions.

As Wintie regretfully sensed, the war had been won at El Caney and San Juan Hill, where Roosevelt and Willie Chanler played conspicuous roles. Willie had sent an account of the July 1 engagement to Elizabeth, honeymooning in the Catskills, writing directly from the "besieging lines around Santiago":

"By this time you must have heard of our 1st respectable engagement. . . . I was in the advance with Gen. Sumner and caught the fire heavily. We had to capture 3 forts by charging up hill under a withering fire. The fight lasted from 6 A.M. till night when we finally established ourselves in the position we now occupy. You will be glad to hear that I did not receive a scratch. I had no idea that modern war was such a dreadful thing. I was really almost made sick by the sight of the men shattered by shot & shell. We lost in killed and wounded about 2,000 men.* Many of my friends were killed. . . . I have told Capt. English (on Gen. Wheeler's staff with me) to send you my little belongings in case of accident. Also the horse 'Jew's Harp' I rode in action. He is a beauty. Now I dont want him turned out to graze; but I want you to use him. Give my love to all & forgive this wretched scrawl. My health is perfect."

Willie's gallantry in this battle was mentioned in dispatches, but several humorous incidents did not get into the official reports. Early in the engagement General Sumner was hampered by lack of knowledge of the Spanish positions, screened by a heavy undergrowth, and Chanler and another aide volunteered to attempt a scout. Riding to a nearby eminence from which they could overlook the terrain, they drew fire from the enemy's sharpshooters, to the disgust of the troops behind them lying flat in the grass. Yells came for those "fool officers" to get away from there, but Willie laughed and made his horse curvet before trotting to the rear.

Much as he admired Theodore Roosevelt, Willie Chanler could not resist teasing his impetuous, barnstorming friend, even in the midst of a battle. Before the attack on San Juan Hill, Roosevelt rode to a hillock to get a better view of the ground ahead. Willie saw him sitting there, squinting into the distance (he was notoriously nearsighted), and as the bullets started to whip uncomfortably close and Roosevelt swung his horse to retire, Willie called out:

"Don't move, Teddy! That's a bully place to be photographed!"

That day's fighting effectually terminated the war; even as Wintie Chanler was announcing his safe return to Daisy, the Madrid government was suing for surrender terms. This would not become known to the public for a while yet, and in the meantime the Chanlers continued to rally patriotically. Lewis was on his way from Europe, intending to enlist, and Robert, at Newport

---

* The official count of U.S. casualties was 1,572.

with Julia, was considering how he might join in the action, although he was not in the least bloodthirsty and had no taste for firearms.

Elizabeth Chapman had hurried down from the Catskills to welcome Winthrop back, and from New York she wrote to Mary Meroney at Rokeby, assuring the old nurse that "Mr. Winthrop's arm is nearly all right again." Margaret, she said, was still aboard the transport, perhaps due to be sent to Puerto Rico instead of landing in Cuba. And on August 4 an urgent note flew from Elizabeth's pen to Mary Meroney:

"Mr. Chapman has secured Mr. Wintie, Mr. Lewis, & Mr. Robert for a family gathering at Rokeby on Saturday the 6th, so buckle on your armor & get Lizzie Hartnett & any of the Mahoney's you can to help. It is short notice for you but Mr. Wintie may go very soon to Cuba. . . ."

But by the time the three brothers gathered in the familiar rooms, word had transpired that peace was at hand, and there was no question of Wintie's returning to Cuba. The war, in fact, had ended for all the Chanlers except Margaret. Upon her the family's attention now became fixed, with pride, amusement, and occasional exacerbation.

Margaret's Way

Margaret certainly was behaving as no society-bred woman of twenty-seven was expected to behave in 1898. Upon her arrival at Tampa, she had found, as the military had found, no provision made for the twenty Red Cross nurses she accompanied. And the reports coming in from Cuba simply angered her.

"The number of wounded on both sides compared to the nurses makes modern neglect seem more outrageously cruel than anything in the helpless Middle Ages," she wrote home furiously.

By bullying the officers in charge, some of whom opposed the whole idea of permitting women near the front, she managed to get her band aboard a converted passenger steamer, the *Lampasus,* and headed for Key West.

From there on progress was slow, inasmuch as the ship was towing a barge loaded with pontoons for the army engineers. Margaret shared her stateroom with the daughter of General Wheeler, whom she had encountered in Tampa, stranded and bewildered in her rueful attempt to reach her father in the field. Such impracticability irritated Margaret Chanler, and with a touch of scorn she described the unhappy lady as "non-professional, as all Southern women are, her one idea [being] to reach her father. I have no intention of appearing in the tent of the cavalry leader during an engagement without being sent for because of illness," she assured Elizabeth.

At Guantànamo the nurses were denied permission to go ashore because of an epidemic in the port. The captain of the *Lampasus* tried to get the whole group shipped back to New York, but Margaret spiked that scheme and then celebrated by attending an entertainment given for the nurses by the men and officers of the U.S.S. *Oregon,* just arrived from the Pacific after its thrilling dash around Cape Horn. Miss Wheeler was trundled off to search for her ex-Confederate father, to Margaret's relief.

Next the *Lampasus* steamed for an undisclosed destination that turned out to be Ponce, Puerto Rico. A task force under General Nelson A. Miles had just occupied that island. Here the Red Cross contingent was requested to accept a dangerous assignment; aboard the transports that had brought Miles's troops were hundreds of men ill with typhoid and other diseases; could the nurses improvise a hospital on the *Lampasus,* they were asked. They agreed to do it if the patients would lie on mattresses spread on the decks instead of in the berths, which would be impossible to keep clean. It was so settled, and the transports *Yale* and *Harvard* drew alongside and sent a procession of tottering skeletons across the gangplanks.

Immediately a series of crises set in. The cooks decamped at sight of the pestilential invasion. Fortunately Margaret had brought a spirit lamp, and this was put into use to boil milk and prepare broths. It was kept burning around the clock.

Patients died, and the corpses were stowed in the lifeboats until dark, when they were carried out to sea and disposed of secretively to prevent a panic. Margaret took charge of the laundry, and hunting up a huge pot, set a stowaway to work boiling sheets and clothing. The officers on the transports kept their distance; whenever one was compelled to come aboard on official business, he would stiffen with horror at encountering delirious fever patients wandering about.

The navy controlled the port, and the naval authorities did not like having a "pest ship" in the harbor. They were convinced that the plague was raging aboard the *Lampasus,* and they kept its decks under constant surveillance through field glasses. Now and then a potshot was taken at the liner during the night; one morning Margaret Chanler found a bullet in her window frame. The navy thought a chance had come to get rid of the nuisance when a lone man apparently quarantined was spotted on the top deck of the *Lampasus*—undoubtedly a plague victim, they said. Actually, the man was suffering from boils, and had been segregated only until the nature of his malady could be diagnosed, there being no laboratory on the *Lampasus*.

A naval officer came aboard and hoisted a yellow quarantine flag, the sight of which threw the patients into acute alarm. Margaret Chanler ordered the patient on the top deck to haul the flag down as often as it was raised by a visiting officer; and the game was kept up for a week, while friends of her brothers aboard other ships in the port laid bets on the outcome. Meanwhile, the burials at night went on, and the army sent new patients to replace those who died or recovered.

The deadlock was broken when orders came for the *Lampasus* to proceed to Fort Monroe, in Virginia; the Red Cross nurses to go with the ship. But this did not suit Margaret Chanler. She was not under official orders, and she quietly went ashore, determined to find some place of usefulness there. With her went a volunteer from New Orleans, Miss Anna Bouligny. Of the twenty nurses who went north on the *Lampasus,* eight contracted typhoid and died.

On shore, Margaret by diligent inquiry learned that there was an "American hospital," but the place to which she was directed proved to be a one-room schoolhouse with a dirt floor. It was crowded with enlisted men, most of them fever patients. Two medical orderlies were the only attendants except for several apathetic Puerto Rican women, who sat languidly fanning the patients, trying to keep off the flies.

Margaret set to work to correct this state of affairs. Although she had no official standing, she sent for an American doctor, then lettered a poster in Spanish and tacked it up at the door of the wretched building, announcing that this was an "American hospital," and as in all American hospitals, only relatives could visit the patients. She knew that would get rid of the fan-wavers, because the only relatives of these patients lived in Illinois and Wisconsin.

Anna Bouligny was sent to the market to hunt up food for light and liquid diets, and after several days the army surgeon in command provided both women with authorization to serve with troops in the field, and the schoolhouse was closed, the patients being transferred to the general hospital on the hill.

Margaret had learned, to her surprise, that whereas enlisted men who were wounded or ill were assigned to definite hospital quarters, officers were allowed to select their own. As a consequence, many officers lay seriously ill in wholly unsuitable surroundings. One, a veteran of the Civil War, Margaret found in a filthy room where pigs ran in and out through the open window, and the flies were thick. The man obviously was dying, and Margaret appealed to a Puerto Rican doctor whom she located nearby to stay with him to the end. The doctor haughtily refused; he had been insulted by the Americans, he said, and he was perfectly willing that they should all die, unattended by him. It developed that although he was a graduate of Bellevue Hospital in New York City, he had been elbowed aside by an American army doctor who called him "only a Dago nurse."

Margaret persuaded the irate man to go with her to army headquarters, where she promised that he would receive an official apology. They drove to headquarters together, and she got hold of a captain who listened to the complaint. At the end, he stood up, saluted the doctor and declaimed:

"I apologize to you in the name of the army, the navy, the Congress, the Senate, the Supreme Court, the cabinet, and the President."

Honor being thus satisfied, the Puerto Rican sat by the dying veteran, rendering such comfort as he could.

Confronted with the need for an officers' hospital, Margaret Chanler rented the largest vacant house she could find, and when the woman owner tried to cancel the lease after she learned the use to which her house was to be put, Margaret bullied her into consent and got the installation under way. She was assigned a couple of medical orderlies, and Miss Bouligny took charge of the kitchen and provisioning; Margaret herself served as nurse from six thirty in the morning until eight thirty at night. She was strict in her schedule, and wasted no energy in romanticizing her work. Implacably practical, she knocked off work at the stated time every evening, and allowed nothing to interfere with her getting a good

Margaret Chanler (right) and Miss Anna Bouligny in Puerto Rico hospital during Spanish-American War, 1898.

night's rest. In this way her Chanler energy carried her along in perfect health and endurance. For relaxation, she would drive into the hills in the evening with Miss Bouligny, who sang French opera arias.

Margaret had left New York with two hundred dollars in her purse, and in Puerto Rico she was obliged to stretch her credit amazingly. Checks were cashed and requisitions were filled by means known to herself, but mainly by simply refusing to accept a rebuff. And she was proud that not one patient died while in her care, although some did succumb later. When one of these died after being taken to the general hospital, his brother asked Miss Chanler to attend the funeral. It was held in a little Protestant cemetery, with a commissary clerk in charge. Margaret offered him her prayer book, but he shook his head.

"Please, miss," he requested, "read a funeral."

And Margaret read the office for the burial of the dead, and after taps had been sounded, went briskly back to her work.

The New York press carried reports of her devotion, and word of her good work spread so far that Cecil Spring-Rice heard about it in Tehran, where he was stationed at the British embassy. He wrote in amazement:

"What a famous woman you are! . . . The Chanler family has been doing pretty well lately and I suppose is perfectly happy at the chance of losing their lives. . . ."

After five weeks, Red Cross nurses came from the United States to relieve her, and when these professionals took over, Margaret and Anna Bouligny moved to Cuamo Springs and later to San Juan, where they continued their volunteer service. On October 18 Margaret Chanler watched with satisfaction the last soldiers of Spain march to the embarkation dock, board their transports, and steam away, while flocks of pigeons wheeled above them in final goodbye. The war was over and her task was finished.

Soon after that, she and Miss Bouligny returned to New York without mishap, traveling in a troop ship with a regiment of engineers commanded by a Colonel Griffin. This formed another link with the past—with her past—with the family tradition of public service. Aunt Tiny Griffin, who at one time had been a guardian of the Chanler children, in her youth had nursed the wounded in General McClellan's army during the Civil War. Margaret Chanler, by then known to the readers of Hearst's and Pulitzer's papers as "The Angel of Puerto Rico," felt that the tradition had been upheld.

With peace in sight, Winthrop Chanler hastened joyfully to his own hearthside, his ebullience unquenched. On the eve of sailing he had informed Cabot Lodge:

"I am off tomorrow on the *Normandie* for Havre. The bad repute of the French line will result in making me much more comfortable than I would be on the other lines as there is scarcely a soul going over on her. I shall take a large revolver; and on the first sign of shipwreck proceed to massacre the crew and then man a life boat myself. One 1st class passenger will most certainly escape."

Lewis Chanler already had returned to Monaco, announcing that he intended to settle in the United States shortly with his family. Robert and Julia Chanler were again abroad, Rokeby continuing to oppress and frighten Julia. On October 3 Willie Chanler was honorably discharged with a citation for bravery. On the distaff side, Elizabeth and Alida were domesticating, happy that the strife was ended. And Margaret got back to Rokeby in time for Christmas. To her Wintie wrote wistfully from Rome:

"Lord! How we wish we could be with you! That's out of the question, however, so we won't waste time over it. Thanks very much for your long & most entertaining letter from Porto Rico. . . . You did good work down there, my dear. You did better than any of us by a long chalk. I suppose Clara Barton trembles on her throne. . . . They tell me you are to have some kind of a monument. I hope it is a husband. Some nice attractive patriot with only one leg & glad to take not only 4 meals a day but even your name if you so insist. Good old Muggins! Never mind my chaff! . . ."

The Chanlers had reason to be pleased with themselves. They had humbled the haughty Spaniard and had served their country well. Indeed, they may have reflected, without their assistance, how would Teddy Roosevelt ever have managed to bring the show off alone?

A Canter in Politics

Captain William Astor Chanler returned from Cuba an authentic war hero. Reports of his exploits had appeared sporadically in the newspapers, and they had often been as entertaining as they were glamorous. Military popularity, added to the laurels that Willie had won as sportsman and explorer, made him a highly eligible political prospect. He was young, handsome, energetic, rich, dashing, and socially impeccable; he was democratic in his bearing, equally at home in his clubs (Union, Knickerbocker, Riding, Metropolitan, and Meadow Brook) and at Tammany Hall; he had received academic honors; and he was the author of a book recounting his adventures in Africa. Roosevelt had prodded him into this last undertaking, and it had been at his friend's virtual command that Willie had retired to Rokeby with a stenographer and dictated the work in a few weeks. Titled *Through Jungle and Desert,* the book had appeared before the war and had been well received.

Willie had often said that he intended to enter national politics, and the opportunity arose when he bade farewell to the army at Camp Montauk a month before the congressional elections of 1898. The Democratic organization of New York offered to run him for the House of Representatives from the Fourteenth Manhattan District—solidly Republican territory. Willie looked over the ground, liked the odds, and accepted the nomination.

The Fourteenth District sprawled over the upper West Side of

Manhattan from 52nd Street north to Spuyten Duyvil, and from Seventh and Eighth avenues to the Hudson River; on the east side of Central Park it took in a slice running from the park to the East River between 59th and 79th streets. An unwieldy territory with a polyglot population, both rich and poor, it contained many Irish and Italians, as well as not a few of Willie's wealthy friends.

His Republican opponent was the incumbent congressman, Lemuel Ely Quigg, who two years before had captured the district from the Democrats. Quigg was the Manhattan deputy of the Republican state boss, Tom Platt, and in 1898 he appeared unbeatable. He was backed not only by the Platt organization but by the endorsement of Theodore Roosevelt, who was running as the Republican candidate for governor of the state in the same election. Roosevelt had long urged Willie to enter politics, even though they were of opposite parties; but as a Republican he would of course have to oppose Willie in this contest.

Captain Chanler threw himself into the campaign as though he were plunging into Africa again. He disappeared from his customary haunts, the clubs and racetracks. He spoke at street rallies and presided at beer busts, keeping the speeches short and the beer flowing. What little he had to say he said with engaging candor, and all the standard devices for whipping up enthusiasm among the voters were trotted out—bands, street banners, posters, circulars, letters to the press, fireworks. The outlay on both sides was heavy, but Willie managed to outspend Quigg ($6,444.85 to $5,998.45).

The press gave the contest good coverage, the Republican *Tribune* sneering at the stress Chanler's camp was placing on his aristocratic background, and the independent *Herald* commending Willie's democratic modesty and earnestness. Both sides admired his good looks—"clean-shaven, tall and slight, with athletic frame and a firmness of features that betokens endurance." His magnetism and genuine accomplishments were not disputed; nevertheless, as election day approached, Quigg held the edge in the betting. Willie's friends were not confident. Stanford White expressed their attitude when he wrote to Chanler:

"I have done most of my electioneering for you personally, as

William Astor Chanler, member of Congress from New York City's upper West Side, 1900.

that, it seems to me, tells more than letters, and I have had some little success, although I do not exactly trust the promises which have been made to me. As far as I can make out, you have a pretty slimy opponent. At the same time, I hope with all my heart that you are going to lick him.''

And Willie did. When the returns were in, Chanler was the winner by a landslide plurality of 6,060 votes. It was a resounding victory, and the press sang his praises. Said the *Herald:*

"Captain William Astor Chanler . . . went through Quigg's bailiwick like a tropical tornado. He saw everybody and everybody liked the looks of the young explorer and soldier. He was full of blood and enthusiasm. He did not pretend to know anything of the political game, but . . . he whipped the Republican county chairman by sheer force of personality."

Quigg was stunned by the result, and the size of his plurality surprised Chanler himself. Toasts were drunk to "Captain Bill" all over town on election night, and Willie told reporters jauntily:

"My late opponent can now go to Mr. Platt and tell him he was licked by a kid."

He celebrated by joining two organizations that seldom were fused in one individual—the Friendly Sons of St. Patrick (qualifying through his Armstrong ancestors, who came from Ireland) and that most blue blooded of New York's honorary military units, the Old Guard. Tammany rewarded him by electing him a sachem, as his father had been before him.

Roosevelt, who had won his own race for the governorship, was delighted by Willie's victory.

"Willie and I had to hide our lurking hopes about each other during the campaign," T.R. wrote to Winthrop Chanler in Rome. "I am awfully glad he is in Congress. I do not like his party associates at all, but on the great questions of foreign policy and the army and the navy, he is just the man to do good work in Washington. I hope he will now have a number of years there."

Wintie also was proud of his brother's achievement. During the Cuban excitement Wintie had entertained a fleeting notion of entering public service, but old habits of aimlessness reasserted themselves when he was back in Italy. But he was full of sage counsel for the brother who was doing things worthwhile, and he wrote to "Muggins" (Margaret) from Rome:

"Tell that handsome gent Captain the Hon. W. Astor Chanler M.C. that I have written & cabled him & also his man George, but get no reply. Where is he now? I hope at Rokeby. . . . Thanks for getting me the Spanish sword & the rum [in Puerto Rico]. Do please keep *some* of the latter away from Willy till I get back. How well he has done, the rogue! I was tickled to death not only at his getting into Congress, but also at the grand fight & victory he put up & won against & over Quigg. It rests now entirely with him whether he goes on or not. Nobody in New York ever got such a chance as he has at his age. Let's hope that he not only realizes this fully but sticks to his job for a while."

To his friend "Amoi" Wintie confided with a tinge of envy:

"Willy is said to be in Congress when that august body next

meets. I'm glad he beat that ass Lemuel Ely Quigg of Quogue, but that is only a detail. He has done dam well and has got there. I wish I were somewhere. I'm blue here & bored, but that's only the reaction after the summer fun [in Cuba]. . . ."

A definite end to their interim life in England seemed in prospect for Lewis and Alice Chanler at this time. Alice's health had improved steadily during their stay abroad, and Lewis was hankering for law practice again. Also, Alice was thinking about a political future for her husband, now that Willie had blazed the trail. Certainly Lewis Chanler had every outward requisite for a statesman: tall and graceful in bearing, with open, boyish features, a resonant voice of singular carrying power, a polished speaker, high-minded, interested in public affairs, and endowed with the abundant Chanler vitality and energy. Alice felt that she was the sort of wife a man in public life would need—a shrewd judge of character, a clever hostess, brainy and ambitious. Wintie Chanler had been hoping for some time that Lewis would get back into harness; Wintie felt that his brother was "rotting in England" but too proud to admit it. There was general satisfaction in the family, therefore, when the Lewis Chanlers headed toward New York.

At the same moment Elizabeth and John Jay Chapman, with the three Chapman boys, headed toward Europe.

Chapman had suffered a traumatic political shock by what he considered Theodore Roosevelt's sellout of the cause of reform, in order to be elected governor of New York State on the boss-ridden Republican ticket. So bitter was the falling-out, Chapman and Roosevelt did not speak to each other for twenty years. John Jay wrote off T.R. as a "muddle-headed and at the same time pigheaded young man," while Roosevelt coined his celebrated phrase, "on the lunatic fringe," to describe Chapman's place in political life and thought, and vented his impatience with all spokesmen for the "extreme left, or Bedlamite, branch of the ultra reform movement."

It was to get her husband away from the fevers of politics that Elizabeth took her family abroad; but even in England Chapman could not hold aloof from political agitation. The Boer War was on, and he *would* take the side of the Boers—the unpopular side.

Elizabeth leased a house in London for the season, but the supper conversations threatened to become acrimonious, with Chapman exclaiming that both England and America seemed to be "mad just now over bloodshed, commercial interests, and jingoism." Finally Elizabeth moved the family to the cathedral calm of Wells, where the summer of 1899 was passed in pursuit of tranquillity.

In Washington, the freshman member of the House of Representatives signing himself "Wm. Astor Chanler" entered upon his duties with characteristic aplomb and energy. Sister Margaret, resuming the role she had filled at Albany, closed her Manhattan home and moved to Washington to function as housekeeper and hostess for her brother. A handsome residence on Farragut Square was leased and quickly became a focus of social and political activity.

Chanler performed his congressional tasks unspectacularly. He was chagrined that he could not run off to join the war in South Africa, on the side of the Boers and against England; and in compensation outfitted a volunteer as his substitute and paid his passage to the front. Life in sedentary Washington went against the grain for active Willie. He dashed up to New York on weekends to watch his horses run on the metropolitan tracks, and during the week would blow off steam by mad gallops through the Maryland or Virginia countryside on a war mount, named Powder. Now and then Roosevelt would encounter him, though their political paths had diverged. Winthrop Chanler, in Rome, heard from Teddy:

"Willie, I met at the Porc mid-year. Before I saw him he had entirely passed through the stage of bigoted sobriety, and I got from him little but the warmest friendship and dark information as to conspiracies through which I was steering my small governmental bark to shattering disaster. I had been trying to see him before and since, but I fear until I become less *anathema marentha* to Croker, Willie is not going to expose himself to any leprous contagion by associating with me. . . ."

Margaret Chanler was creating a reputation of her own in Washington. Her work in Puerto Rico during the war was widely known, and a resolution was introduced in Congress to award her a medal expressive of the nation's gratitude. But this she promptly squelched by her curt observation that other women deserved just as much honor, and the resolution was shelved.

Margaret's self-sufficiency (that abundant Chanler trait) came to the surface in numerous ways. As her brother's hostess, she fulfilled all the requirements imposed by custom and etiquette, while expressing her opinion that most of these observances were sheer nonsense and a waste of valuable time. At her weekly "at homes" for congressional wives, while her guests chatted, the hostess would withdraw to a corner and take out her knitting. This gave her "time to think," she explained. And she took a senator's wife's breath away when she remarked brusquely, in regard to the social parade:

"You are not interested in me, and I am not interested in you; we come to these affairs because we feel obliged to, that is all; it's the custom."

Time and energy could be saved, she pointed out, if a number of congressional wives—say those coming from the same geographical region—instead of holding their separate, individual "at homes," should band together, rent suitable quarters in a hotel, and once a month hold a joint reception. The purpose would be served, and much bother and expense would be eliminated.

The senatorial dame repeated this revolutionary proposal to a society reporter, and Miss Chanler's daring originality provided grist for newspaper commentary for weeks thereafter.

When Doctors All Agree—

Watch Out!

Through all this period, the confusion into which Armstrong Chanler's affairs had been thrown by his confinement in Bloomingdale asylum had snarled the affairs of other members of the family, with their interlocking interests and joint sharing in the income from properties held in trust. Henry Lewis Morris, the family lawyer, upon whom rested the main responsibility for wise administration of the family's finances, had been pressing for a termination of the muddle. This would require a precise defining of Armstrong's rights and position under the law.

Theoretically Archie was in charge of his own affairs, inasmuch as he had not been declared incompetent by any court. As a practical matter, however, he had no control over his estate whatever. Stanford White still held power of attorney to act for him in business transactions, but there was a large area not covered by this authorization. The anomalous situation had become insupportable, and in midsummer of 1898—just after the end of the war and Winthrop Chanler's return to Rome—Lewis Chanler and Morris urged upon White the desirability of having Archie ruled legally incompetent. But White declined to be a party to such a step. A year later, however, Winthrop and Lewis Chanler took action on their own responsibility, overriding White's objections.

The procedure called for the hearing of testimony by a sheriff's jury, which on the evidence submitted would rule as to Armstrong's competency and sanity. If he should be judged incapable of administering his affairs, the court would be petitioned to appoint a conservator to manage his estate for him. The legal phrase for such a court appointee was "a committee for the person and estate."

This step—applying for a sanity hearing before a sheriff's jury—had been suggested to Armstrong himself several times as the most expeditious way of vindicating his sanity, if he could; but he had refused to accede. First, he feared a trap by his relatives, and second, he had lost confidence in the justice dispensed by the courts of New York, especially when interests as pervasive and as potent as those of the Astors and their business and social allies were involved. Archie believed that the correct way to go about obtaining his release was to petition the federal court for habeas corpus protection.

On June 13, 1899, New York newspapers published an account of the hearing obtained by Armstrong Chanler's brothers. It had been held before a sheriff's jury in the Supreme Court the day before. Armstrong had not appeared nor had he been represented by counsel. Three medical witnesses had testified—Dr. Samuel P. Lyon, the director of Bloomingdale asylum; Dr. Carlos F. McDonald, an eminent alienist; and Dr. Austin Flint, an even more celebrated neurologist and medical authority.*

Dr. Lyon, a pleasant-spoken person, testified first. He said that Chanler had been notified of the hearing, but had declined to attend, averring that a chronic backache, which he claimed to have acquired in Bloomingdale, was so painful he could not stand the jolting twenty-mile ride into the city. Dr. Lyon believed that while Chanler did feel pain, and really had a backache, it was not extreme enough to incapacitate him. Chanler's disease, he swore, was clearly paranoia, and there was no hope of a cure. Citing the delusions which he said Chanler harbored, Dr. Lyon said he imagined himself to be a magnet and his stomach a Leyden jar; also, at times he believed himself to be Napoleon, and at other times

---

* This Austin Flint, son of another Austin Flint even more eminent, and father of a third Austin Flint, was a member of a medical dynasty. He was the author of *The Physiology of Man* and *The Physiology of the Nervous System,* two of the most widely circulated and respected medical textbooks of the century. He commanded an immense reputation and was much sought after as an expert witness in medical lawsuits.

imagined himself to be a greater man than Napoleon, reserved by destiny to carry out some brilliant mission in the world. Dr. Lyon also swore that several times Chanler had evinced a desire to kill him, and that he was under the delusion that people were trying to poison him, refusing to eat the institutional bread for that reason and ordering bread brought in from outside; yet even so, he was never satisfied, but switched from one bakery to another, denouncing the products of each in turn as "rank poison."

Just before the war with Spain, Dr. Lyon recounted, Chanler had been preparing to bring his case before the public, saying the people of Virginia would come to his rescue as soon as they learned of his unlawful detention; but after the start of the war he had changed his mind, saying he did not wish to add to the nation's anxieties. Chanler had compiled a statement of his case, said the doctor, so voluminous it "filled a book more than three inches thick." He also had taken to literature and was writing a book of poems, mostly sonnets, of a satirical and enigmatic nature.

Dr. McDonald gave corroborative testimony, stating positively that Chanler's malady was incurable. He, too, dwelt upon Chanler's asserted delusions, saying that Armstrong had once showed him a silver box which he claimed had been tarnished by magnetic emanations from his body. The jury listened attentively as the alienist gave his unequivocal opinion that John Armstrong Chanler was suffering from "progressive paranoia, or chronic delusional insanity. It is an incurable form of mental disease."

He emphasized this opinion, stating:

"I would say that Mr. Chanler is the most typical, classic case of paranoia I have ever seen. I have seen thousands of them. It presents all the essential and diagnostic signs of that disease."

"In your opinion, doctor," the questioner pressed, "is he now of unsound mind?"

"Yes, sir."

"Is he capable of attending to his person or estate—his affairs?"

"Absolutely not," came the response. "There is no shadow of doubt in my mind, and I think . . . any experienced examiner in lunacy would reach that conclusion without any history of the case whatever. . . . It presents all the earmarks of typical paranoia. In the physical and mental condition there is no symptom lacking to make it a perfectly typical case of paranoia. If one wanted a case for teaching or describing a case in a textbook, you could not describe it more graphically than by simply taking his case as it presents itself. It is the most striking case of paranoia that I have ever seen in my life." *

Then Dr. Flint added the weight of his prestigious authority to the findings of his colleagues, upholding Dr. McDonald's stated opinion without reservation. Yes, he swore, John Armstrong Chanler was suffering from progressive paranoia, and his disease was incurable.

The jury made no attempt to examine Chanler, either by fetching him from Bloomingdale or by interviewing him there. On the contrary, since the hour was late and the jurors were impatient to get away (the hearing had been called, for some unexplained reason, at the unusual hour of four o'clock in the afternoon, the time when New York courts were normally closing), the evidence was accepted quickly as sufficient and a verdict of insanity and incompetency was returned.

Press reports of this hearing, brief and factual, identified John Armstrong Chanler as "formerly the husband of Amélie Rives," and mentioned that he was thirty-six years old. They did not mention that he had already been in Bloomingdale more than two years; nor did they point out that the verdict of the sheriff's jury was in effect a sentence of life imprisonment without hope of reprieve. The testimony had been given by highly respected and accredited medical experts, who agreed unanimously that Archie's derangement would grow progressively worse until he died.

Archie's brothers, Lewis and Winthrop, as executors of their father's estate, promptly applied for appointment of a "committee for the person and estate" to administer Armstrong's affairs, and the case was marked closed; to be reopened, it seemed, only upon receipt of word of Archie's merciful deliverance by death.

---

* From transcript of testimony. In a similar hearing several years later Dr. McDonald would testify that he could identify a paranoiac at a distance of several feet by the shape of his head.

In Which We Take French Leave

One subject upon which Margaret Livingston Chanler felt qualified to speak, and did, was the nursing of soldiers in the field.
Except for male nurses, who really were only medical orderlies,
the army relied upon Red Cross volunteers. A bill was before
Congress to create a corps of nurses in the army, and Margaret
was heartily in favor of it, not alone for its utility, but because
any action that tended to break down the barriers raised against
equal opportunity for women commanded her enthusiastic support.

The bill was encountering stiff opposition. The Surgeon General, George M. Sternberg, who although a distinguished bac-
teriologist and a skillful administrator thought the admission of
women into the army revolutionary and uncalled for, was against
it. With a number of women holding views similar to her own,
Margaret organized a lobbying campaign on behalf of the bill,
but soon realized that its passage was being endangered by rumors
coming from the Philippines regarding the supposed frivolous
conduct of Red Cross nurses assigned to the army there. When her
co-workers became alarmed, Margaret undertook to go to Manila
and find out the truth.

On May 24, 1900, therefore, she set out from New York for
San Francisco, to embark there on an army transport. She was
equipped with letters of introduction to army commanders in the
Far East and intended to make a thorough inspection of the army

hospitals there. The trip was to last six months, and would take her not only to the Philippines but to Japan and China during the Boxer uprising

The voyage across the Pacific was dreamily placid, and Margaret outdid herself in writing long, almost undecipherable descriptions of the passage to her sister Elizabeth and to Mary Meroney, steadfast at Rokeby.

From Manila she wrote cogently about conditions in the hospitals—deplorable in many respects, she thought. Before leaving Washington, she had been authorized by Secretary of War Elihu Root to report to him directly any delinquencies that she thought he should know about, and she took him at his word. The rumors about the Red Cross nurses were groundless, she stated; they had been studiously circumspect and efficient, and the doctors were singing their praises. On the subject of the need for a corps of nurses, "the fear of the Surgeon General" was keeping the military noncommittal, she reported, and she noticed many inadequacies in the hospitals, particularly in the service of supply, even necessities like bed sheets being lacking in some instances. All this she embodied in a hasty report addressed to Root, and then went on a tour of the islands, noting conditions with a stern eye but enjoying herself enormously. She attended the trial of a head-hunter and shuddered at tales of savagery. When an officer handed her a Malay kriss, after making sure that he had "wiped all the blood off it," she was thrilled.

As her transport had entered Manila Bay on arrival, other transports had been steaming out carrying troops to China, to relieve the Peking legations besieged by Boxers. Margaret debated whether to follow them, and when a fair chance arose, she did sail for Nagasaki. At that port she found no facilities for receiving the wounded coming from China, and on her own initiative she rented and fitted up a house as a depot hospital, with beds for thirty patients. Great was her indignation when the first transport bringing casualties declined her hospitality, and sailed directly for San Francisco. "Fear of the Surgeon General" again, she surmised; and she was not surprised to hear later that every one of the patients, denied a brief rest ashore at Nagasaki, had died during the long, taxing voyage.

Pressing ahead, Margaret made her way to China, where the

outbreak had finally been suppressed. Visiting battered Peking, she toured the imperial palace, and saw its treasures strewn about just as the fleeing dowager empress and her court had left them. She noted the sandbags that the women of the British legation had sewn for a breastworks during the siege; at the start these had been made of coarse cloth, but later sumptuous brocades, woven for the imperial use, had been pressed into service. A British officer snipped swatches of these priceless brocades for Margaret to add to her collection of souvenirs for Rokeby.

At Rokeby, Mary Meroney, aged but still very much in charge of the household, trembled for her mistress, alone in heathen lands; but Elizabeth reassured the old nurse, writing:

"If ever there was a human being capable of looking after herself, it is Miss Margaret. I don't know where she is at this moment, but think it most probable that she is sitting on the wall at Pekin, telling Mr. Conger and General Waldersee how far superior the view of the Hudson and Catskills from Barrytown is to anything she has seen on her travels. She last wrote from the Philippines . . . where she had been to one town in the interior where no white woman had ever been before. She was having the time of her life, apparently, and I don't see why she shouldn't keep it up and go to China. . . . The papers said she was there and they probably got it right, and letters will come from her soon. . . ."

The old nurse was not comforted. And she wrote, combining news of the estate with her foreboding:

"Dear Miss Margaret, as I could not get all the bills by the first of the month i thought it best to wahte. . . . Miss Aspinwall as married a rich old man with 6 children and with her four ther will be a very large family . . . the new stable is getting along nicely the green house not so well . . . i dont get any letters from Miss Alida i dont know why . . . this as been a long summer i wish you were at home never to leave it for so long a time you may see many places but none more faire . . . the house looks fresh and home like . . . your affectionate Mary Meroney."

Such letters provided the "Antaeus touch" with the ancestral earth that could always revive and sustain Margaret.

Having seen and done all she had come for, Root's unofficial inspector of the medical establishment in the Far East sailed for home. She reached Washington in late November, and found a storm raging over her confidential report to the army secretary on hospital deficiencies at Manila and elsewhere; somehow the letter had leaked to the press, and she was being berated for "meddlesome interference" with military concerns. Root lectured her, saying she should have known that "there is no such thing as a private letter to a public official," and the nurses corps bill was defeated. However, the cause was saved, for Root embodied the plan in his general reorganization of the army, and in that form it was adopted.

Watching this turmoil from the sidelines was John Jay Chapman, home from Europe with Elizabeth and his sons. To Chapman, his wife's family was a constant source of astonishment and entertainment. As an "inward creature, wandering about in worlds unrealized" (his own self-characterization), he was fascinated by the extroversions of the many-sided Chanlers.

"There is always one Chanler in the newspapers," he observed. "The Chanler theme dies in the bassoons and is dropped in the pathetic drum solo—but hark the flute!"

Back from England with the Chapmans were Lewis and Alice Chanler, settled in the house at 190 Madison Avenue belonging to their Aunt Laura Delano. Lewis had picked up his law practice without difficulty; he told Margaret with satisfaction that "within 26 hours of landing from England I had a criminal case on my hands & have been very busy ever since."

The press signalized Lewis's return by reporting an incident in the courtroom of Recorder John W. Goff. A man acquitted of a stabbing charge was before the recorder for discharge. Chanler happened to be present. It was December, bitterly cold, and he noticed that the man was shivering. The lawyer handling the case said the poor devil, who had been in the Tombs since summer, had neither hat nor coat, and so far as counsel knew, not even the price of a night's lodging. Following the man into the corridor, Chanler threw his own coat around his shoulders, with, "Here, I don't need this, you take it. And here's five dollars and an odd nickel for your fare home. Let me hear how you get on." Thrusting the money into the man's hand, he brushed aside the stammered thanks.

Alida's new baby girl, named Margaret, born in her aunt's home on West 74th Street, was not the only recent addition to the family. Wintie and Daisy Chanler were adding to their section of the pride, a son having been born to them in Munich. Since Wintie was hunting chamois in Switzerland at the time, the boy was christened Hubert, after the patron saint of hunters.

Roosevelt envied Winthrop's athletic freedom, and wrote wistfully from Oyster Bay:

"I only wish I could be with you for a shoot but I should need at least six weeks of conscientious work in the open before I should be in fit condition to cope with a cow, let alone a chamois. . . . Upon my word it makes me feel rather shaky to hear about Mrs. Winty jumping. I know that I could not hunt now and jump anything that was not very small. . . . I am both old and fat (and stiff to boot)."

Wintie himself was in tip-top trim. "In hard training all summer," he told his friend French. "Chamois shooting and mountain climbing; and . . . never a time to drink." He had inaugurated the new century by a hunting expedition in Asia Minor, as the guest and enlivener of his cousin and former guardian, Rutherfurd Stuyvesant, on the latter's yacht, *Arcturus*. The hunt had been organized at Alexandretta, and Wintie enjoyed himself thoroughly, bagging plenty of game and poking through the rubble of centuries that littered the landscape, from ruined castles of crusaders to the stronghold of a "wicked bey" who had once ruled the town familiar to Harun al-Raschid.

Wintie had sold his Tuxedo Park house for $60,000, and this windfall had temporarily lifted him out of the money doldrums. Business in connection with the sale had brought him to New York for a brief visit, and during this crossing he had pondered seriously on his marriage and the woman to whom he had been married nearly fourteen years.

"Fourteen years ago I dragged you to the altar by the hair of your head & I've been happy ever since," was his conclusion. "As

I walk the deck my thoughts race along back & forth from you in Rome to me here at sea—& then they go darting into the past & come skipping back from year to year like a flat stone thrown on a smooth sea. You seem (tonight) so much more mine & real to me, than you do (tonight) ten years ago. As if I hadn't really known you thoroughly then. You seem like a sort of pale vision to me, a sort of Lady of Chalotte, passing before me, and I think of you now in Rome and I really see you as if I had just left the room. Heigh-ho—'I am half sick of shadows' . . . There is a man playing the 'fire motif' rather well on the piano. Is it the fire motif? No—it is what you play so often: Dum dum dumty dum *twice*. You know what I mean. Good night."

That Easter in New York, Wintie arrayed himself "like a lily of the field" and betook him to the Sunday service at St. George's Church, on Stuyvesant Square—the church of his and Willie's hunting companion and friend, Dr. Rainsford. ("Old Rain-in-the-Face" Wintie dubbed him.) Writing from the Knickerbocker Club afterward, he set down a jolly account for Rome-bound Daisy:

". . . Such a crush! I could only just get inside the door which is bad English but the truth. The whole circle behind the altar— I never remember the name of the place—was one wall of red roses with a white cross in the center. Of course, lots of lilies about. Old Rain-in-the-Face loomed up as big as ever & bullied his congregation as well as a man can. The singing was bully—mixed choir, men, women, & boys. I left when the sermon began. He gave a trumpet call for alms, saying, 'I won't trouble you with the object of your offering today; let it suffice that I never wanted money more (and be damned to you)!' "

Margaret Chanler had been persistently begging Winthrop to settle in America, and during this visit he had almost promised. Luther Terry had died at a ripe eighty-seven, and there was nothing further to hold him or Daisy at Rome. The notion of digging in permanently, say at Cliff Lawn in Newport, was inviting; but not quite yet, he decided; and as he sailed back to Italy Margaret grieved that her jumping-jack of a brother had eluded her again.

Willie, too, was proving a disappointment, for he was abandoning politics. The life was simply too tame for him: he required action, combative action, for contentment. He had confessed this to his companion of Africa, Lieutenant von Höhnel, who was now serving as naval aide to the Emperor Franz Josef in Vienna. In October, 1899, Willie had written:

"Once when (in Africa) I told you of my plans in civilization (reform & other things) you laughed. You were right. I have not changed & possibly cannot. Without action I am no good; & the past years (except the Cuban episode) have found me more than idle. . . . I am tied to politics till 1901 & then I'm free and off again. I chafe, just now, for the Transvaal fight is on & I cannot be in it. Never again will I be tied down to any work but exploration of some sort. . . ."

The gerrymandering of his congressional district's boundaries furnished Willie with a plausible pretext for not accepting renomination by the Democrats in 1900. He was impatient to get away, and as the time of his deliverance drew near, his conversation, always ready to crackle and glow in the presence of attentive listeners, glittered with reminiscence and cloud-castle building. Christmas found him with the family at Rokeby, helping to launch the old house on the new century. Rokeby hummed and clattered with grow-ups and children. Around the table on Christmas Day of 1900 were ranged the Chapmans and their sons; the Lewis Chanlers with their children; and Alida and Temple Emmet with theirs. The hostess was Margaret Chanler, radiantly returned from the Orient; and it was she who gave the toast that thenceforward would be considered the crowning toast to be drunk at ceremonious Rokeby gatherings:

"To all who have been here; to all who are here; to all who would like to be here."

And although she lifted a glass of cider, the others present drank the toast in beverages more to their taste.

Willie, as Willie would, took fire as the dinner progressed, and held the group entranced by tales of adventure in Arabian Nights-like lands. Believable or not (were the tales of Scheherazade supposed to be literally true?), the stories glistened like jeweled tapestries. Jack Chapman, new to the performance, with his knack for impromptu versifying, fixed the scene in a rhyme entitled "The Snake Charmer." The stanzas ran:

The tide of victuals was running slack
(My interest failed at the canvasback),
And still the waiters circulate
With wine on wine and plate on plate;
And the glasses yellow and red and green
On the distracted board are seen,
Like an autumn garden, stalk on stalk,
When Willie Chanler began to talk.

What he said I'll not repeat. . . .
For could a mortal understand
How he reached his sacred heat,
Or what the meaning of his hand
As he raised it, and the eyes of all
Followed its movements magical?

He talked of Egypt—how he slew
In an afternoon ten thousand men,
And half a thousand women too!
(The last to frozen rivers grew,
For they looked too long on his eyes of flame,
And returned to their consorts never again!)

And next a lion he did tame,
And with the skin old Kruger smote,
Till the mane grew fast to Kruger's throat,
And Cecil Rhodes gave up the game!
Now touching lightly on the Czar—
And the Duchess of the Alcazar—
And what he won from the Shah in a fight
And lost at faro in a night.

And ever the visitors craned their necks,
And the waiters listened behind the door
To catch but a word if they could no more
Of that marvelous stream that might perplex
The brain of a Plato to unravel,
Of history, legend, intrigue, travel.

Now a whisper about doth go,
"Does he believe it—is it so?
We don't know and he don't know!"
And still the continuous stream doth flow.
"Is it opium? Is it wine

That makes his glassy eye to shine,
And tinctures yours and dazzles mine,
Until the decanters seem to dance
In tune with the flashing of his glance?"

He is telling the laws of the Boogla-Goo,
The secret clique that rules Bombay;
He himself was the chief, they say,
The very Pyjam of the How-do-you-do,
That poisoned the Princess of Cathay
And won the bride and turned the tide
Of the Mongols in Baffin's Bay.

One at a time they came up the pass,
One on an elephant, one on an ass,
While he with sorceries manifold—
A handful of silver, a pound of gold—
And the hair that the witch of Atlas gave
When Genghis Khan came out of the grave—
Did frighten them all away!

He talked till the brain of the men that night,
Like absinthe mixed with dynamite,
Gave off blue sparks, and the lamps burned low,
And still the murmur about doth go:
"Did he do it and is it so?
We don't know and he don't know
If it be false or if it be true."

Nobody living ever knew,
Or in eternity can find out—
We only obey his call;
He is merely weaving his charms about—
Till the snakes crawl in, and the lights go out—
The charmer has charmed them all.

There was need of Willie's verbal hashish on that Christmas night of 1900, for the minds of the Chanlers gathered around that festive board were not at ease. Three brothers were absent from the circle. Wintie once more was shooting in Sardinia. Bob was in Paris, from where he sent brave but homesick greetings. And Archie?

It had required Willie's spellbinding exuberance to exorcise, for a few hours, the cloud of anxiety that had overhung all the brothers and sisters for weeks. The fact—at first discreetly hushed but now blazoned by the newspapers to all the world—was that on Thanksgiving eve John Armstrong Chanler had disappeared from Bloomingdale asylum, and the most diligent search had failed to turn up a single clue to his whereabouts or fate. Had he perished? Many people believed he had. Or was he at large? And if so, where?

That his disappearance was voluntary and premeditated seemed indicated by a note found in his room—an odd sort of note to have emanated from a man whose wits were supposed to be addled. Addressed to Dr. Samuel P. Lyon, the medical superintendent of Bloomingdale, it read:

"My dear Doctor:

"You have always said that I am insane. You have always said that I believe I am the reincarnation of Napoleon Bonaparte. As a learned and sincere man, you, therefore, will not be surprised that I take French leave.

"Yours, with regret that we must part,

"J. A. CHANLER."

The enigma was impenetrable, and as the Chanlers entered upon a new century—one that would be portentous for them—they had need to draw tighter their bond as a family to await its unfolding. Many turns of the wheel of fortune awaited them. None guessed, for example, on that Christmas night in 1900, that restlessly adventurous Willie would one day be roaming the Sahara as a Moslem holy man inciting an Arab revolt; or that Wintie would carry his unquenchable light-heartedness into a grimmer war; or that Lewis would gallantly win and lose a political fortune and start a future President toward the White House. None dreamed of the sensational and ludicrous role that Bob would play in an international comedy of love and money, nor could they envision the tenacity with which year after year Margaret would strike roots deeper into the home soil of Rokeby. Least of all could any foresee (although all apprehended) the course that fate would take with Archie. Monumental disputes and fantastic reconciliations lay hidden in the impenetrable future. Meanwhile, thanks to such spells as Willie momentarily wove, life would go on for some time still in much the same channels as before.

The Curtain Falls—The Author Speaks

Who were the Chanlers, and why should their story be told? Theirs is not a famous name, and biography, according to some, should concern itself only with the familiar or the great of the world; although the lives of the familar too soon become a tale twice told, and those of the great sometimes are singularly devoid of much interest aside from their celebrity.

There are numerous reasons why the lives of the Chanlers are worth telling. The first is the same reason that makes *Cinderella* and *David Copperfield* worth telling—because they are good stories, and a good story is always worth telling for its own sake.

There are other reasons, however (though certainly none more solid), for recounting the lives of the very lively Chanlers. These reasons have to do with the evolution of the American social structure, and the ways in which the Chanlers uniquely illustrated its successive transformations.

The Chanlers—a group of brothers and sisters bearing the indelible stamp of kinship, yet at the same time exhibiting extreme individuality—stand in a peculiar position historically. Born into the class of inherited wealth, privilege, and assured social position, in many ways they adhered to the conventions of their surroundings, and to that extent were truly representative of their milieu. Truly but not consistently, for impelled by a superabundance of vitality, imagination, and extraordinary independence of spirit, again and again they burst through the constrictions of their conventions and became wholly untypical of their social class.

These dramatic departures from the accepted norms throw a

strong, often unexpected, light of contrast on their background, giving it a vividness of relief and a clarity and firmness that are lacking when it is viewed in subdued generalities, in the mass. It is difficult to name another family that fulfills this function so strikingly and with such a variety of interests.

The class of which the Chanlers were members by birthright shaped and guided America for nearly three hundred years, politically, socially, and culturally. It was the class that set the standards of the times; its forms and ideals were paramount in fields as widely divergent as philanthropy and privateering. In this class the Chanlers occupied a strategic middle position, neither too high to lose touch with their inferiors, nor so low as to render them uneasy in the company of their superiors. They could respond, in varying degrees, to influences from both ends of the social spectrum. Their ideals and habits were not bourgeois in the classic economic sense; as basically country gentility, they corresponded roughly to England's landed gentry—patricians, not aristocrats, and American patricians at that, with nuances setting them apart from any European near-counterpart. The very ideals of equality and democracy on which the United States was founded were formulated by these patricians, men like Jefferson, Washington, Livingston, Adams.

The values which they and their class cherished were those of a patrician society. They valued courtesy, and moderation, and simplicity in manners and in one's style of living. They took very seriously the obligations of their position, with personal responsibility. In the intellectual field they cultivated learning, literature, and music, together with the "approved" arts, but they were appreciators, not innovators. Yet their minds were not closed to innovations, which they accepted slowly. Incapable of showing subservience to those in authority or stationed above them, they never condescended, and were jealously loyal to the interests of those dependent upon them. They welcomed graceful living, but desired that it be contained within the bounds of decorum; showiness and ostentation they reprehended, and in conversation they insisted upon a decent reticence. Their inherent pride and untroubled self-sufficiency they wore with modesty.

These are the attributes of a patrician society, and into this world the Chanlers projected themselves both as mavericks and as conformists. And long before the last survivor of their generation would leave the earthly scene, they and their social setting would vanish, displaced completely by the plebeianism and aggressiveness of an all-encroaching plutocracy. The Chanlers themselves would become anachronisms.

Further advantages are held by the Chanler story for the student of the effects of heredity and youthful environment upon character and action, advantages that probably are unique, for identical conditions are little likely ever to occur again. The Chanlers were the grandchildren of Sam Ward, one of his century's most expansive and imaginative spenders; but they were also the great-grandchildren of the same century's foremost acquisitor and hoarder of wealth, William Backhouse Astor. Mingle the genes of these two mutually repellent personalities, and the result is apt to be a volatile mixture about as unstable as nitroglycerine. In the Chanlers that mixture exploded in all directions, the detonations being heightened by the bizarre circumstances of their early environment.

These are considerations for the scholar; the chief concern of the present author has been telling the human story of the Chanler family. It is a story that is as extraordinary as it is instructive, and as instructive as it is entertaining. Linked by inseparable bonds of legacy, tradition, and loyalty to a shared ideal, this family might and did dispute famously among themselves, quarrel with affection, and reconcile with fervor, yet, to the last, a united band of orphans, present to the unorphaned world a united defiance; and through it all, through storm and serenity, they were never mean, never dull, and never defeatist.

The even tenor of our days. Summer afternoon on Rokeby's porch during the Nineties. From left, Elizabeth Chanler, with guitar; Edith Folsom, a cousin; Margaret, and Alida Chanler.

ACKNOWLEDGMENTS

This narrative obviously could never have been put together without the generous and unreserved assistance of the various heirs, descendants, associates, and friends of the subjects with whom it deals. Since principal reliance necessarily has been on private and personal data, contained in family memoirs or conveyed orally—sources not yet accessible to the public—the burden of debt owing to these contributors is unusually heavy.

In one way or another, the Chanlers (or at least the generation here treated of) touched upon a bewildering array of fields of human activity—society, finance, religion, politics, law, art, sports, literature, agriculture, war, exploration, reform, philanthropy, education, bohemianism, occultism. The Chanlers impinged upon all these fields, and in some instances not insignificantly. Consequently the record, public and private, which they left is of staggering dimensions. In the category of published sources alone, so deft and knowledgeable an authority on the Chanlers' world as Mr. Louis Auchincloss has ventured his opinion that no other family in America, except the Adamses and the Roosevelts, has had so much written about them (mainly by themselves) as the Chanler-Ward-Astor connection. To list a complete bibliography documenting these works at this point would be burdensome.

However, some expression of the author's gratitude to the many individuals, members of the family and others, who have contributed directly to the enterprise will admit of no deferment. And first acknowledgment should be addressed to the memory of two of the book's subjects whom it was the author's good fortune to meet and from them glean facts that could have been obtained from no other source. These two last survivors of "the eight" were the late Margaret Livingston Chanler Aldrich, and the late Alida Beekman Chanler Emmet.

Others who have aided materially by both their cooperation and their hospitality include:

First and foremost, John Winthrop Aldrich, whose outlay of time and enthusiasm throughout the protracted task has been enormous; and with him, his brother, Richard Aldrich, and his sister, Mrs. Rosalind Fish Aldrich Michahelles, the present proprietors of Rokeby; with their mother, Mrs. Richard Chanler Aldrich, and their aunt, Mrs. Byron DeMott.

Also: Mrs. William Christian Bohn; Mr. Porter R. Chandler; Rear Admiral and Mrs. Hubert Winthrop Chanler, of Sweet Briar Farm; Mrs. Lewis Stuyvesant Chanler, Jr.; Mr. and Mrs. William Astor Chanler, Jr.; Mr. Sidney Ashley Chanler; Mr. William Chamberlain Chanler; Mr. Chanler Armstrong Chapman and his late wife, Mrs. Helen Chapman, of Sylvania; Mr. and Mrs. Conrad Chapman; Mrs. Charles H. Clarke; Mr. Christopher Emmet; Mr. Thomas Addis Emmet; the Rev. Allie W. Frazier, Jr.; Mrs. Julia Chanler Laurin; Mr. and Mrs. G. Francklyn Lawrence; Mrs. Kiki Minervini; Mr. William Platt; Mrs. Kenneth Robertson; Mrs. Julia Ward Stickley; Mrs. Pauline Petchey; Mrs. Lawrence Grant White; Mr. Peter White.

Others whose assistance has lightened the burden are:

The late Allan Nevins, whose readiness to share his stories of historical knowledge was a stimulus and inspiration;

Mr. John C. Willey, whose sympathetic support as editor and adviser surmounted obstacles and smoothed the path of the author;

Mr. Robert Lescher, but for whom the project would never have been conceived, undertaken, or carried to completion.

Appreciation is extended to the staffs of the following libraries for cooperation cheerfully rendered:

New-York Historical Society; New York Public Library; Henry E. Huntington Library; Museum of the City of New York; New York Society Library; Franklin Delano Roosevelt Library; Houghton Library; Harvard University; Alderman Library, University of Virginia; San Francisco Public Library.

The principal manuscript sources consulted (many of these in private custody) include:

Margaret Livingston Aldrich Papers, at Rokeby.

Elizabeth Chanler Chapman Papers, at Sylvania.

Robert Winthrop Chanler Papers, courtesy of Sidney Ashley Chanler.

William Astor Chanler and Beatrice Astor Chanler Papers, New-York Historical Society, with accretions in the custody of William Astor Chanler, Jr., and Sidney Ashley Chanler.

John Jay Chapman Papers, at Sylvania, courtesy of Mr. Chanler Armstrong Chapman.

Margaret Terry Chanler Papers, Houghton Library.

John Armstrong Chaloner Papers, Alderman Library, University of Virginia.

Rives Family Papers, Alderman Library, University of Virginia.

S. L. M. Barlow Papers, Henry E. Huntington Library.

Franklin Delano Roosevelt Papers, at Hyde Park.

Over Land and Sea, unpublished manuscript biography, by Ludwig von Höhnel, courtesy of Mrs. Byron DeMott.

Because the house and estate of Rokeby exerted so critical an influence on the youthful Chanlers and left its impress upon them indelibly for the remainder of their lives, as a curiosity, a detailed account is appended of how the estate acquired the name so appropriate to its sturdy dignity. Among Rokeby's distinctions, which are many, is the fact that it is the only one of the stately river houses lining the banks of the Hudson that has never been out of the possession of the family, and is still occupied by direct descendants of the builder. Its traditions thus have flourished in unbroken continuity for more than a century and a half.

The Name and Provenance of Rokeby

Mortham Tower, in Yorkshire, England, was built at the end of the fifteenth century to serve as the fortified manor house of the Rokeby family. Ralph Rokeby, master of requests in the reign of Elizabeth I, wrote a family history for his nephews which he entitled Oeconomia Rokebeiorum.

After the battle of Bannockburn (1314), the victorious Scots swarming over the border overran most of the northern counties, and, among much other damage, burned the home of the Rokebys. And so the structure which evolved into the present-day Mortham Tower was built to replace the original, "where [in Ralph Rokeby's words] yet unto this day continueth—God be thanked—the house of our whole family and parentage."

However, with the passage of time, the Tower and surrounding lands were sold in 1611 to William Robinson. A Robinson descendant in 1730 built a very large, handsome Palladian house close by, which he named Rokeby. In 1769 the whole place was sold to J. S. Morritt, whose son, J. B. S. Morritt, M.P., was an intimate friend of Sir Walter Scott; and it was Scott's frequent visits to the ancient seat of the Rokebys that gave rise to the epic poem, written in gratitude for the hospitality Scott had received there.

It was Scott's description of the ravines at Mortham, through which the Greta and Tees run to confluence, that inspired Mrs. William B. Astor to name her Hudson River home after the original Rokeby.

In 1810 J. B. S. Morritt gave Rokeby a certain celebrity by purchasing from the Spanish statesman Godoy a famous painting by Velasquez, representing Venus. His descendants sold this prized work of art to the National Gallery in London, and it is known throughout the art world as the "Rokeby Venus."

At Rokeby on the Hudson there is a leather fire bucket from the English Rokeby, marked with the name.

Although the Rokeby family seems to have disappeared, both Mortham Tower and Rokeby still stand and are inhabited.

Besides the estate on the Hudson, two other houses in America are known to be named Rokeby, although as a result of what circumstances is not clear. One is a pleasant old house in western Vermont, which once served as a station on the Underground Railroad aiding the escape of southern slaves. The other is the Virginia estate now owned by Mr. Paul Mellon, which has furnished the title for the Mellon thoroughbred interests (Rokeby Stables)—an association of name and activity that the Chanlers on the Hudson would have considered eminently appropriate.

INDEX

Index